THE MYSTERY OF HEALING

BY PAUL RYMNIAK

CENTER FOR PEACE
P.O. BOX 2206
MARIETTA, GA. 30061

(800)-245-9846
(770)-425-5803

ISBN: 0-9651738-0-1
Library of Congress catalog number: 96-92160

Table of Contents

DEDICATION

This book is dedicated to St. Therese of Lisieux, the Little Flower. By her intercession, she has watched over, guided and brought about the writing of this book. A first degree relic of hers sat by the computer for the entire writing. She promised, in her memoirs, that she would do more good for people after her death, from Heaven, than while she was alive here on this earth. As far as this book is concerned, her task is complete.

A TRIBUTE TO GEORGE ORENSTEIN

There is a special tribute that needs to be acknowledged in this book. It is to the memory of a good friend George Orenstein. I knew this man only for a short period of time, but in that time, a special bonding occurred. All of you reading this book would never have had the chance to do so, if it were not for the generosity and benevolence of this man. He BELIEVED in me.

I came to know George in a very unusual manner. How that happened is not necessary to explain here. I talked with him many times, and I visited with him twice. In this brief period of time, I found a true gift from God. I really perceive George as that gift. God puts all kinds of people in our lives, some we remember and some we forget. Some we cherish and some we do not. George will always have his own special category with me.

I knew nothing of his past, and he knew nothing of mine, but that was the beauty of our relationship. It was UNSPOKEN. We knew each other. We only had to look at each other to understand how life had treated us to that point. It was UNSPOKEN. Somehow our minds were able to think without the ability of words. It was UNSPOKEN. Our hearts would, in some way, beat together with the realization of the pains we knew each of us had endured in our lifetime. It was UNSPOKEN. More important, our souls were able to have a level of communication, even that was UNSPOKEN.

I will never forget George Orenstein because of an even greater reason. January 1, 1996, I finished the last chapter in this book. I ran it through a grammar and spelling program.

The printer printed the final 11 pages, and there, on my desk, sat the complete manuscript of my life in the healing ministry. The book, for all practical intents and purposes, was finished. I shut off my computer and went to bed.

This same day, I got a call from Maxine, George's wife, around 5:00 p.m., and she informed me that, a moment before, George died. She asked me to say the last prayer I would with him. She put the phone to his ear, and I told Jesus to take my friend into the realm of His Sanctity. George was gone, but Maxine let me have the best memory that I will have of him. She let me stand before Christ, with George one last time, and say good-bye.

George, I know God has you. Your pains are gone. You're free at last. You will be missed, but you will never be forgotten. I say to you as a final tribute, it was a pleasure to know you, my friend, and I want you to know that I will always LOVE YOU.

All the stories in this book are true. Names and places were changed to protect the privacy of those individuals involved. Some of the stories, at times, have been slightly altered for even further protection. Please remember that this book is compiled totally from experiences that I have had since the beginning of my Healing Ministry. If anyone is offended by the contents of this book my apologies go out to you. If the conclusions I draw in some of the chapters bother you, I truly hope you overlook them. My intent was **NOT** to write a controversial book. My intent was to help you along in your spiritual journey of this life. I can only hope that my task is accomplished.

INTRODUCTION

This book is a map. It is a guide for some territory which I have explored. As with any map, you will find some very good uses and some limitations.

A map of a region of the country, let's say the Northeast, shows you a big picture of that area. It can be useful for a general travel plan. However, if you try to use it to find a specific address in Pittsburgh, you will be wandering around for a very long time. You will have to find your own way, ask questions of the people along the way, take some chances, and maybe make some wrong turns. This book is similar to that big map in that it provides a broad picture. The details contained here are individual experiences and stories that may or may not spark something in you. Ultimately, it is **YOUR** story, **YOUR** journey with which you must be concerned. I hope the common ground that we can cover together will be of benefit to you.

It is worth noting here that I am a Christian, specifically Roman Catholic, and this orientation colors the book.

I have written the book from the perspective of my experiences and beliefs about healing. If something in this book works for you, **take it**. If something doesn't work for you or goes against your personal beliefs, **leave it**. I am not a theologian. I have tried to present this information in a way that is consistent with Christian teaching and with the Bible. I know that by taking a stand with some things I will not be able to please everyone.

The "territory" of HEALING is a fascinating, challenging and elusive one. If it has called you either through your own pain or illness, through that of a loved one, or through your choice of a profession that involves some form of healing, you probably feel the urgency and power with which it can draw you. I hope you will find, as I have, that to answer the call to heal or be healed is to set off on a journey of discovery and surprise.

Healing and Cure are not the same thing, although they often occur together. Webster's dictionary says that although these two words have similar meaning, cure implies the ridding of a disease or condition, while healing suggests a process of returning to soundness and wholeness. If you are chasing a "Cure", this book may not be for you. If you are searching for Healing, you have in your hand a guidebook to find your own healing path. I give you this blessing as you start your journey:

> May the Lord bless you and keep you. May
> the Lord make His face shine upon you. May
> the Lord take your Life and Live through it.
> May He take your Voice and Speak through it.
> And may the Lord take your Heart and Set it on Fire.

IT ALL STARTED HERE

February 10, 1987, I found out about Medjugorje, the small village in what was then known as Yugoslavia where the Blessed Mother had been allegedly appearing to six children since June of 1981. This was going to be a time I would never forget. I was going to begin a personal MINISTRY, and I was going to find a new spirituality. Little did I know what was about to happen, but all I can tell you is that I am extremely happy about how things evolved.

Let's go back to February 10, that infamous day. Several weeks before this day, my church, was starting a new program. It was called Renew. The pastor at the church, for several weeks, had been making the same announcement, repeatedly. He kept reminding everyone to make sure that they signed up for the program. Personally, I was becoming bored, listening to the same announcement week after week. The program was designed to bring small groups together, once a week, in someone's home, to learn more about God. Yeah, right...this was the idea that kept running through my mind as I sat listening to the priest's chatter. This program was only going to gather six to eight couples to have an evening out. That was what I was perceiving all the program to be. Nothing more than glorified coffee klatches for men and women. How boring!

Well, as luck would have it, on the last Sunday the announcement was made, I sat thinking, "Boy, what a waste of time that's going to be!" As I sat there daydreaming, I slipped off into oblivion thinking about mindless, idle tripe. The announcements were over, and I stood up to receive the final blessing. Shortly after that, I started for the door just like everyone else. You know the time; it's in the middle of the recessional hymn. Later, I came to find out that someone had signed me up for that foolishness, without my knowing it. I do not have to tell you how annoyed I was.

The night of the first meeting, I was led, under false pretenses, to a beautiful residential section, in the north end of town. The person I went with kept telling me I was going to have a wonderful time. All I had to do was be trusting. As we approached the house, I said, "Why are we here?" The person said nothing. The car was parked, and we got out and went up to the door. We were greeted by a very warm and friendly gentleman, who was the owner of the house, and for the first time I realized what was going on. As I glanced at the person who brought me, if looks could kill, as they say, death would have occurred instantaneously.

I went into the house and was introduced to all the people. There were six couples, including us, involved in all of this, and the whole evening I just sat there seething. How could this have happened to me? The evening started around 7:00. The general topic for the evening was devotions, not any specific ones, just those we grew up with in our early life. I guess I should tell you that at the time of this happening, I was 45 years old. This is significant because I grew up with pre-Vatican II ideology. Religious devotions held a prominent place in my life, especially those devotions to the Blessed Mother.

The man sitting next to me the whole evening piped up and said, "I wish the Blessed Mother would do something here in America, like She is doing in Medjugorje." I just looked at him. I asked him, "What's Medjugorje?" The word meant nothing to me.

He proceeded to tell me that Our Lady was, supposedly, appearing to six "Commie" kids. That's how he phrased it, six commie kids.

I let out a roar. I said, "What?"

He said these children had been receiving messages, daily, just like in Fatima and Lourdes, two other famous apparition sites in the world.

I sat there spellbound. The more he talked, the more excited I became. After several minutes of this, I simply stopped him and said, "Where did you hear about all of this?" He told me about a book called Queen of Peace. This was the first definitive book written about Medjugorje, at the time. It was written by a priest and a nun.

I asked him where I could get this book, and he told me his wife had a copy with her. Well, I immediately jumped up, ran to the kitchen, found his wife, and all I said was, "I want to see this book about the Blessed Mother." She reached in her purse and took out a small gray paperback book and handed it to me. I asked her if I could borrow it, if I brought it back next week. She made me promise, and I did.

This is where it all began, because that evening when I got home I sat for a few minutes on the couch and tried to clear my head. I picked up the book on Medjugorje and I started looking at the pictures. This was a big mistake. Why? I never put the book down until I finished reading it from cover to cover...almost seven hours. I was hooked. I sat and thought about what I had just read. This was the first time, in a long time, that reading material was so captivating to me I was numb.

I started towards the shower to get ready for the day, after no sleep, and a full day of work to look forward to. It never bothered me. I got through the whole day in a breeze. All I could do that day was think about what I had read. I kept envisioning my body sitting on a plane going to Yugoslavia. The thought haunted me all day. I went home and spent most of the evening pondering my next move.

I should tell you that most of my life had been spent owning my own businesses. At the time, I owned a travel company, and that's how I managed to go to Medjugorje. The following day, I started lining up the exact people to contact to get me overseas. I first called Yugoslav Airlines. Next I called the biggest ground operator in Yugoslavia. Ground operators are companies that handle everything associated with the land portion of trips. I made those two calls, things started to fall into place. I had appointments with them. All I had to do was wait.

Two weeks later, I was sitting with a gentleman from the airlines and a woman from the travel company. Plans were being made, I was "IN" as they say. In a matter of a few hours, I had procured passage on the airlines, and booked accommodations for my whole stay throughout the trip. As a side trip, I elected to go to Rome, and to my surprise, I made it there for the opening of the Marian Year. I even got to see the Pope. I thought I was clever in setting all of this up. Little did I know who was really planning all of this. I am sure most of you have guessed that, in hindsight, Our Lady's hand was in all of this. Here I was thinking how skillful I was, and never did I realize what a great travel agent, Our Lady could be.

Before going to Medjugorje, I had several weeks to prepare. Not only did I read the book I got from the Renewal Program, but I saw several videos. I read more, anything I could get my hands on. I contacted all sorts of people who had made this trip. I talked to anyone who knew anything about Medjugorje. I was totally enthralled. I cannot remember wanting to be any place as much. I wanted to go to Yugoslavia. I counted the days until the trip. I was like a five-year old waiting for Christmas to come. I was so excited all that I could think of was being where a true apparition was occurring. Not only was I thinking that, I was feeling it also.

I had been to other apparition sites, especially the ones approved by the church. Now, not only could I be there and experience all of it first hand, I could be part of it, also. This was going to be great. I read all about the Miracle of the Sun, Rosaries turning gold, and being with the visionaries. All this was intriguing to me. I was going to do it all. I wanted all these things to happen. The best part was I was going to be able to make money doing planned pilgrimages to Medjugorje. I know some people could say how wrong I was to think like that, but that's what was running through my mind. I was, after all, a business man.

SIGNS AND WONDERS

Running after signs and wonders. That's what I was doing. I do not demean anyone who does this sort of thing, but, I have met many people who do just that, run from apparition site to apparition site, clamoring after this visionary's message and that visionary's message. I see fanaticism beyond your wildest beliefs. This type of activity is not what Our Lady wants, not only from me, but for anyone. She tells us constantly that we should not worry about the future. She doesn't even know when the Chastisements are going to happen; only God the Father knows. She has made this point evident to us many times. The Bible even says not to worry about the end times, and I am sure those who do are missing out on all the good things of this life. Jesus promised us abundant life, and people who constantly worry about the doom and gloom of this world look forward to the future, not with anticipation, but with remorse and fear. How pitiful this seems to me.

One of the things I tell these fatalistic people is what Our Lady told Maria, one of the young visionaries. In 1989, on Easter Sunday, during an apparition, She said we should pray to God, the Father, with special thanksgiving prayers that day, because the Heavenly Father was granting Her more time. Think of that. She was receiving more time to be with us.

Why was this so important? Our Lady told Maria that the Chastisements of Medjugorje were supposed to have started by Easter of 1989. Think of that, the chastisements were to have already started, but Our Heavenly Father decided against it. Why? Our Lady said it was because of all the prayers and Rosaries being offered up...It was because of our prayers.

What else do we have to be told? The Father in Heaven hears and answers our prayers. Why should we worry about the end times? Maybe if we prayed instead of worrying or talking about the end, maybe it could be averted also. Did you ever think of that? I hear of people building shelters, hoarding food, etc., and for what? Yes, it's good to be on guard, but not if the guarding is all-consuming.

Our Lady says, month after month, Pray, Pray, Pray. Why do you think She says that? Why do some of us become bored with the same messages, over and over? Why are we waiting for the axe to fall? Why don't we direct this energy towards praying? We should. I would ask any of you who are reading this book....STOP...put it down, and thank God for what you have. Do it right now. Maybe if we took this approach more often, we would have less to worry about.

THE BEGINNING OF THE TRIP

The trip was about to happen. Things were in place. My passport was valid. I didn't need any shots. I had spend money. All I needed was the day to come.

Well, it came. I boarded the flight to LaGuardia, from there to Rome, three days there, and then on to Medjugorje. I arrived late in the day, in Dubrovnik, Yugoslavia, and was greeted by a pleasant young man. Soon we were off for our three-hour car ride to the village. The drive up the shoreline of Yugoslavia, along the Adriatic Sea, was fantastic. The scenery was superb, and I was in seventh heaven. For the next three hours, as tired as I was, I must have asked my personal tour-guide a million questions, and he had all the answers.

I asked him about the six children, two of which he knew personally. I asked him about the government. I made him tell me almost everything he knew. I am sure that at the end of that car ride he was glad it was over, and so was I.

We arrived in Medjugorje around 9:00 p.m.. Everything was dark. As we went over the small bridge (people who have been to Medjugorje know what bridge I am talking about), we made a right turn and my heart leapt into my throat. There, directly in front of me, was the church of St. James with its two gigantic spires, which were lit, reaching up into the night sky. I was so excited I didn't know what to do. I almost cried. We drove past the church, up past a row of small houses, and then all of a sudden everything got extremely dark. My guide knew exactly where he was going. It did not seem to matter much to him about what was going on in Medjugorje. I realized this when he said he had made the trip almost 60 times.

We arrived at the house where we would be staying. We went through the gate up a narrow, winding path, and finally stood in front of a small but modest house. I was simply beside myself. My guide knocked on the door. Immediately it opened, and the traditional greetings started to take place between us and the whole household, mother, father and children. They stood there smiling at me. I smiled back. Food and the drinks were placed on the table, and for a moment I thought I was sitting back at one of the Ukrainian Christmas Dinners out of my past. You know the kind of dinner I am speaking of: food everywhere. Well, not wanting to be rude, I ate.

Finally, I was escorted to my quarters. I walked into the room, which was very small. One large bed, one large dresser, and one small night stand with a small lamp with a

20-watt bulb; that was it. I looked around, smiled and started to unpack. As I did, I could think of only one thing: I was finally here, and I couldn't wait until tomorrow. This was going to be the big day. I was going to be with the Blessed Mother. That was all I could think about. It was the only thing going through my mind.

I finished unpacking. I even tried to do the impossible. I tried to sleep. As you can probably guess, sleep did not come. I looked at my watch. It was 1:30 a.m. I kept lying there trying to sleep. I remember looking at my watch for the last time, finally, at 5:15 a.m. Somewhere in the next moments I feel asleep.

Unfortunately, I was rudely awaken at 6:15. I didn't even get an hour of rest. Most of you would never guess in a million years what the rude awakening was. It was the noise of every animal that God ever made, and they were all outside my window. There were chickens, ducks, a cow, a goat, a horse, a pig, two dogs, a cat, several sheep, crickets, and a blaring rooster, all making noise. This was my first morning in Medjugorje.

I got out of bed, grabbed a towel and my shaving stuff and started towards the bathroom. Did I say bathroom? When I made it to the door, I realized where I was. I got outside my room, and the first person I ran into was my guide. I was never so happy to see someone as I was to see him. I asked him to show me the way to the bathroom. He just laughed. He pointed towards a door about 15 feet away, and said, "It's in there." I walked towards the door, and when I got inside, another rude awakening. There was no sink or tub. There was just a lavatory and a spigot coming out of the wall. The spigot was the shower. I turned it on and immediately got very cold water. The home's only source of hot water was an eight-gallon tank, which was outside the window. The bigger problem was that four other people had already made it to the bathroom before I did, before 6:30 a.m. All the hot water was gone. I washed and shaved and got back to my room as quickly as I could. Not only was the water freezing, so was I.

I shared the house with four women from New Orleans, whom I eventually became friends with, and until this day, when I go to New Orleans, I stay with one of them, and the other three usually show up to visit.

I got dressed and started off to have breakfast. Ah, breakfast. I could hardly wait. The women from New Orleans were sitting at the kitchen table, and I sat down to enjoy my food with them. Boy, was I surprised. Now, I like my coffee strong, and I only drink one cup a day, usually, but let me tell you, when I put my lips to the small cup, I was shocked. The coffee was so strong that the spoon stood up in it. I smiled. The woman of the house smiled back. My guide was there at the table, and I asked him what we were having for breakfast. He asked me what I wanted. I was gracious. I said whatever they have would be fine with me.

Well, for those of you that have eaten in a European country, you will know what I'm talking about. Breakfast is not the same as in the U.S.A. It is not eggs, bacon and toast. It was cold cuts, hard bread, cheese and more strong coffee. I was so hungry that I just sat there and ate. I didn't complain. I couldn't. I didn't want the Blessed Mother to think ill of me. I know She is smiling right now. I was very gracious. I didn't even ask for more.

I ate quietly, and after I finished, my guide asked me, "Well, what do you want to do first?" I wanted to get outside and look around, but my reply was that I wanted to meet Fr. Slavko, the priest in charge of the visionaries. He was also in charge of who could get into the apparition room. I remembered that from all my reading, watching videos and talking to the people who had been there. My guide just shook his head, mostly in dismay. He could not believe that was what I wanted to do first. I pleaded, and after much discussion, my guide relented. We started off for the church to find Fr. Slavko.

Meeting Fr. Slavko

We got outside, and it was a beautiful morning. The sun was shining. The air smelled exceptionally clean, and I was happy. As we walked towards the church, which was about a mile away, I looked all around. Everything was just as it appeared in the books and videos. I could see Cross Mountain directly behind me. I could see the two tall spires of St. James church directly in front of me. The road was hard dirt, not pavement. The crops that had been planted were just starting to grow. It was early June. I walked at a brisk pace, with my guide, and I talked feverishly and almost non-stop. I was asking him to point everything out to me.

He pointed towards Apparition Hill, just off to the right, and I could already see people starting to climb the hill. It was only 8:00 a.m., and the whole village was already very much alive. As we walked along the path, we passed people coming and going in both directions. I told my guide that I wanted to talk to Fr. Slavko about getting into the Apparition Room. He just looked at me, and told me that was going to be a very difficult task. I asked him why. He told me that he had been coming to Medjugorje for three years. He brought people like me, who owned travel companies, about two or three times a month, and in all that time, he had never been granted that request. He asked each time, sometimes twice, but to no avail. The answer was always "NO!" Fr. Slavko never relented.

You must remember that this was 1987, and many Americans were starting to come here. We Americans like to have things done our way. I felt sure that I could accomplish getting my way. As luck would have it, as we approached the church, who was walking from the rectory, but none other than Fr. Slavko. My guide got excited. He called out to the priest. Fr. Slavko stopped. He recognized my guide and started to walk towards us. I was "IN." This was the omen that I was sure was from Our Lady. The first person I was going to meet was Fr. Slavko himself. This was destiny.

My guide made all those customary greetings that they do in Yugoslavia, even the kissing on each cheek, and after several minutes, he introduced me to the priest. I shook his hand and smiled. I said hello, and he smiled. I immediately turned to my guide and asked him to see if he could get permission for us to get into the Apparition Room. He did, and my heart sunk. I could see almost immediately that Fr. Slavko started shaking his head in a very distinct and vigorous, NO. My heart sank even deeper. I got scared. Here was my chance, going out the window.

I have to interject something here. Before going to Medjugorje, I had been writing for my church newspaper. This publication was several pages, and it was almost the size of a tabloid paper, but not quite as thick. It came out every other month, and the stories I wrote were all about the approved apparitions in the Catholic church....Fatima, Lourdes, Guadalupe, La Salette, Knock, Banneux, Beauraing and the apparition about the Miraculous Medal. I had written about all of those, and the very last article was about my preparations for Medjugorje. I had closed that article by saying that when I returned I would let everyone know about my trip. This little item was going to be my wedge into the apparition room. This was going to be the "Clincher."

I regained my composure, looked at my guide, still trying to convince Fr. Slavko of why I should be getting the chance to be with the visionaries, and I kept seeing Fr. Slavko still shaking his head, "NO." I was not going to give up. I told my quide to mention that I was a journalist, and that I wrote for a very large Catholic newspaper in the United States. My guide just looked at me, very astonished. I poked him in the ribs, and told him to ask. He did. This was when my heart skipped a beat. Fr. Slavko quit shaking his head. He just stopped and looked at me. I smiled. He smiled back, but the look on his face was very quizzical.

I stood there staring this priest down, as if he were an animal. All he did was stand there looking back at me. Finally, with a disgusted look on his face, Fr. Slavko relented and said, "Okay." I didn't know what to do. Should I smile? Should I run? Should I grab the priest and hug him? For a moment I just wanted to scream with delight. With a quick whisk of his hand, Fr. Slavko said to be back at the rectory at 5:30 p.m., and I would be let in to the Apparition Room. I couldn't believe my ears. I was going to get in. I grabbed my guide by the arm, and started pulling him away. I didn't want anything to happen. As I was backing away, I told the guide to tell this priest that I was extremely pleased, and that I would be back that evening.

When we finally got away from Fr. Slavko, I stopped to catch my breath. My guide even stopped. He couldn't believe it. The priest was going to let me in. He was more surprised about all of this than I was. What a morning! It wasn't even 9 o'clock, and I had accomplished what I set out to do, get into the room with the children. I didn't know what to do next. I looked at my guide and asked him what we could do. He suggested going up on Apparition Hill. I said, "Okay," and off we went.

APPARITION HILL

This was the first time that I could really take everything in. I went very slow. I didn't want to miss anything. As we approached the hill, I could see many people had already had the same idea, get to the hill before the crowd. A hundred people had gathered at different points on the hill. As I started up the small path, I could see the very jagged rocks that were coming up out of the ground. For the first time, I understood what all the books and videos were explaining about how treacherous these hillsides could be. The rocks jutted out of the ground.

As I walked very slowly, I soon came upon the Blue Cross. This is seen very quickly as you start up the hill. Our Lady, supposedly, first appeared to Ivan here on this spot. I stopped for a moment and took a picture. As I did, for the first time I could look out over the village from my vantage point. Even though I was not very far along, the vision I had of the village was beautiful. I kept walking up the hill and every so often I stopped and turned around to look. The higher I got, the more impressive the view, until, finally I reached what was considered the top of the hill. There, in a cleared out area, stood a gigantic Cross made out of wood. It stood on the ground where the Blessed Mother stood, when She appeared to all six children. I stopped there for a moment, gathered all of this in and almost cried. I couldn't believe I was standing right where Our Lady appeared. I was speechless.

I stayed on this hill for a considerable time. I had never been somewhere so awesome. Not only was the sight impressive, but the peace that overcame me was too much to put into words. I sat and watched people come and go. Some people were gripped by tremendous spiritual intensity. Some cried. Some were there in a transfigured posture staring at the sky, the village below, or the Cross. Some were as I was, just looking around. Every once in a while, someone looked at me and we smiled at each other.

The most amazing experience I had that morning was listening to people praying in almost every language known to mankind, and it didn't matter what country they called home. There was a sense of camaraderie that permeated the hill. The common denominator was that we were there to pray, and that's what all of us were doing. We were praying.

I finally walked down off the hill and met my guide, who was sitting in a small restaurant having coffee with a fellow countryman. He saw me coming, jumped up and came towards me to ask what I wanted to do next. It was about 1:30 in the afternoon, and I was getting tired. The lack of sleep was starting to take its toll on me, along with the excitement of the morning. I told the guide I was going back to my house and take a nap. He offered to escort me back. I told him that I wanted to walk back leisurely and just be quiet. He said he would pick me up at five o'clock. He assured me he would have me at the rectory in plenty of time to be admitted into the apparition room. I told him that he didn't have to worry about that. I wouldn't be late. He could count on it.

THE APPARITION ROOM

Well, four o'clock came and I was ready to go. I left my house and started towards the church. I knew I would be early, but I didn't mind. Much to my surprise, when I got to the rectory people were everywhere. There must have been 500 people gathered in and around the small house.

I found out that Fr. Slavko sometimes picked one or two people from the crowd to go into the room. This explained the large crowd. I looked at my watch. It was 4:30. I scanned the crowd to see if I could find my guide. I spotted him standing some distance from the rectory. We saw each other and waved. He worked his way over to me, and we stood there waiting.

At approximately 5:30, I started to look for Fr. Slavko. I expected him to be there, but he wasn't. Time passed, and I started to become anxious. Where was he? Another priest came to the steps of the rectory and started letting only priests and nuns into the room. I took this as a cue to move forward in the crowd towards the rectory. When I finally got to the priest, I had my guide explain to him that we were given permission to enter. He told us he knew nothing about it. He said Fr. Slavko had said nothing to him about any lay people who were to be let into the Apparition Room. I started to get angry, but that made matters worse. It was approaching 6:00 p.m.

I kept looking at my watch, and as the minutes ticked on, I became more nervous. The possibility of not getting into the Apparition Room started to loom bigger and bigger. It was about 6:10 when Fr. Slavko appeared. My heart skipped a beat. He saw me and waved. I grabbed my guide's hand, as a father would, his two-year-old son, and I pushed through the crowd towards the priest and the Apparition Room. It took me all of five minutes, but I made it. I was about to enter the rectory and go into the room to be with the Blessed Mother. How exciting!

Fr. Slavko motioned for me to go up the stairs, and as I did, I grabbed my guide's hand. This time I pulled him abruptly. The priest yelled out to me, "STOP!" He was yelling only I could go in the room, not the guide. I said, "Father, what if something happens and I am the only one in the room that speaks English? I couldn't ask any questions. I was trying to make it clear that I might need an interpreter.

The priest said, "You're not going into the room to talk, you are going in there to pray." All of a sudden, I realized Fr. Slavko could speak English. I kept resisting his demand and kept pulling my guide with me, one step at a time, up the stairs. He finally relented. He waved his hand at me disgustedly, and pushed us both along. I could hear him mumbling something about those "Crazy Americans."

I ran up the stairs with my guide close behind me. We got into the hallway of the rectory and were directed to the Apparition Room by the same priest who tried to stop us from entering earlier. I smiled a giant grin of satisfaction and walked into the room, along with my guide.

As I entered, I could see approximately 40 people, smashed into the tiny room, and almost all of them were priests and nuns. With the exception of three or four other people, my guide and I were two of six, lay people, allowed in the room that afternoon. I was elated. We stood for several minutes and then Fr. Slavko came in and started to explain how things were going to be conducted. My guide and I listened intently.

We were told we would be praying the Rosary until the visionaries arrived, and we would only stop when the actual apparition was occurring. Almost immediately we all knelt and began praying. As we started into the prayer, I couldn't help looking around the room. It was just as it looked in the video. There was a large bookshelf against the one wall, and a small altar set against the other wall where the children would be kneeling. Various statues were scattered throughout the room. It was all there, and the best part...so was I.

Twenty minutes elapsed, and I could hear a commotion outside the building. I heard someone say two of the visionaries had arrived. Not only could I feel my heart pounding against my chest, but I could feel the veins in my neck throb. For a brief moment, I was in suspended animation. I looked towards the doorway and in came Maria and Jakov, two of the children. As luck would have it, they came towards me and knelt down almost directly beside me. I cannot tell you how I felt, it is impossible to describe. Not only was my body pounding, but my mind started concocting all sorts of outlandish scenarios. I thought because the children had elected to kneel beside me, maybe this was a sign from heaven, and something spectacular was going to happen. I even foolishly thought I was going to see Our Lady. That's how far my state of mind was taking me. I must tell you that never happened, but I think most people put in this situation would probably react the same way.

Everyone stopped praying for a moment. Maria and Jakov, after kneeling, resumed the Rosary, and everyone followed along. Ten minutes went by, and both children got up, stepped towards the little altar, and knelt directly in front of it. Everyone was still praying. The two children raised their heads, simultaneously, towards the ceiling. They transfixed their gaze upon a spot somewhere on the wall and remained that way for about 5 minutes, the entire length of the apparition.

It was explained to me that when they raised their heads towards the ceiling, they see a small white light, about the size of a baseball, and it keeps getting bigger and bigger untill Our Lady is standing in it. Then the light goes away. When the apparition is over, the light returns and engulfs Her. It continues to get smaller and smaller until it disappears. This happened that day, because after the apparition was over, the children told Fr. Slavko the same story.

I must explain one phenomenon that occurred. Even though the room was crowded and it was a warm June day, the room was never unbearably warm for the first half-hour. However, when the apparition started, everyone felt an intense heat, and it left when the apparition was over. It was explained to me that this occurred quite frequently. To this day, I cannot give anyone an explanation for this occurrence.

The apparition ended. Maria and Jakov immediately got up and left the room. It was all over. I thought I had missed something. I really had expected more. I looked around and everyone was starting to leave. I, of course, decided to take as many pictures as I possibly could, but I was disappointed about the way things turned out. I really had expected some fantastic spiritual happening. In hindsight, though, I realize I should have never anticipated anything of that nature, because that led to my disappointment. I think that this is how we all get ourselves into trouble, because for the most part, we all search for Signs and Wonders, and I'm no different.

I left the room, went outside and started down the steps of the building. I was deluged by people asking me what happened. One man even took me aside and videotaped all the replies to the questions he asked me. It was probably the dullest event he ever taped. I could only stand there and blandly state what had occurred. I had almost no emotion, but this was only because of the expectations I had set up in my mind before entering the room.

My guide, in his own stoic way, was beside himself. He was still reeling from just having been able to be in the room. He acted more the way I should have been. We made our way back to the house where we were staying, and dinner was waiting for us. After several hours of eating food and drinking homemade wine, I went to bed. The next day, I was going to tackle Cross Mountain.

Cross Mountain

The next morning came and it was a beautiful day. It started for me at 6:00 a.m., but only because I wanted to start then. There was method to my madness. I wanted to be in the "bathroom" first, and I accomplished that feat. It felt good to stand in hot water again. I did remember how I felt the day before, and I knew others would be using the facilities, so I stood with the hot water running down on me for only about 30 seconds. You really don't appreciate something until you have to do without it. I was starting to appreciate a lot of things I had previously become accustomed to, but that I was now doing without. The only problem: I'm like everyone else. Once I got back home, that keen appreciation vanished after I was able to get back into the swing of things. I wonder why we do that?

I showered, shaved and dressed, and I went to the kitchen to have my breakfast. I was feeling so good the cold cuts and cheese didn't bother me. I even enjoyed the extra strong coffee. I was sitting there daydreaming, when in walked my guide. I had a second breakfast with him.

I told him I wanted to climb Cross Mountain by myself. He didn't seem to mind. He told me he would use the time to do some work he had brought with him. I made him feel even better. I told him I was going to do it later in the day, so he could have not only the morning but part of the afternoon off, also. He gave me a big smile.

He did ask me if there was anything I wanted to do besides going up on the mountain. I asked him for some suggestions. He said he would try to see if he could arrange personal audiences with some of the visionaries. I started to get excited. I asked him to explain just what that meant. He told me he would try to see if Maria would talk with us, just him and me. I told him I really would like him to see if he could accomplish that task. He said he would really try. We sat there for a few more minutes and then went our separate ways. My guide went to do the work he brought with him, and I went off to visit the souvenir shops.

I spent the entire morning wandering around the village, in and out all the small shops, and there were plenty of them. I must share with you an experience that was quite interesting, but not of a religious vein.

After a good 30-minute walk from the house where I was staying and several hours of walking around, I went looking for a restroom. Everyone I asked kept guiding me to a facility behind the church, and I finally found it. Some industrious young man had bought portable toilets and installed them to provide restroom facilities for the pilgrims. What was so enterprising was he charged to use them, and if you came out of the facility and started to walk away, he chased you down and made you understand you had to pay. He caused such a commotion that people would pay him just to shut him up. I was not immune to this man either, so when I came out of the facility, he started after me. His foolishness didn't bother me. I merely smiled at him and, as people in foreign countries have done with me on occasion, I shrugged my shoulders, pretended I didn't understand him and walked away. If only that man knew all the satisfaction I was getting for all those times I had to put up with my own frustrations of people claiming ignorance.

Feeling wonderful, I started off on my journey towards Cross Mountain, which loomed on the horizon a few miles away. As I walked towards the mountain, it didn't look all that big, but I found out that it was bigger than I thought. I finally reached the base of the mountain, and by then it looked like Mt. Everest. I took a deep breath and started up the path.

I remembered from the books and videos that the Stations of the Cross had been erected on the Mountain. As I walked those first hundred yards on the path, I came to the first Station. Each area had a cross that had the picture of the station on it. Walking up the mountain and stopping to pray at each station was not only a way to meditate, it also gave me a chance to enjoy the fantastic view of the valley. The higher I went in the climb, the more breathtaking it became. Years later, those crosses were replaced by beautiful bronze sculptures donated by an artist from Italy.

As I continued my climb, my mind raced as it had in the Apparition Room the day before. I figured because I didn't get my religious experience in that room, it would occur on that mountain. My head became filled with thoughts of reaching the top and seeing visions of angels and saints. I became so engrossed in that thought that at one point, I knew in my heart I was going to be greeted by a host of celestial beings, including Jesus and His Mother. Again, looking back in hindsight, I can see the potential danger of getting too caught up in the thirst for having a religious experience. For me, in those times, God becomes less spectacular in presenting Himself to me, but that's only because He knows how I am.

Well, I finally got to the top and there in all its splendid glory stood the gigantic cement cross that had been there for years. Men of the village had erected it, and its completion and dedication took place on September 14, 1933, the Feast of the Holy Cross. Medjugorje lies in a valley susceptible to devastating hail storms. The people of the village decided to erect the Cross to ask Jesus to spare them of the destruction of the violent storms that often destroyed not only their homes, but their crops. This area of Yugoslavia is known for its superb tobacco leaves as well as its grapes used to make wine. It is no coincidence that since that September date, no further storms have occurred. This story is not merely a legend. It was confirmed to me by many people, including the priests of Medjugorje.

I looked at this Cross, and I wondered how hard it must have been to carry all the materials up there to build. I never found out how long the project took, but I'm sure the work was back breaking. At this point, I realized I was the only person on the mountain. I also realized no celestial being was there, either. I sat down to wait for my own personal, private revelation. I knew that I was going to be spoken to by someone from Heaven. I knew I was going to see something special. I knew the experience was going to be one I could take back home for everyone to enjoy.

As you probably guessed, this never happened. I did enjoy the two hours I sat there and looked out over the entire countryside and relished God's handiwork. The sight was awesome. I was at last in Medjugorje, on Cross Mountain, wondering why I was really there. Little did I know.

Meeting the Visionaries

I came down from the mountain very excited about the possibility of personally meeting one or two of the visionaries. It took me about two hours to get back to the house where I was staying, and as I went through the door, there sat my guide, waiting for me. He told me he had contacted Maria and Vicka, two of the visionaries, and both of them had granted us an audience with them, and we had to leave then to make it to their homes. I didn't care about being tired. I simply turned around and went back out the door, and my guide followed me.

As we approached the main road again, I became keenly aware of how much I missed my car. As I had mentioned before, I thought about all the other things I took for granted, also. As quick as these thoughts came into my mind, I pushed them back out. I was going to meet two children who where allegedly seeing and speaking to the Mother of God. How exciting that must be for them!

We stopped at Maria's house first. I watched as my guide climbed the steps to the second floor. He knocked on the door several times. Maria finally answered it. She stepped out to greet my guide, and after two or three minutes, he motioned to me to come up. I tried to hold my emotions in check and remain as calm as possible I walked slowly to the top of the stairs. A thousand questions flashed through my mind, and I was going to ask her every one of them. When I finally got in front of her, I did what all American people usually do: I extended my hand to shake. She just stood there and looked at me. I put my hand down. Why did I think she had to be cognizant of that American custom? I felt awkward.

My guide introduced me to her, and I stood there as Jackie Gleason used to do, with those big wide eyes and saying hum-a-na, hum-a-na, hum-a-na.

My mind went blank. I felt like a schoolboy, all of a sudden, standing in front of a girl I secretly loved. I stared at her for what seemed an eternity. My guide must have been aware of my loss for words, because he said, "Is there anything you would like to ask Maria?" Guess what I said. I told him, "NO." Both of them looked at me, as if to say, "Well, what did you come up here for?" I stupidly stuck out my hand again, and this time Maria took it and shook my hand. Somehow she gained full knowledge of that American custom instantaneously. I told my guide to take a picture of Maria and me, which he did. I thanked her again and we departed. We got to the bottom of the steps and my guide asked me why I was so nervous. I told him I didn't know. He smiled. I promised to do better at Vicka's.

MEETING VICKA

We left Maria's house and walked a very short distance to Vicka's home. Everyone who ever traveled to Medjugorje knew where Vicka lived after visiting her the first time. Her house was painted a very noticeable blue color. It became a landmark in Medjugorje.

Meeting Vicka for the first time was different from meeting the other visionaries. Vicka had a personality everyone enjoyed. She was always in a good mood. I cannot remember ever seeing her without a smile on her face. Even during the apparitions, she occasionally smiled while talking with Our Lady. I made eight trips to Medjugorje, and each one of them included either visits or private audiences with this young woman. Everyone always insisted I make sure that we stop and see her.

My guide walked through the iron gates in front of Vicka's house and knocked on her door. Much to my surprise, she answered the door. Again, I stood in awe. This time though, I was not going to be embarrassed. My guide called me over and introduced me to her. I was astounded. She stepped forward and gave me one of those European greetings. She held my hands in front of her and touched the cheeks of her face to mine. This was the way Vicka greeted everyone. It seemed so natural. I felt no embarrassment at all.

My guide told her I was from America. She turned her gaze back towards me and smiled. I nodded my head and returned the smile. There we stood, Vicka, my guide and me, smiling at each other. Although I didn't know what to do next, I felt comfortable. I asked her a few trite questions about the Blessed Mother. They were the common ones everyone asked her. We finished. I said good-bye, and we hugged again. That was my first encounter with Vicka.

I must share with you a future experience visiting Vicka's. I took a woman with cancer to visit privately with her at home. The woman, my guide and I were escorted to a balcony to wait for Vicka. A group of Italian pilgrims came to see her while we were waiting. Approximately 75 people crammed into the little courtyard in front of Vicka's house. As they were listening to an answer Vicka was giving to a question, a woman in the group started screaming. This woman's screams became so intense she appeared to be convulsing. Everyone in the group immediately turned their attention towards her. The woman was led up the stairs to where we were waiting. The priest in her group came with her. When she reached the top of the stairs, the screaming started again. This time she began throwing herself on the ground and was thrashing around. Our guide, who could speak Italian, told us she was cursing God. The old priest didn't know what to do. He even got scared. He looked at me as if to say, "Please Help." I rushed to this woman's side.

Vicka came up the stairs. The old priest, Vicka and I huddled around this woman, praying.

The woman would scream and thrash around, then become calm. We continued praying. At one point, she appeared to be calm enough to sit up. We lifted her up and sat her on a bench near us. She sat there for about five minutes. The priest backed away from her, and so did I. Vicka went back to the group and answered more questions. All of a sudden, the woman became agitated. She jumped up and rushed towards the priest in a violent rage. The anger in her face was so strong it was scary. I jumped up and ran towards the woman. The priest did not see her coming. He was startled. I grabbed this woman and almost had to wrestle her to the ground. Her rage gave her super-human strength. It was almost impossible for me to keep her in my grasp. Two other men from the group saw what was happening and came to my assistance. The three of us were able to contain this woman from harming not only the priest, but herself. She fell to the ground.

While she was lying there, we all started praying for her again. Vicka rushed up the stairs again. We huddled over this woman one more time and prayed. I placed my hands on her head and began praying prayers to St. Michael and any other Saint that would come into my mind. Vicka held the woman's wrists, closed her eyes and started praying. The priest took a crucifix from his pocket and held it in front of the woman's face. Her body tensed. She arched her back. She clenched her teeth so tightly I thought they were going to crumble in her mouth. The woman let out one more scream so loud it hurt our ears. She tensed her body very tightly again and then collapsed. She went limp. Whatever had caused the anger in this woman seemed to leave her. She lay there, on the ground, exhausted. We released our grip on her. She lay still for a moment. Tears welled up in her eyes. She placed her hands over her face, as if she was embarrassed, and continued to sob quietly. Several minutes passed and she sat up. Again we placed her on the bench. This time she sat there and slowly regained her composure.

I stepped back and looked around to find my guide and the woman who had come with me. They were both on the other side of the balcony, safely watching everything that had happened. I rejoined them, and sat down to catch my breath. Then I started to realize what had just happened. Had I just taken part in an exorcism? Was that poor woman possessed? Was she really possessed, or was she just mentally disturbed? What happened?

I found out later, from my guide, that the woman's hysteria was prompted by an abusive relationship she had with an uncle who dressed up like a priest and tormented her. For most of her childhood, he even pretended to be different saints. While in a disguise, he molested his niece. No wonder she acted deranged. No wonder she cursed God. No wonder she tried to attack the priest.

At the moment, however, I looked at this woman, and I could not believe what had just occurred. What was even more unbelievable was that I participated in what had gone on. I became numb. I sat there as the woman and her group left the area. Vicka and the priest hugged each other. He departed, making the Sign of the Cross over all of us.

Vicka's attention then focused on the woman I brought to see her. My guide explained to Vicka that the woman was dying of cancer and wanted her prayers. Vicka immediately placed her hands on the woman's head and started praying. She finished praying and we left.

An hour later, the realization of what happened on that balcony gripped me. My guide was impressed with the way I responded. So was the woman who came with me. I wasn't impressed at all with what occurred. I spent most of the day reliving the event of that morning. Occasionally I think about that woman and shudder.

Well, back to my story. We left Vicka's house and went back to our house to rest. I wanted to be at the church that evening for Mass. After Mass, I returned home for the final night in Medjugorje. I felt the sorrow of having to leave. I also felt disappointed because I didn't have a sign or a spectacular story to bring back home. I did get into the apparition room. I did meet two of the visionaries. I did have most of my expenses paid. I did get to see Rome and Medjugorje. Somehow, all that was not enough. I would not be able to tell anyone of a tremendous revelation. The links of my Rosaries had not turned to gold. I had not experienced the Miracle of the Sun. I had not smelled roses. No divine being manifested itself to me. I felt empty. I was hurt. How could the Blessed Mother do this to me? I packed for my trip to Dubrovnik in the morning. I did all that I could, and I went to bed.

The Rose

I awoke the next morning and prepared for my departure. I went to Mass the next morning. I made one last trip through all the souvenir shops, and I went back to my house. My guide was packed and ready to leave. So was I. We said our final good-byes and started for Dubrovnik.

As we left the village, I turned around to get one last look at the spires of St. James Church. Somehow, I knew that I would return. The drive to Dubrovnik took us three hours. I hate long car rides, but that trip I didn't mind; the scenery was spectacular. As we drove along, I started to feel guilty about trying to coerce Our Lady into giving me a sign. I told Her I was sorry. I thanked Her for giving me the chance just to be with Her.

We arrived in Dubrovnik, at 1:30 p.m. My guide told me he would be back at 8:00 p.m. to take me to dinner. He had arranged for another guide to take me on a tour of the old city. He told me to be ready at 3:00 p.m. The tour was over at 6:00 p.m., and I arrived back at the hotel at 6:30 p.m.

I went directly to my room to get ready for the evening. I opened the door of my room and found it to be totally dark. I searched for the switch on the wall. I couldn't find it. I stumbled through the room and made my way to the large curtains that covered one entire wall. I drew the string, and the curtains opened to give me a view of the city that was absolutely breathtaking. I stood for several minutes simply looking at the water. Dubrovnik is on the Adriatic Sea.

I went to sit down and relax. A vase sat on the coffee table with three red roses in it. In front of the vase was a card, the same type of card you see in flower arrangements. The difference was It was not signed. The card merely rested against the vase. As I looked at the flowers, my heart began to pound against my chest. Was this the Faith Experience due me? Was this the gift the Blessed Mother had for me? I had heard stories about roses and the Blessed Mother. This had never happened to me before. The story doesn't end here.

After dinner, and upon returning to the hotel, I started to pack for my trip home. I decided to take one of the flowers home with me as a memento. I pulled one of the roses out of the vase and carefully wrapped it in paper. I placed it in the side compartment of my travel bag. I hoped it would last the long trip home. I got up at 6:00 a.m. the next morning and went to the airport. The trip home took 24 hours. I arrived at my house and started to go through all the homecoming rituals. I opened windows. I watered all the plants. I even stopped to pet the dog, but that was only to keep him from mauling me. I then unpacked my bags. I went through all the compartments of every bag to make sure I got everything.

As I was putting my bags away, I remembered the rose. I reached in the bag to take it out, and much to my surprise, the rose looked as fresh as it did when I put it in the side pocket. I immediately put it in water and set the vase on the kitchen window sill. The flower stayed there for several weeks. Every morning I checked the rose for signs of stress. Finally, one morning, the rose collapsed in the grasp of my fingertips as I tested it.

Some of you are going to read this and laugh. Some of you are going to dismiss this with no thought at all. Many of you will feel the way I do. I was looking for all the bells and whistles, and I was even trying to manipulate Christ's Mother into doing what I wanted. She showed me when I least expected it, She was there all the time. I can honestly tell you that you should never let what you believe ever be changed by your, or anyone else's, mind. Remember what Jiminy Cricket said in the movie, "Pinnochio." "Always let your conscience be your guide."

The Real Beginning

Returning home was delightful. I had a beautiful experience in Yugoslavia, and had a lasting memory at home with the rose. I was on fire from the trip. Everyone who goes to Medjugorje comes back with this same enthusiasm. It manifests itself in different ways with each individual. Your prayer life changes, because you want it that way. You seek conversion within yourself. You strive to be more Christian in your attitude towards others. In fact, the change is evident to everyone. They see something new about your attitude. You still will get emotional. Your life will still have its ups and downs. The difference is you have a peacefulness within your soul. You always come back to the fact that you were touched, in some way, by the experience of Medjugorje, because it will never leave you.

My spiritual enthusiasm was running very high in my mind and heart. I wanted to share my experience with everyone. The trouble was that not everyone shared my enthusiasm. I thought that after my first trip to Medjugorje everyone was going to fall down and listen to what I had to say. That was not the case. People were interested about what was going on in Medjugorje, but most of the time their curiosity made them interact with me. People wanted to see my pictures of the trip. They kept asking me the same questions. They wanted to know about the children. They were generally caught up in the sensationalism of Medjugorje, and not the true reason the apparitions were occurring.

From the beginning, the message of Medjugorje was there is a God, and we should strive to get back to Him through Conversion, Prayer, Faith, Fasting and Peace. I was trying to do that with everyone I met. I talked to anyone who wanted to listen. I went to people's houses and spent evenings with them. I felt the urge, deep within me, to spread the messages of Medjugorje.

This struggle with what I should do was hard for me. I spent many months wrestling with the choice I was about to make. My second trip to Medjugorje, I took a group of people with me. I was happy I was going a second time, but my attitude was different. I was going back with NO anticipation of anything. I was not expecting my Rosaries to turn gold. I was not interested in seeing the Miracle of the Sun. I was going back to give thanks for the changes occurring in my life. My prayer life had deepened. I was praying more. The most important change was my heart was softening. I started to be more compassionate towards others. Without my knowing it, I was slowly turning my life over to God. I only say this in hindsight, because while I was going through it, I wasn't aware of what was taking place.

The Second Pilgrimage

The second time I went to Medjugorje, I took a fairly large group. I was excited. I was going to get a chance to give the Medjugorje experience to others. The trip started all right, until we got to Belgrade, Yugoslavia. We were only supposed to have a three-hour layover. It turned into a nine-hour stop over. We finally got to Dubrovnik, and then came the three-hour bus ride to the village. Things finally got quiet on the bus, and I had a chance to relax. At this point, I began to tell Jesus and, especially His Mother, I was coming with no expectations. I told Mary I would not coerce Her or Her Son. I was simply coming in thanksgiving, and I was happy I was bringing people with me.

Needless to say, we were all tired when we finally arrived in Medjugorje. It was 11:00 p.m. when we climbed off the bus. The guides met us, and we put everyone to bed. The group gave me no trouble. Everyone was simply happy the traveling was over. I went to sleep around 2:00 a.m.

I awoke the next morning and made sure everyone was up and functioning. They were a bit tired, but their spirits were high. I had everyone ready to board the bus when it arrived. We started off on the very short ride to the church. I was starting to get excited myself. The bus went over the small bridge and made a right turn. Then I could see the two tall spires of St. James Church. I pointed this magnificent sight out to everyone. You could only hear oohs and ahhs.

Everyone got off the bus in front of the church. The Mass was going to start in 20 minutes. As I walked towards the church, I saw a small group of people staring into the sun. I said to myself, "Paul do not go over there." As you can guess, I did. As I approached this group, I promised myself I was not going to try to experience any phenomena. I was going to church. My intent was not to see the sun dance around the sky. I looked up anyway. Much to my surprise, I was able to look directly into the sun and it didn't hurt my eyes. For almost 10 minutes, I was mesmerized by what I was seeing. The sun seemed to be pulsating. The center of the sun was blocked by a disk-shaped object, which made it possible to stare at it without it hurting my eyes. I finally stopped gazing at the sun and went into church. I did get to meet the visionaries again. I even had the privilege of being with them the second time in the apparition room. What was even more amazing was the chain links of my Rosary had turned gold before I left Medjugorje.

As I analyzed the happenings of the second trip, I realized everything I wanted on the first trip was given to me on my second trip. The big difference was I went with no expectations, and I got everything. Needless to say, I went home very pleased, and even more on fire spiritually.

I went home and immediately started planning my third pilgrimage. During the next seven months, I tried to tell everyone I met about Medjugorje. I gladly took any opportunity I was given. The whole experience became totally consuming. I was a devotee.

THE THIRD PILGRIMAGE

The third trip was the most important out of the eight I made. A year had elapsed since my first visit to Medjugorje. One thing was becoming very clear to me. The harder I tried to spread the messages, the less responsive people were becoming. Everyone wanted to see my pictures. Everyone wanted to ask me questions. Everyone's curiosity was high, but that was it. I'm not sure what I was trying to accomplish, but I wasn't having much success. Eventually, interest started to diminish, not only from the clergy, but from the people. I became discouraged. The only interest I got was from people in other states.

I published a monthly newsletter strictly devoted to the Medjugorje messages. It was reaching about 800 people all over the United States and Canada. From this newsletter I was able to put together my third pilgrimage. I had a total of 63 people. The preparations for this trip were exhaustive. Most of the 63 pilgrims were coming from other states, so the pre-planning was also extensive. Long distance phone calls. Making sure people had passports. Securing visas for everyone. Deposits and payments. Making sure I had medical histories for everyone. Making sure everyone had travel checklists. Making sure everyone had the seats they wanted on the airplanes. What amazed me was that, all of a sudden, everyone had a reason why they could not sit in the middle seats. That was my worst headache. The list goes on forever; I'm sure all of you appreciate my dilemmas. Even though the other trips were explained to you, in the previous pages, I am going to go through it one more time so you will get the full impact of this particular journey.

The big day arrived. I met those people from the Atlanta area and went with them to New York. Once in New York, my frustrations were intensified. I was like a sheep dog trying to gather and corral the herd. People were coming from San Francisco, Los Angeles, Denver, Phoenix, Chicago, Florida, New Jersey, Virginia, and New York. I even had a couple from Ottawa, Canada. I finally got them all into the departure area and boarded on to the plane. The fun was just beginning. It was 11:00 p.m. The day had started for me at 7:00 a.m. I was in my seat watching the flight attendant go through the safety explanations, and all I had to look forward to was a grueling nine-hour flight. I don't sleep well on airplanes, so collectively I got about two hours of cat naps.

We arrived in Belgrade, Yugoslavia, at 9:00 a.m. We had a three-hour layover before the short flight to Dubrovnik. We arrived in Dubrovnik and I got everyone through customs and on the bus. It was now 2:00 p.m. The bus ride to Medjugorje normally took three hours. With the stops, we finally arrived in the village at 6:00 p.m. The irritations and frustrations, the complaining, the whining, the sheer craziness all goes away when the bus crosses the little bridge and makes that right turn. Again, my breath was taken away. When directly in front of me stands the two giant spires of St. James Church, all I can do is sigh. Those of you who have been to Medjugorje know exactly what I am talking about. Somehow you feel as if you have just stepped on to sacred ground.

I was greeted by our assigned guide and a representative from the tour company, and we were all dispersed to our quarters. The tour company was great. They kept everyone within a few houses of each other, and they kept me right in the middle, where I wanted to be. Everyone unpacked and ate their first real Yugoslavian meal. The food isn't that different from American cuisine, although, it's bland, but anything hot will taste good after 40 hours of traveling.

I had everyone meet to brief them on the upcoming days. We talked about 10 minutes, and then I dismissed them. Everyone promptly got up and went back to their rooms to sleep. That was the end of the first day of the trip.

MORNING IN MEDJUGORJE

The second day started off great. I was up early and I had already made the rounds. Everyone was bright-eyed and bushy-tailed. The previous day's travel seemed to have no effect on anyone's spirits. Everyone's energy level was extremely high.

I had everyone gathered and moving towards the church by 9:00 a.m. By 9:30 we were all in front of the church. I instructed everyone to meet me at a designated place after the Mass, and I let them go on their own.

In the next half hour, the turning point of my life occurred. I mentioned I was becoming extremely discouraged with everyone's ambivalence back home. I was prepared to take the matter up with Our Lady and Jesus immediately. I boldly walked over to the stature of the Blessed Mother in the front of the church, and with no disrespect to Her or Jesus, I told them my dilemma. I also told them if I did not get their help, I was going to quit promoting Medjugorje and what it stood for. This sounds rude. It may even appear to border on blasphemy. I was just being honest. I told them I was tired of feeling as if I were beating my head against a wall. I wanted them to tell me what they wanted. It was that simple. I stood there for 25 minutes explaining my problem, and I left it in their hands. I told them they knew I had 63 people with me to contend with, and I didn't have time to discuss the matter anymore.

Although I was being bold, I was concerned Jesus might have been disturbed with my attitude. I then gave my undivided attention to the people I had with me. Jesus and Mary knew my request, and they knew I had pilgrims to attend to. I was simply going to wait for my answer. It didn't take long. It came that very evening. I got my answer in a dream.

THE DREAM

The day finally ended. I made my final rounds to each house. I left everyone to relish their first full day of Medjugorje. I finished all my tour conductor chores. I had a good meal. I took a shower, and I was going to relax in my room and be quiet. Someone gave me a book to read, and I laid down and began reading. Now you must pay attention and follow the happenings in the next 20 minutes.

A 20-watt bulb hung from the ceiling. That was my reading light. Things were still primitive in the tiny village, and modern day conveniences were at a premium. As I read, as I always do, I got sleepy. I let the book fall to my chest. That was always my clue to get up, put the light out and go to sleep. Again, I did as I always do, I went to sleep...Now here comes the dream.

My dream was very vivid. You have all had that kind of dream. I could see clearly. I could hear everything that was going on. It was one of those dreams so good that if you wake up you try, desperately, to fall back to sleep and pick up where you stopped; if it was bad, you lie there for the next four hours thanking God it was only a dream.

I must tell you I did not see or hear Jesus or Mary. They were not part of the dream. Even to this day, I have never heard or seen Jesus or Mary.

In the dream, I got up to shut the light off. As I did, I looked out the door and I could see everything as it was in real life. I could see St. James Church off to my left. I could see Cross Mountain that was directly in front of me. And I could see the other houses to the right of me. I was on a balcony of the house looking at all of this. I looked down and I could see many people below. The strange thing was that they all had different types of afflictions, diseases, ills and infirmities. I walked to the top of the stairs and went down to the lower floor. When I got to the bottom of the stairs, I did not recognize where I was. I could hear the Rosary being prayed. As the prayer continued, all those sick people kept stepping forward in front of me, and when they did, I touched them, and whatever their problem, they were healed. That seemed to go on for hours and hours. I finally stopped to take a break. I turned to go up the stairs, and when I got to the top, I was back in Medjugorje again. I went to the bathroom, and then I went to my room to rest. I laid down on the bed, and I was going to close my eyes to sleep, when I remembered that I should shut the light off. I turned in bed, in preparation to get up, and that's when I really stirred and woke up.

At that moment, I did not know where I was. I wasn't even sure if I was dreaming or not. As I opened my eyes, I realized that I was dreaming. I even got up and went to the door to look out. When I did, everything was normal. There were no people standing below the balcony. I tried to gather my thoughts. What had just happened? The dream was so real I really was surprised to see no one below the balcony. I didn't know what to do. Was that my answer from the heavens about what they wanted me to do? Was I supposed to react to this dream with enthusiasm? Was it nothing more than a sensationalistic dream that I should just forget? All those things kept running through my mind. I laid in that bed for the next four hours mulling over the dream, and I finally got so weary I got sleepy. As I closed my eyes, I told myself to get some sleep and I would think about everything tomorrow. It took a while, but I finally fell asleep.

The rest of the time in Medjugorje was filled with beauty. I do not want to go into any of that. I could write a book solely on the eight trips I took. That may be my next project...Who knows?

I got back from that trip still wondering about that dream. I was still not certain about my involvement. What was this Healing thing I saw? How was I to respond? At first, I did nothing.

Healing in Phoenix Arizona

Months went by and I put this Healing thing on a back burner. If I was supposed to heal people God would clear the way. I casually let it slip from my mind. To be honest, I forgot about it.

Several months later, I was invited to Phoenix, Arizona, to give a talk to a group about my testimony on accepting Christ. A thousand people came to the gathering. I gave my testimony, led the group in the Rosary, and I walked off to the side. A lady came up to me and asked me to pray with her. I was surprised that she would come to me, so to avoid disappointing her I prayed with her. I guess the rest of the people there thought that was what I was going to do next. So, a line started to form where I was standing. The longer I stood there praying the longer the line got.

I was praying with the people for almost an hour, when a blind woman came up to me, led by her family. I was told the woman thought she was going to get her sight back if I prayed with her. I stood there in utter amazement. I couldn't believe my ears. That woman actually thought her sight was going to be restored. I thought she was crazy.

I closed my eyes and bowed my head. I was not laying hands on people in those days. I prayed with them, but I had a hard time with this "touching" thing. During the prayer, the woman moved towards me, expecting me to touch her. I felt the movement, and when I opened my eyes, she pushed her head into my chest. I was startled. I was so surprised I almost fell over a platform I was standing in front of. I reached up to grab the woman's head, to keep from falling, not to lay my hands on her to pray. There I was clutching that woman's head, trying to keep from falling and praying at the same time. My prayer was simple. I said, "Jesus, help this woman." I quit praying and I pushed this woman away from me. I turned to catch my balance. I turned around and saw the woman had tears streaming down her face. She was crying because she could see. I felt shocked.

Everyone ran to see what was happening. I looked at the woman. She looked back at me. We hugged. She stood there thanking God for a long time. So did her family. I continued to pray with people. I stood there for the next five or six hours until everyone was prayed with. I left that evening in disbelief. What had happened? Was it real? Was I dreaming all of that? No, it was real. I wasn't dreaming. I went to the motel and collapsed on the bed and went to sleep immediately. I was exhausted.

The next day, I boarded a plane to return home. I had plenty of time to think about what happened the previous day. I still couldn't believe it. I got back home wondering whether to mention any of this to people I knew. I was embarrassed to know what they might think. I wasn't sure how to handle what had happened.

I continued to go to people's houses and show my pictures and pray the Rosary. One of those places took care of my dilemma. At the end of one of these evenings, a woman I knew came to me and asked me to pray with her. I said I would. That was becoming common-place. I wasn't even self-conscious anymore about praying in public.

The woman told me she was going into the hospital to have her breast removed because of a malignant lump. I prayed with her that evening. I told her I would continue to keep her in all my prayers for the next few days. She thanked me. Four days later, I got a call from that woman, and I was surprised how enthusiastic she sounded. I remarked to her that she sounded great for having just gone through major surgery. She informed me that the surgery never occurred. She said that after we prayed that evening, she felt different, but she couldn't explain it. She went to the hospital and went through all the pre-op testing. When an additional X-ray was taken to see if there was any further involvement, the doctors were surprised. They couldn't find a tumor. Our praying together, was the only thing that she could attribute the miracle to. Again, I listened with intensity and disbelief. It was happening again. Healing. I was praying with people and Jesus was healing them. It started to dawn on me, maybe that was what the dream I had in Medjugorje meant. Maybe that was truly what I was destined to do.

I don't have to tell you what happened after that woman's tumor disappeared. I was flooded with calls. People started calling me to pray with them. They even started coming from other states. That was the beginning of my new job, working with the Lord...the start of my **HEALING MINISTRY.**

CHAPTER 1

THE MYSTERY OF HEALING

I am going to start this book straight off by telling you I don't understand very much about healing. That's right, I have the audacity to write a book, even with the help of another person, about something I admit I don't understand very well. I can only offer you the benefit of my experience to help you forge your own way with some clarity and insight.

One thing I do understand is that healing has something to do with energy. Science has proved that our bodies have electromagnetic fields around them that can be influenced by thought, touch, and prayer. We can influence those fields from within; they can be similarly influenced by external forces. The "laying on of hands" spoken of in the Bible probably has something to do with this electromagnetic field. We are beginning to understand how our thoughts can affect this energy field, too -- our own thoughts and those of other people. Jesus even felt that with the woman who had a bleeding problem. He didn't know who touched Him, and He even asked who did it, because He said He felt the power go out of His body. (Mark 5: 27-34, Luke 8: 43-48)

Randolph Byrd, a practicing cardiologist in California, set up a study a few years ago with some heart patients at San Francisco General Hospital. The study was a randomized, double-blind trial to see if prayer affected healing. None of the 383 heart patients in the study and none of their doctors or nurses knew which patients were being prayed for daily and which were not. Findings were published in the Southern Medical Journal in 1988. Patients who received prayer needed fewer antibiotics and had fewer complications. I find that interesting.

However, when we look specifically at individual cases, sometimes the effects aren't as clear. Some people search for healing and take a very long path. They frequently report what they learned on their journey was worth the effort. Some never receive the healing they say they wanted. Some of them become bitter. Some accept their problem and say they have, in spite of their suffering, learned a great deal about life. Some receive healing quickly and they may be grateful and humble or they can get a little cocky because they think they have it all figured out. BE CAREFUL! I have been working in this area for a long time, and I can't begin to explain it all. There's no "HOW-TO." Anyone who tries to tell you there is one way to heal is oversimplifying the process. The healing power of God flows wonderfully and beautifully. It resists prediction and judgment, however.

I could tell you only the delightful, magical stories about people who have dramatic, life-changing, happy experiences with God's healing touch. That would be fine, but I want to do more than that. I want to include a few puzzling stories that make us stretch our thinking, that challenge and even trouble us, because I would prefer God's ways to be rational, logical, predictable, comfortable and easy. Sometimes we want to rush to solutions, solve the problem, get it all over with quickly and neatly. We want the quick cure, not the deeper healing. The Spirit resists the demands of our rational minds, and takes us on wondrous journeys full of adventure, danger, joy and surprise.

Consider the following examples:

A woman in South Carolina had a tumor the size of a baseball on her head that disappeared immediately with prayer and laying on of hands.

A five-year-old boy developed cancer. Many people, including myself, prayed with and for him. For five years he suffered with painful chemotherapy treatments and difficult surgeries. He would appear to get well, then the cancer would come back. Finally, the doctors stopped treatment and said he would not live more than a few months. Prayer continued. He regained vigorous health and the cancer disappeared.

A drunken man came into a church to a healing service. He was yelling and distracting the group. I went to him and prayed with him. He had had surgery on his chest, and the incision never healed properly. The wound was severe. Doctors had not been able to help him, and he was in considerable pain. During the prayer, the man's pain left him and the wound disappeared completely. The man became emotional and thankful for what happened, but the priest reports he never changed his lifestyle.

A woman has a rare auto-immune disease she has prayed to be taken from her. It has disfigured her body and impaired her ability to do many daily activities. She is 38 years old, and has had it since she was 14. She has prayed; her family and friends have prayed. She has received anointing of the sick. She has attended healing services. She has tried to understand it. She says she has surrendered her problem to God. The disease, so far, has not left her.

A woman with a history of cancer relapses. She has two children and says she wants to live. She prays. Her friends and family pray and ask God to heal her. She attends healing services. She continues to believe that the healing is possible up to the last few days of her life and asks to live at least long enough to see her children grow up, but she does not receive an extension of her life. She dies at age 48.

A boy with a broken back from a diving accident came to a healing service in a body cast. After prayer he said he felt warm all over and knew he was healed. He wanted to remove the body cast immediately, but his mother and I persuaded him to see the doctor first. The doctor was surprised to see an X-ray confirmed the boy's belief that the bones have healed. The doctor had expected him to wear the cast for several more months. The doctors had believed he would never walk normally again, but when the cast was removed, he had no restriction of movement.

Reading these stories, some of which will be covered more in depth in this and the following chapters, one might get the impression that healing can be an unpredictable, whimsical thing. You might even surmise it is "unfair." The people who appear to deserve the healings sometimes do not receive them, and the people who appear to be dirty, rotten rascals sometimes get cured mysteriously. Sometimes they don't even change their lifestyle! Is God's healing a capricious and arbitrary phenomenon? Of course not, but then why does it seem so?

Some people will try to tell you some of those people didn't receive healing because they lacked faith or had some other fault that obstructed the healing power of God. I do not believe this to be true. I know many people who have been hurt by this "faith cure" approach to healing. Although faith may be an important factor in a person's spirituality that needs attention, it isn't necessarily the only avenue to healing.

After many years of working in this field I believe healing can be truly classified as a MYSTERY. That means it cannot be fully understood through human reason or completely explained in words. It can be observed, experienced, lived, and enjoyed but, as with many things of the Spirit, it resists being made into a recipe or a "one-size-fits-all." If you are searching for healing, you are like Dorothy in the Wizard of Oz: you have a journey ahead of you to find your heart's desire, but you may come to the end of your journey only to find that your answer was always there within you, as close to you as the shoes on your feet!

As with most mysteries, a searcher can delve into its depths and discover its truths. As with all mysteries, human reason cannot unravel its meaning or harness its power. If you have chosen to seek out this mystery, if you have an open and sincere spirit, you should find it a fascinating, comforting and powerful path to the heart of God.

TERMINAL DIAGNOSIS OPENS A DOOR TO SPIRITUAL AWAKENING

Do you want to seek from God life abundantly, as He promised? Do you want to find pleasure in what can be given to you by coming to God humbly, like a child? Do you want purpose and meaning in your life? Are you ready to start the journey that will lead you to untold treasure?

I want to tell you about one of the very first dramatic healings with which I was involved. On Sunday, February 14, 1990, I was in a church celebrating a reunion of the people who had traveled with me on religious pilgrimages I had led to Medjugorje, Yugoslavia. During the festivities, a friend of mine came over to me and asked if I would go outside and pray with someone. The temperature outside was cold, and I was reluctant to venture out, so I asked my friend to tell the person to come inside. He told me that for some reason the man did not want to come into the church but urgently wanted prayer. I grew curious about who the man was and decided to go meet him.

As I started for the door, I asked my friend to tell me more. He told me the man's name was Bill, and he had just learned through a company physical that he had cancer. He hadn't told anyone in his family yet. Bill's wife didn't even know. She was out of town visiting with their daughter, who recently had given birth to their first grandchild.

I got outside and saw a man who looked distraught. He stood in a recess of one of the outside walls of the church. As I approached him with my friend, I could see another gentleman standing near him. I walked over to them, introduced myself, and shook Bill's hand. I asked him what he wanted from Jesus. He briefly disclosed the story of the company physical and even told me about the doctors' diagnosis and the grim prognosis.

I stepped forward and placed my hands on Bill's chest and back. My friend and Bill's friend did the same. As we prayed Bill burst into tears. I kept on praying.

I'd like to stop the story here for a moment and tell you that a tearful response frequently happens when I pray with people, especially when they are facing death or some deep sorrow. The tears are easy to understand. The people are focusing on some deep pain or fear, and perhaps that is the first time they are being honest with themselves and God. I have also been told the power of the Holy Spirit may be cleansing them through their tears.

If I may digress, I also want to tell you about a time when I experienced uncontrollable tears as a spiritual phenomenon. I was at a prayer service in 1983. I had gone to Jim Bakker's Heritage U.S.A. strictly out of curiosity. I had little conscious awareness of my own spiritual life then. I wandered into a service and sat down to see what it was like. After being there for about 10 or 15 minutes, for no apparent reason and with no warning, I suddenly burst into tears.

The crying lasted for almost two hours, and it stopped as fast as it started. To this day I cannot tell you why I did that, but everyone at the prayer service told me it was the power of the Holy Spirit washing my soul. I really loved that explanation, and I felt it was true.

Maybe this washing of the soul was what was happening to Bill. Perhaps the tears of fear over his new diagnosis mingled with the tears from the Holy Spirit. Outside in the cold, a great intensity held the four of us as we stood praying. Although it was a very serious moment, you'll have to permit me to wonder with some humor what people driving by must have thought seeing four grown men standing together in the cold, three of us looking as if we were holding the fourth in place as he stood there crying. I'm sure it looked as if we were mugging him.

As we prayed, I felt heat go through my hands, a sensation I frequently feel when I pray with people. Bill calmed down. We stopped praying, and without further conversation, I said good-bye to Bill and his friend. That night I couldn't get Bill out of my mind. I decided to call him. We talked for a little while, then I gave him my phone number and told him to feel free to call me any time. He seemed reluctant to have further contact with me. He thought his wife wouldn't understand having someone like me involved with a medical situation.

The following Tuesday, I got a call from Bill's wife, who said Bill was in the hospital and he wanted me to come and pray with him. When I got to his floor, Bill's wife greeted me with obvious and understandable skepticism. As I thought about the situation from her point of view, I sympathized with her. One day she was happily enjoying the arrival of her first grandchild and the next day she was being told her husband is dying of cancer. A week later she was meeting me in the hospital and possibly thinking, "Who's this nut?"

Fortunately, she was able to put her skepticism aside because Bill wanted me there. I went into the room and he was propped up in bed waiting for me. He told me he had been having some pain and decided he should go to the hospital. When I put my hands on Bill's shoulders to pray, he told me he could feel the heat in my hands.

The next day I had to leave for a business trip to Los Angeles. When I checked with my answering service for messages, they informed me I had six messages from the same person. When I heard the calls were coming from a hospital, I had the strong feeling it was Bill again. I was right.

I called Bill from L.A., and he hurriedly asked me when I would be back in Atlanta. When I told him I'd be arriving that Monday, he asked me to call him when I got in so I could come and pray with him again. I feared the worst had happened and thought he must be calling because he was still having pain or because his condition was deteriorating. I asked him with great concern how he was doing and he told me he was getting BETTER! A large node under his right arm was gone. The severe internal bleeding, diagnosed as a possible perforation of the stomach or intestines, had completely stopped. Even the doctors were amazed. I was, too! The healing business was all new to me, and I felt so privileged to be part of something so fantastic. Bill couldn't wait for me to come back to Atlanta so we could pray for the eradication of the rest of the cancer. I promised I would call him as soon as I returned.

As the plane set down on the runway in Atlanta, I was thinking about seeing Bill again. I decided to go to the hospital that very evening. My visit was brief. My main intent was to pray with him, and it only took a few minutes.

Several days later, Bill contacted me to say further tests revealed more of the cancer had disappeared. Over the next few months, through oncology and prayer, Bill was freed of his cancer. I was privileged to get to know Bill during that time, to hear stories about his life and how he believed God was reaching out to him.

Today Bill is working again at his old job, and he has returned to a normal life. He has reached and surpassed that magical "five-year mark." As any cancer patient will tell you, when cancer stays in remission for five years, the patient is put into a special category. At that point, research shows, the incidence of relapse is greatly reduced.

Bill had been to the edge of life, faced death, and come back. What a paradox that this journey into suffering gave Bill; a rebirth into new life! That is the paradox of Christianity and a recurring theme in the mystery of healing.

HOLY HUMOR

One of the things I love most about the way the Holy Spirit works, in healing and in many other spiritual avenues, is the way God's sense of humor is expressed. Some of my favorite memories from my healing services are those that made me laugh. Is there humor in heaven? I believe so. You tell me what you think. I love this story.

Don, a long-time friend of mine, arranged for me to go to several churches in his area. I had done many healing services there over the years and he frequently attended them with me. That particular church was the fifth or sixth I had visited that week, and Don was there, assisting with the service.

The parish spoke French, the church was crowded, and I was a little nervous because I do not speak French. Eighty per-cent of the people were bilingual, and even though most of them spoke English well, communication was more of an issue than usual. I have a strong Pittsburgh accent, and sometimes people have a little trouble understanding me. When a second language is added, well, sometimes it's a problem.

However, that night I was doing a superb job of enunciating my words, and I was pleased there had been no major misunderstandings. Two fellows came forward from the prayer line. They had come to the healing service together and were good friends. Their names were Pierre and Francois, two prim and proper looking young gentlemen. Francois didn't speak English very well, so Pierre had come along to interpret for him.

I asked Francois what he wanted Jesus to do for him. Pierre interpreted the petition and then he walked over and sat down in the pew to wait while I prayed with his friend. I started to pray with Francois, and as soon as I touched him, he became rigid, toppled over and hit the floor.

Most of you readers probably have heard of the phenomenon "slain in the spirit". It occurs more frequently in charismatic churches than in more traditional settings. Some of you may have witnessed it in church or on television, or even experienced it personally. It doesn't happen frequently when I pray with people, but I have seen it happen. Apparently the power of the Holy Spirit overtakes the person, and they fall down and appear to be resting. They frequently report their perception of time is distorted. Sometimes they believe they have been resting only a minute or two, when in actuality it has been much longer.

In Francois' case, when he hit the floor, he went into a very deep and relaxed resting. When Pierre saw his friend hit the floor, he became frightened. He had never seen anything of that nature. He surmised his friend was in trouble. He jumped up and hurried to Francois. Several people stopped him, and as I listened, they explained to him in beautiful-sounding French what had happened. They assured Pierre nothing was wrong and suggested he could go back and sit down, because everything would be okay in a few moments. Pierre sat down. Meanwhile, oblivious to the inconvenience and worry he was causing his friend, Francois stayed on the floor, sleeping like a baby.

Moments dragged into minutes. Minutes dragged into an hour. An agonizingly long hour dragged on further, and Pierre could only look at his buddy lying on the floor, wondering, "What the heck is going on here?" Finally, Pierre got up and knelt beside Francois and shook him gently. That was when I first became amused at the situation. My amusement was not at Francois lying on the floor. It was how Pierre looked trying to revive his friend from this deep spiritual happening. The more he shook Francois, the less responsive Francois seemed. Several people cautioned Pierre against trying to wake his friend. I could observe what was happening easily, because it was only a few feet away from where I was attending to people in the prayer line. Pierre reluctantly went back and sat down in the pew again.

Finally, Pierre became agitated. He looked as if he was going to burst. It was getting late, his friend was out cold on the floor, and it didn't look like he was going to get up any time soon. Pierre started speaking in his native tongue out loud, then he left the area. I was a bit concerned he might be fed up with his friend and about to abandon him.

Pierre returned several minutes later with a cup of water. He sprinkled drops on Francois' face. This ploy did not work. He then poured the whole cup of water on his friend's head, thoroughly drenching him. This revival technique did nothing to awaken Francois. He remained motionless.

Pierre was becoming more distressed by the minute, and I was beginning to giggle almost every time I looked their way. Other people in the service were noticing the ongoing sideshow, and although it was rather disruptive, it was serving the purpose of entertaining the people as they waited in the long line for prayer. I glanced at the distraught Pierre and the sleeping Francois. It was all that I could do to contain myself.

Finally, I saw Pierre grab Francois as he bent over, and with one last ditch effort, give him a giant swat on the cheek. In heavily accented English, he said, "Get up Francois, damn you, I want to go home." Everyone within 20 feet of the two men burst into laughter. Pierre seemed unaware of the laughter and gave Francois a second hefty swat. My friend, Don, and I decided it was time to intervene.

I found myself wondering what God thought of all this and thought that He probably was enjoying the humor of it. Nonetheless, I felt responsible to help Pierre with his dilemma, and I really didn't want the healing service to become chaotic. I suggested my friend Don try to get Francois off the floor and move him, and perhaps with Pierre's help they could get Francois out to the car. Pierre and my friend Don successfully lifted Francois, and as they did, he opened his eyes a little bit, but he didn't really wake up. They sat him up in a close by pew and watched expectantly to see what he would do. Almost immediately, Francois slumped over on his side and almost fell off the bench seat. I had to look away and especially be careful not to make eye contact with Don, or we both would have fallen to the floor laughing. I tried to be respectful of the people standing in the prayer line. I sincerely concentrated on their needs and prayed in earnest for their petitions. I don't believe the quality of the healing prayers was diminished by this ongoing drama of Francois and Pierre, but rather the event was a gift from God to help us all lighten up. Sometimes God does that.

Poor Pierre tried to explain to everyone that he had to leave because he and Francois had big plans to leave the next morning for a retreat center where they would be spending the weekend. Apparently, Pierre wanted to get back, make a few last-minute preparations for the trip and get a good night's sleep. I even saw a little humor here in the Holy Spirit's timing. We plan things like retreats, and they can be a wonderful way to reflect on our lives and seek God. One of the things we might hope for is a profound spiritual experience. Perhaps these two guys already were having a religious experience right there on the spot, but it certainly wasn't happening according to their plans. I thought to myself, "God sure does work in mysterious ways!"

I watched Pierre and Francois. They were staying with Francois' mother, and I conjured up a picture of Francois' mother waiting nervously for them, possibly getting angrier by the minute. I could see her listening to Pierre's explanation of where they had been and why he was bringing her son home in a semi-conscious condition. I could see Pierre or possibly the two of them (if Francois was sufficiently recovered by the time they got home) desperately trying to convince that woman they had been in church for almost four hours. I kept thinking about that, and I wanted so badly to give in to laughter. I thought about how my own mother would have reacted to such a story and had to stifle more laughter. I could envision Francois' mother standing at her front door, a frying pan in her hand, listening to that explanation from the two young men and saying, "Yeah, right. I'll show you resting in the spirit!" I could imagine Pierre and Francois both being bopped on the head until they fell to the floor and rested in the spirit of a different kind.

Finally, the two men were ushered from the church and I was able to regain full composure. However, the story doesn't end here. When Francois was helped into his car, he still wouldn't wake up. Don and Pierre had to lay him down in the back seat so he wouldn't slump over. Pierre, who did not have a driver's license, wound up driving the car home. My friend, Don, learned later Pierre was still unable to revive Francois when they arrived at his mother's house, so Francois spent the night in the car! The images of that evening stayed in my mind for many weeks. I thought of these two men frequently. Every time I did, I smiled.

AN INSTANTANEOUS HEALING

Some of the healings I have witnessed, like the one in this story, have been instantaneous. I want to say for the record that I do not believe that an instantaneous healing is better than a gradual one, even though I know that is the type people prefer when they make healing prayer requests. Again, the Spirit moves as it will. God works in His own time.

A good friend of mine, who asks me occasionally to pray for people, called me one day and told me of a friend of hers who had a malignant lump on her breast. Surgery was scheduled, but the woman also wanted healing prayer. My friend asked me if I would go to her home to pray with her. I told her I would, and the arrangements were made. I called Mary and asked her to go with me, thinking the woman might be more comfortable with another woman present.

We drove to her house in a lovely neighborhood. When the door opened, we saw a sweet-looking lady who welcomed us in and introduced herself as Ann. We sat down in her living room, and she began to tell us about herself.

Ann explained she was not Catholic and seemed a little reticent at the beginning, but we quickly established a common ground. If people want prayer and they are not Catholic, I will use the language and symbols of their faith. The only thing I insist upon is praying in the name of Jesus. In Ann's case, I left out references to the Blessed Mother and Saints because she was Protestant. After she explained the whole story about her illness, I asked her if she was ready to pray. I placed my hands on her shoulders and began to ask God for healing. Ann told me she could feel the heat in my hands.

I finished praying with her and I asked her how she felt. She told me she could still feel the warmth in her body. I told her to go into another room and check the lump to see if anything had changed. She left the room and was gone for some time. Then she called out to Mary and asked her to come back to the room were she was.

Mary went into the room and found the woman with a shocked expression on her face. She appeared to be feeling for the tumor and was somewhat confused about the fact that it seemed to be completely gone. When the two of them returned to the living room, we said a prayer of thanksgiving. Ann was excited, but we encouraged her to keep her appointment to see the doctor.

Our mutual friend has kept me updated on Ann. As of this writing, her tumor has not returned.

THE "RIPPLE EFFECT" OF HEALING

The following two stories illustrate what I call the "ripple effect," which must have occurred during Jesus' time, too, because one person's healing is bound to affect the people who know and love him. The healing event itself becomes real to people when they know the person who has received the healing. Skepticism can melt away when you know Aunt Sue had arthritis yesterday and today she's moving around like a 20-year-old and, well, Aunt Sue just wouldn't lie. Sometimes a physical healing has obvious repercussions in a person's personality, spirituality and emotions. Uncle John sure was a mean old cuss until he got that healing. If God can sweeten him up, maybe I ought to pay attention! It's beautiful to watch the Holy Spirit move among people, and it is one of the things I most enjoy about what I do.

I was at a church in Indiana a few years ago. A woman stepped up to me in the prayer line and said she was going to have surgery and was frightened. She had a large cyst on her waist that needed to be removed, and she was scared because it could be malignant. She was hoping, through prayer, surgery could be averted. I asked her, "Do you believe Jesus can take care of this?" She said she did believe.

She turned and placed my hand on her waist to show me where the tumor was, and I could feel a lump about the size of a golf ball. I started to pray. As I spoke her petition and asked for God's healing, I could feel the tumor get smaller and disappear. No matter how many times that happens to me, I will always be startled and delighted by the experience. I stopped praying and drew my hand away. As I did I told the woman to feel for herself what had occurred. Immediately she started yelling for her friend, who was standing farther back in the line, to come to her side. As her friend made her way toward us, all the woman could say was "It's gone...It's gone...It's gone."

The woman placed her friend's hand on the spot where the tumor had been and they shared an ecstatic moment of relief and joy. I asked the woman, as I sometimes do, if she would be willing to give her name and phone number to the person selling my tapes at the back of the church. I assured her all I wanted was to follow up with her, because I like to document some of the healings people experience - how the person feels later, what the doctor says, etc. I am glad that she did leave her name and number, because I enjoyed hearing the rest of the story.

I called the woman, whose name was Judy, about a month later. She told me she was happy about the healing she received. However, she described her visit to the doctor as less than enjoyable.

When the doctor examined her, he told her he must have made a mistake in his diagnosis. Maybe the tumor wasn't there to begin with, he said, and when Judy told him about attending a healing service, he looked at her as if she had rocks in her head. She knew what she had felt on her waist, and I knew what I had felt, so we weren't concerned about the doctor's skepticism. I should add that although most doctors tend to be skeptical about dramatic healings, most of them do believe that a person's emotional and spiritual state does affect their healing. Some doctors are supportive of healing prayer, but it sure hurts when you run into one, as this lady did, who has no belief in it whatsoever..

Judy also told me she had a relatively slight case of polio when she was in high school. The disease left her with one leg shorter than the other, loss of muscle tone in that leg, and some loss of the use of her left hand. She had experienced intense pain, especially in her back, since 1959. The pain was so bad she couldn't lie on her back, and she often cried herself to sleep at night. After the healing service, not only did the cyst disappear, but the severe back pain she had lived with all those years was gone. She saw this as a greater healing.

Judy told me the pain had been so intense it was becoming too hard to endure. She had been losing mobility and energy, cutting back on many activities and unable to devote herself to work she loved. She explained she was the vice president of an organization that worked with abused children. With the pain gone and her energy level up, she could return to her work with vigor. She also reported that being out from under constant pain had changed her personal life. Now, what about that "ripple effect" I referred to earlier? It seems this all started with Judy's friend, whom we will call Linda.

Linda read about the healing service in the newspaper and wanted to go, but she didn't want to go alone. She asked her husband, but he refused. She asked a few friends, but had no luck. Then, out of the blue, Judy called and asked Linda if, by any chance, she would be interested in going to a healing service. Linda thought that was an amazing coincidence, especially knowing Judy had not been to church in quite some time. Both were delighted to have someone to go with them, and they made their plans to attend.

One of the things that impressed Linda about the healing service was the emphasis placed on confession. Having grown up in the Catholic church with confession an important part of her tradition and upbringing, she decided to return to that sacrament. In so doing, she examined her conscience and realized she wanted help with a habit she had developed - being judgmental of others. She experienced an emotional and spiritual cleansing from her confession.

Linda admitted she thought her friend Judy was exaggerating about the severity of the tumor and its disappearance. Linda even shared with her family that she was suspicious about Judy's healing. Her family reminded her that she had asked for God's help to be less judgmental, and suggested perhaps she needed to be less critical of Judy's experience. Even Linda's husband, who had refused to come to the service with her because he didn't believe in faith healing, told her to keep an open mind. When Judy went to see her doctor and the tests showed that the tumor on her waist was gone, Linda's skepticism softened.

Linda then told me about another ripple that occurred within her family. The newspaper article she had read included my schedule of churches and dates for the week I was in her area. She noticed I would be in a church near her son and daughter-in-law. She called them and suggested they go. Her son called Linda back the next day to tell her they had gone to see me and that he had gone to confession, also. Linda was surprised, because it had been several years since he last went. He told Linda it wasn't as he remembered it as a kid. Linda was happy, because her son not only went to church that evening, but he started attending Sunday Mass again regularly.

Yet another story emerged from Linda's family. Her daughter-in-law and I prayed together that night for a lifting of grief. Her brother had died two years earlier in a car accident, and she still felt the loss deeply. Linda reported her daughter-in-law's grief did begin to lift shortly after our prayer.

I see emotional healing as a process, not like a disease or something bad to be eradicated. Grief, as well as many other emotions, is normal and healthy. Trying to bypass normal grief through prayer would not be desirable. After two years, Linda's daughter-in-law may have been ready to move out of her grief and embrace life again. Ideally, her prayer for the lifting of her grief was simply giving voice to her soul's readiness to accept her brother's death and fully enjoy her own life again. Then the Holy Spirit could move into the space she made, comfort her and give her peace.

The above story started out simply because a woman came to a healing service with a tumor on her waist. It eventually wound its way around several people in two different cities. It began with a physical healing that brought freedom from physical pain and renewed energy and vitality. Tolerance, joy, open-mindedness, and spiritual balm for long-held grief ensued. I'm sure the story is still going on today with those people. The Ripples of God's Pond.

In my next story, the ripples were fruits born of sorrow. As you undoubtedly know, God will use all life situations to touch people.

Several years ago I prayed with a young woman named Tess who had cancer. The cancer did go into remission for almost a year, but then it came back. I didn't hear about the relapse until she was dying.

I got a call from Tess's husband, who did not believe in healing prayer. He did not want Tess to be praying with me, perhaps because he feared she would be disappointed if she did not get better. He definitely was bitter toward God because his wife had cancer. I understood him. He and Tess were in their mid-thirties and had two children, 14 and 12. He couldn't understand why God allowed his wife to suffer so. Tess had been in the hospital for several weeks. She had lapsed into a coma, but had come out of it and was coherent. During that period of lucidity, she asked her husband to call me so I could come pray with her. That made the husband angry, but he complied with her wishes. He asked me if I would go to the North Carolina hospital where Tess was staying.

I knew Tess, and I wanted to be there to pray with her if I could. I decided to go, even though it was a four-hour ride. I was not looking forward to the long drive alone, but God sent me one of those little "coincidences" that day. A friend of mine whom I hadn't seen in a couple of years called and asked if we could get together. Did I have any free time? Could we go somewhere together for a day? I said, "How 'bout North Carolina?" He said, "Why not?" and the next day we set off.

The drive was enjoyable with someone along to talk to and crack jokes with, but once I got to the hospital, the mood turned serious. When I went into Tess's room, a greeting party was waiting to meet me. Tess's two children, her husband, Tess's best friend and Tess's older sister all turned their eyes to me when I walked in. Tess was lying there with her eyes closed, not moving. She was near death.

As I approached Tess, she stirred and opened her eyes. She smiled and thanked me for coming to pray with her. I prayed, and before I left, I put a scapular around her neck. For those of you who are not Catholic, a scapular is a sacramental or sacred object that Catholics believe can be an instrument to invoke God's grace and protection, especially at the time of death. I didn't stay long with Tess. She was easily exhausted. Out of respect for the family, I made my visit brief.

When I arrived home six hours later, a message from Tess's husband said she died about an hour after I left. I was extremely happy I had been able to see Tess one last time and put the scapular around her neck. Her husband later told me that just before she died, she grabbed for the scapular and seemed to derive great peace from it. He said she took her last breath clutching the scapular in one hand, and his hand in the other.

The ripple effect begins to be evident. Tess's husband was so happy at the contentment and peacefulness of her death that he was able to let go of his anger at God.

He realized that his 14-year-old daughter, however, was having a difficult time with her mother's illness and death. She didn't want to hear anything about the mercy of God. She hated God.

One day while housecleaning, the daughter came across the same scapular her mother wore at the time of her death. It was lying on the dresser. The daughter felt drawn to it and picked it up. As she held it, she was overwhelmed with tears. She told her dad as she cried she felt an assurance that her mother was happy in heaven. A calmness came over her, and the bitterness left her heart.

Tess's sister was in the room with Tess's daughter that day, and she had a revelation. She realized that although she was only 37 years old, the same thing could happen to her that happened to Tess. She felt awareness of the fragility of life. She decided to go back to church after being away for almost 15 years and reports having found a more peaceful approach to life.

So, did Jesus answer our prayers that day? Some would say it would appear He didn't, because Tess died. Another way of looking at it is that God saw a way to use the death of Tess to reach her family members. That is the way I look at it.

In my final story about the Ripple Effect, the reverberations were felt over several states. It began when a young woman came to a two-day mission service I was doing at a church in Houston. She complained of almost constant neck pain because of a problem with the cervical vertebrae. I prayed with her and she felt a complete release from the pain.

She came back the next night, this time to pray for a friend who was living in Florida. She asked, "Can you pray for someone who is not physically here with us?"

While it seems logical to the human mind that we have to go to a service, and although the Bible does tell us that "laying on of hands" is an effective form of healing prayer, in truth God's healing power cannot be limited by physical distance. "Sure," I said. "Let's pray for your friend." (Remember the Centurion in the Bible: Matthew 8: 5-10)

The woman told me the man was a good friend of hers. She said he was like a father to her. He was suffering from cancer in his bladder, and she wanted to pray for him to be cured. We lifted this man up in prayer and asked for God's healing. I never expected to hear from that woman or her friend in Florida again.

Several weeks later, I got a call from a man who introduced himself to me as George. He told me someone had come to one of my healing services and had prayed for him. He wanted to know if I might be able to recall the person; honestly, I had trouble recalling the incident, so I told him I was sorry, but I just couldn't remember. (Sometimes I pray with several hundred people in one evening, and I can't always pull up a specific person into my memory.)

George refreshed my memory about the prayer for his bladder cancer and disclosed to me that on the evening when his friend prayed for him, he felt somewhat different. He couldn't put his finger on what exactly was different at the time, but he came to believe he had received a healing. I was happy for him and invited him to tell me his story.

George went on. He told me he was diagnosed with bladder cancer in May 1993. He was living outside the U.S. at the time, and decided to go to a clinic in Florida to have the surgical procedure done. Unfortunately, when the doctors started the surgery, they discovered that the cancer had spread too far to be operable. They closed him up and told him the prognosis was not at all hopeful. They estimated he had only about 6 more months to live.

George was left with a decision. He could let things stand or he could have chemotherapy. The thought of having chemotherapy was abhorrent to him. Cancer had visited his family before. His beloved daughter had died of it at a young age. He had lost friends to the disease, also, and he remembered those people saying they regretted taking chemotherapy that had made them sick, left them with diminished quality of life, and hadn't cured them. He made a clear decision not to receive chemo and launched himself on an adventure with holistic medicine. He researched treatments and learned about where he could go to get them. He began a regimen of vitamins, herbal teas, natural serum injections, and other holistic treatments for his condition. The treatments seemed to be helping. The cancer was not spreading. However, cancer was still present in his bladder at the time his friend and I prayed for him.

When George finished telling me his story, I offered to pray with him. After we finished praying, we chatted awhile.

Several weeks later, I got another call from George telling me he had been back to see his doctor. A CT scan and MRI confirmed no visible trace of cancer was present in his bladder. George reported the doctor was amazed, and he even gave George written confirmation of the surprising turn of events.

FOR THE DOUBTING THOMAS

Although the work of God's hand is apparent in all of these stories, it is difficult to document and qualify the effect scientifically every time. We will never be able to remove skepticism about faith healing. There will always be people who either resist this kind of faith or whose intellect requires scientific proof in a way we cannot provide. There will always be doubting Thomases who love the Lord but who cannot believe in healings without proof.

Unfortunately, there will also always be people who pose as healers but who are really charlatans, who prey on the misfortune and ill health of others for money, power and their own notoriety. Those people may erode the faith of many who might otherwise believe. My research will never lead to "undeniable proof," but I am hopeful it will lead to further understanding. If you have seen the movie "Leap of Faith," you might reflect on the power of the Spirit to move even through the charlatans who pose as "healers." The Spirit of God cannot be contained.

To summarize:

**FOR THOSE WHO DO NOT BELIEVE,
NO EXPLANATION IS SUFFICIENT.**

**FOR THOSE WHO BELIEVE,
NO EXPLANATION IS NECESSARY.**

CHAPTER 2

DEVELOPING A PERSONAL RELATIONSHIP WITH GOD

Okay, I know the subject of developing a personal relationship with God has been dealt with many times before. You've probably heard your priest or ministers talk about it or read a book or article about being in a relationship with God. Personal. Intimate. Real. Something you put your SELF into. A relationship that takes effort, but one rich, deep and full.

Even though this subject is talked about in church and written about repeatedly, I believe it is so important I must add to the volumes already written. The more I read and talk to people on this subject, the more I learn about ways of being in relationship with God. Books, articles and seminars have been done on how to develop this relationship with God. The main thing I have to say is that there is no recipe for this, any more than there is a set formula for any other kind of relationship such as marriage, parenting or friendship. There are some guidelines, but as soon as the relationship becomes routine the heart can go out of it. It should be an adventure.

WHAT DO YOU MEAN AN "ADVENTUROUS" RELATIONSHIP WITH GOD?

I think this is one of the things God was talking about when he said if you are lukewarm, He will spit you out of His mouth (Rev. 3:16). Who wants a lukewarm lover? Who wants a lukewarm friend? He wants you to be passionate about life, anticipating the adventure He has for you. He wants you to come to Him like a little child (Mark 10: 15), with your arms and heart open. (Too bad this natural openness is usually lost at an early age.) I think He wants us to approach this life as a fantastic gift, and that He'll be waiting at our death to ask, "Well, what did you think of it? What was your life like? What did you learn? What was fun? What was hard for you? I loved you so much and I wanted you to have the chance to experience this unique creation of Mine. I wanted to put your soul in a body so you could more deeply know Me and yourself. There's nothing quite like it! What adventures have you had?" Can you picture His face at that moment as full of expectancy and hope?

Perhaps that could be what our judgment day will be like. I don't know, of course, but perhaps it could be going to God and being able to say we made mistakes but we learned from Him, we had sorrows, but we sought Him, we sinned, we missed the mark, but, oh, what an opportunity this life has been! What an adventure! Imagine His dismay when, upon death, a soul comes to him and says, "My life was hard. I had a lot of troubles. Yeah, there were a few good times, but I think life could have been better." Now, some would argue that life isn't meant to be pleasurable or easy because we live in a fallen world, etc. We're not talking about having it easy here. We are talking about grabbing hold of life to experience it fully, learn from it and enjoy it - not because it's easy or full of pleasures, but because it's an opportunity that should fill us with wonder and awe!

What sorrow there must be in heaven over the soul that can't get past the hardness of life and becomes closed and bitter. That state can lead to depression and despair, exactly the state of every soul where suicide occurs. Life is too hard. It's not worth it. It won't get better. The soul believes it is cut off from Grace. That is only one step from what hell is like.

BUT -- there is good news! That state of mind is an illusion! We can never be cut off from God's grace (Romans

8: 38-39), and one strong and healthy way to connect with this state of Grace is to develop a relationship with God. (You probably knew I was going to say that!)

Adventure is difficult to plan for. Have you ever tried to plan a fantastic vacation that turned out to be less than fantastic? Have you ever had an "unplanned" adventure unfold beautifully before your eyes? A priest tells a story of a secretary who worked for him who had a car breakdown in a rough section of Chicago. As she described her experience, her fear, no one helping her, clambering up a hill and climbing over a chain link fence to get to a telephone, the priest said he felt anxiety rising in him. He thought it sounded horrible. When he expressed concern for her, she surprised him by saying, "Oh, but Father, it was exhilarating!"

"What? That woman must be a fool," you might say. Maybe. Maybe she faced danger and felt afraid. Maybe she persevered with God at her side and felt the exhilaration of it all. Maybe she let go of fear a little and rode out the adventure. Maybe she learned something about herself. Maybe she learned something about God.

Okay, so what does this have to do with having a relationship with Jesus? That's a fair question. I think most of us are trying to eliminate the element of risk in our lives and that hampers a deep relationship with Christ. Think about it - life insurance, health and disability insurance, homeowner's insurance, savings accounts, IRA's, annuities, bonds...Sometimes these things get to be about reducing the risk of life. They can have the effect of a wet blanket on life as an adventure. Now, don't get upset -- there's nothing wrong with any of those things listed above, but if you put emphasis on them as a way to get security and get rid of your anxiety, you might be headed for trouble. This is probably what Jesus meant when he said it is easier for a camel to get through the eye of a needle than for a rich man to enter the kingdom of heaven (Matt. 10:24).

Remember the rich young man who went to Jesus and asked what he must do to be saved? Do you remember His reply? He said, "First, sell everything you have and then follow Me." The young man walked away sadly, "because he owned many things." What does that tell you? Is your need for security and reducing risk standing between you and your relationship with God? Can you let go of that need or are you at least willing to loosen it up a little?

Mary had an experience that taught her something about risk. This is how she explains it. "I was at a point in my life where I was very afraid. Nothing was going right. I had moved to another state to be with my nine-year-old son, Patrick, while he had a bone marrow transplant. I was worried about whether he would survive, and if he did, what the quality of his life would be in the future. I was worried about finances. I had to quit my job to care for him and his hospitalization was expected to last months. How would we pay for the costly treatment? Of course, I was also frustrated that the wonderful healing he had received two years before had not lasted. The cancer came back. I was leaning on God and praying a lot, but my fears were extreme.

The first week of treatment involved tests and radiation, so we tried to fill the afternoons with trips to the zoo, movies, whatever Patrick felt well enough to do. My mother stayed with us the entire time. She had recently retired from teaching, and her presence there for the entire four-month ordeal was a gift from God. One day, someone from the hospital gave us tickets to the circus, and the three of us decided to drive to the county fairground where the circus would be performing.

When we arrived at the fairgrounds, we were less than impressed with the little ragtag circus that awaited us. The fairgrounds were shabby, the circus didn't even have a tent, and the concessions food looked like an invitation to ptomaine poisoning. The free tickets appeared to be worth every penny we spent on them, and our enthusiasm was gone, but we shrugged our shoulders and decided to stay awhile. What else did we have to do?

My mom bought us drinks and popcorn. We walked up the rusty bleachers to a wide choice of seats. Few people were there. Three rings sat in front of the gravel path where people walked, trickling in to see the show. Behind the three rings, screens separated the performers and their equipment from our view. The ring to our far right had equipment set up for the high wire and trapeze acts. The show was about to begin.

The circus master came out and began introducing the acts. We laughed at the animal tricks - comical dogs dressed in costumes pushing baby carriages, monkeys performing like clowns and horses whirling around the ring with acrobats doing tricks on their backs. The quality of the acts surprised us, but nothing prepared us for the high wire act.

A man came out in white tights and bowed. You would have thought from his grace and presence that he was about to perform for a royal audience. And what an audience we were! Common, ordinary folks sat in those old, broken-down bleachers in the open air. We didn't look as if we deserved much of a performance, nor did we expect one, but that circus performer stood with perfect posture and bowed low. Then, with amazing energy, his head held high, he ran over to the ladder and climbed to the platform of the high wire. Then I realized there was no net below him.

I've been to quite a few circuses in my life, and they usually provide safety nets for the high wire and trapeze acts. The flashy circuses turn down the house lights and focus spotlights on the performers so the audience won't pay attention to the fact that the act is really quite safe. If you can't see the nets, the illusion of danger is created. Unlike those glittering big tops, this little circus had no spotlights and no nets under the high wire. The wire was high enough that a fall would have resulted in serious injury, or worse. My anxiety went up as I realized this was no act, this was real.

Being a rehabilitation counselor, fears about head trauma, spinal cord injuries and other physical effects of falls flashed into my mind. I thought to myself that the act shouldn't be allowed, the risk was too great, but I was powerless to stop it at that moment. I watched in awe with my mouth open and my heart racing.

The performer pranced on the wire as if he had wings. He had a twinkle in his eye, and with every turn and jump he performed, the audience gasped. The more we responded, the more he seemed to enjoy his show. He had his moment to shine, and he stunned us all.

As I watched, I was mesmerized by his mastery of fear. He seemed to be saying, "Look at me! See me strut and risk my life. I can go to the edge and look over into the abyss. I can spit in the devil's eye and laugh. I can jump back on the platform, safe for now, and hear you cheer in wonder for the chance I have taken. It is exhilarating for both of us. Do you envy me? Do you wish you could take chances, too?" The impact this event had for me was profound - one of those things that passes into your life and changes you forever. I was ready for the lesson.

I found myself thinking about that high wire act over and over through the coming months. As I spent long nights sleeping in a hospital chair, dozing for 20 or 30 minutes and then getting up to help my son when he awakened in pain, I thought about the high wire act. I felt as if I was working without a net, too. I was facing death, the death of my son. I was stretching myself to the ends of my own endurance. I prayed all the time for the strength and energy I needed as his main caretaker, but whenever I felt fear about to overtake me,

I tried to act like the man on the wire. I tried to remember I was not a victim, but an artist! The difficulty I was in was not a cruel twist of fate, but an opportunity to see what I could endure, and a test to see if I could do it with grace and finesse. I had prayed for it to be removed, and it had not been taken from us, so I had to face it head on with energy and enthusiasm. I had to find a way to dance through it and take my bow at the end."

Sound strange to you? Perhaps this is a strange way to look at adversity. Even though Mary had many tears and trials then, she kept trying to exemplify that lesson she had learned at the circus.

"You gain strength, courage and confidence by every experience in which you really stop to look fear in the face. You are able to say to yourself, 'I lived through this horror. I can take the next thing that comes along.' You must do the thing you think you cannot do." Eleanor Roosevelt

"Whosoever tries to keep his life safe will lose it, and the man who is prepared to lose his life will preserve it." Luke 17:33 (Phillips)

WHEN EVERYTHING YOU THOUGHT YOU WANTED ISN'T ENOUGH

There is an expression that says, "You can't get enough of something you don't want." What does that mean? Well, if you've put too much emphasis on material things, when your true heart's desire is in the spiritual realm, you will never get enough material "stuff" to make you happy. House, car, money, clothes, the finest schools, title and position, sumptuous food, fancy vacations -- they can be wonderful, but if you have the feeling soon after getting them that they're not enough, you may be experiencing a spiritual reaction to material "feeding." You find you have a gnawing feeling that there is something else...this isn't quite what you wanted. We're sure this is what Jesus meant when He said to seek first the kingdom of God and the material things would be taken care of (Matt. 6:33).

I am not saying to go out and sell everything you have and give it to the poor. If you feel inclined to do that, go ahead, but that's not necessary. The point is you can't enter into a trusting, adventurous relationship with Christ if you believe that your security comes from shuffling around your material world.

Give it a try. Put your concerns about your material things, or lack of them, on the shelf. Take the leap into an adventurous relationship with God! By the way, this includes everything in the material world, including your physical body. Preoccupation with your health or appearance, for example, can be equally as distracting to your spiritual growth as preoccupation with money or having enough insurance, or any other "worldly thing." Throw off those shackles and get ready for your adventure!

"Life is either a daring adventure or nothing. Security does not exist in nature, nor do the children of men as a whole experience it. Avoiding danger is no safer in the long run than exposure." Helen Keller

"SPIRITUAL TRAVEL AGENTS"

Some people find it helpful to set the stage for their adventure in a certain way. When they want to encounter Christ, they have special things they do. It could be a place they like to go to do this, a room in their house, a special chair, a chapel. It could be a state of mind or special prayers they say, such as the Rosary or a favorite chaplet. Some people don't need any of these things. There's no right or wrong way.

Remember what I said in the introduction? (What do you mean you didn't read the introduction? Well, that's why I'm saying it again.) I said this book is a general map. If you went out into the wilderness, you would want to talk to people who had been there before, wouldn't you? You'd want to know if they had a map of part of the territory, at least. They might give you a map of their journey. They might tell you where they went, there were bears, the sun was unbearably hot, and a rock slide over their path made them hurt their feet climbing over the rocks. Based on their experiences, you might take precautions to make your journey better than theirs.

What if it rains during your time on the trail and your shorts, baseball cap and sunscreen are no help at all? Their map covered only part of the area where you were going. (Well, at least you didn't get blisters on your feet, and you were on the lookout for those bears!) No one could take your journey for you or prepare you completely. At a certain point you must go and discover for yourself.

I was in the travel business for many years, and I eventually owned my own meeting-planning company. Not only would people come to me for help in planning their vacations, but business men and women also depended on me to give them answers about their trips. After I had been in the business for 10 years or so, I developed a reputation as someone who knew how to advise others so their travel plans had less risk of failure, disappointment or "unhappy surprises." I enjoyed the work, and I believe I was really good at it.

I could plan a vacation for a family and consider their likes and dislikes. I could tell a business person the "ins and outs" of a certain city, so they could move around more easily and feel in control of their trip. I even handled groups of 800 to 1,000 people, coordinating everything from flight and hotel reservations right down to meals and color coordination of decor. I took groups to foreign countries. I covered every aspect of travel you could think of, but eventually the time came when I had to stop planning things, hand people their travel documents, hope for the best, turn control over to the people taking the trips and let them launch off and make it theirs.

Consider what I am trying to tell you. You have to take everything you have learned from all the planning, all the book reading, all the tape listening, all the seminars, all the retreats, all the religious pilgrimages, all the church services and all the life experience you have under your belt and apply it to your spiritual journey. Eventually you have to get into the driver's seat and say, "I'm ready." You might not feel ready, but you have to start living what you believe. You say you believe the engine is tuned and the tank's full of gas, the tires have proper pressure and the oil and brake fluid are at the proper levels? "Yes, but what if something's wrong that I don't know about?" Well, you can't reduce all the risk. You might never take a trip if that's what you're trying to do. Come on! Turn that key! Step on the gas! Give it a whirl! I want to be your "spiritual travel agent," but I want you to take the trip and come back and tell me about it!

"We don't receive wisdom; we must discover it for ourselves after a journey that no one can take for us or spare us." Marcel Proust

TREAT GOD LIKE YOUR LOVER

Now I will try another metaphor -- a pair of lovers. When a couple is romantically involved, they might really enjoy allowing their relationship to blossom by going to an expensive restaurant and having fine food and wine. Another couple might be equally as happy going to McDonald's, and sitting in a booth and gazing into each other's eyes. Yet another couple might stay home by the fire or go hiking. Your relationship with God can be as personal and tailored to your individuality. Some people truly do find God most profoundly out in nature. Some have their deepest spiritual moments in church. Others find Him in private prayer when they are alone. Where do you find Him? Have you ever experienced Him in a special way? Do you associate that experience with a place or a ritual? Think about it.

Some people who have strong relationships with God say they experience Him mostly in everyday life. "He's always there." They talk to God as they go through their day and they find this satisfying. They feel God is ever at hand and available to them in their need or in their joy. This is another way, and it's beautiful!

When do you feel God reaching out to you, guiding you, or speaking to you? This is another personal preference. Some say they feel Him speaking by reading the Bible or by going to church. Some say He speaks to them through other people. How does He speak to you?

An interesting note here is that God can reach out to us and try to guide us, to be with us, but sometimes we don't listen. We're not in a frame of mind where He can pierce through and get our attention. Imagine yourself sitting and thinking about a close friend you long to see. You are thinking about them intently and trying to feel close to them in your mind because you love them so much. Then, that special person comes to your door and knocks. You may rush to the door and say, "I'm sorry, but I don't have time to see you right now. I am very busy. I'm thinking about you." Then you close the door in his or her face and go back to your meditation. It's a silly story, but sometimes that's the way we are with God. He is at the door knocking, but we are too busy to let Him in and be with us. We might be saying prayers or meditating and miss God altogether.

How do you find your special way to be with God, to experience your relationship with Him? Find out what works for you. Then do it with sincerity. Do it regularly and with enthusiasm. Do it with your whole Heart and you may be surprised with the results.

YOUR OWN SECRET, HOLY PLACE

I have a favorite way to feel close to Christ. I sit in front of the Tabernacle in church. Most of the time I merely sit there quietly. For non-Catholics, I will explain that the Tabernacle is the container that holds the consecrated Host that we use for communion. It typically sits on the altar in older Catholic churches, and off to the side or in a side chapel in newer churches. Catholics consider this Tabernacle to contain Christ in a very real presence, so we consider visits to the tabernacle to be visits with Jesus. I like to go on weekdays when the church is quiet. I have had many wonderful periods of time spent in meditation or simply "being" with God. I have also had some times when I have not felt the presence as much as I would have liked, but I never felt the trip was for naught. I always believed the time was well spent.

If you think about those special friendships or important relationships you have had in your life, didn't the ones that meant the most usually take time and cultivation? Think about an old friend; think about the person who was or is your "true love;" think about a teacher who, once you got to know him, became a strong influence on you. Getting to know God develops in the same way. Your relationship with Him is enlarged and enhanced over time. It is a process. This relationship is one you can grow into. The more time you put into it, the better it will be. The more you broaden your capacity to experience and enjoy the relationship, the more you will grow and develop as a person.

I thought I would include an exercise for you to try if you feel your relationship with God could use a new perspective. (Mary does this frequently) Again, this is not a formula for everyone, but a suggestion some people like and that may be a little different from what you have already tried in the form of prayer, meditation and scripture reading.

Imagine a place that has great appeal to you, a place where you feel safe and at peace. You can be alone in this place when you want to unwind. You can ask Jesus to be present with you there. You can ask Him to talk with you or sit and be with you.

Use your imagination to make this place exactly what you want it to be. It could be a quiet place to sit in a meadow. It could be at the seashore. It could be a rustic cabin or a beautiful house. It could be your own private chapel with the exact interior you would love to look at as you rest in God. What appeals to you? Fluffy clouds and angels? Balmy breezes by the ocean? Make it exactly what you want. Think about when you were a kid and you asked Santa Claus for something for Christmas. You didn't say "I really want a big, red Tonka truck, but you probably won't give it to me, so I'll settle for a matchbox car. You didn't say, "I want the Barbie camper with all the trimmings, but you'll probably just give me a Raggedy Ann." You knew exactly what you wanted and you asked for those things with full intention of getting them. When you used your imagination about your heart's desire, didn't you feel a joy inside? When did you stop believing in your dreams? Who taught you not to trust your heart?

We all have answers to those questions. Life probably threw you down at least a few times. You probably have had your heart broken at least once or twice. Kids probably made fun of you and called you names sometimes. For some of us, that happened often and childhood is a painful memory. Someone probably laughed at your dreams and ridiculed your ideas. For some of us, ridicule was a way of life and hampered us. Did any of these things ever happen to you? Did you get embarrassed? Did you become ashamed of your dreams?

Well, your Quiet Place should be that sacred place where no one can intrude to hurt it or you. It should be that place where you can take all your dreams, hopes and ideas and share them with God. I recommend you not tell anyone else about it, so it stays safe and sacred and only for you. You can call it something else if you want -- your Inner Chapel, your Sanctuary, your Heart Altar. Use your imagination! Remember this is your place, and it is only for you and God.

Do you feel as if you are wasting your time doing this? If you find you are strongly resistant to trying this exercise, then skip it. Be gentle with yourself. However, consider that spending a few minutes with God each day isn't a waste of time. The benefits you can get from closeness to Him, as well as stress reduction for your body and mind, are significant. If you try this, the time you spend will be taken because you want to, not because you have to. Who taught you time spent this way was wasted, anyway? Give yourself permission to make up your own mind about what is good for you and what is a waste. Remember also what St. Paul said in second Colossians: 6 -10.

And now just as you trusted Christ to save you, union with him. Let your roots grow down into him and draw up nourishment from Him. See that you go on growing in the Lord, and become strong and vigorous in the truth you were taught. Let your lives overflow with joy and thanksgiving for all He has done.

Don't let others spoil your faith and joy with their philosophies, their wrong and shallow answers built on men's thoughts and ideas, instead of on what Christ has said. For in Christ there is all of God in a human body. So you have everything when you have Christ, and you are filled with God through your union with Christ. He is the highest Ruler, with authority over every other power.

If you have a thirst for God, you can have a deeper relationship with Him, even if you do not consider yourself religious. I favor religion and all it implies - the church services, creeds, religious education classes, projects for the needy and pot luck dinners - but the relationship you have with God is not dependent on those things. Your relationship with God may be enhanced by these things, but the trappings of religion can feel shallow and pointless, if you do not have a vital spirit.

For clarification, the American Heritage Dictionary defines these terms as follows:

Religion - 1 : an organized system of beliefs and rituals centering on a supernatural being or beings / adherence to such a system

Church - 1 : all Christians regarded as a spiritual body 2: a building for public worship 3 : a religious service 4 : ecclesiastical power / clergy

Spirit - 1 : the animating or life-giving principle within a living being; soul 2 : the part of a human being associated with the mind and feelings as distinguished from the physical body 3 : the real sense or significance of something

If you marry someone, does that mean you will love him or her? If you get a medical degree, does that ensure you will be a good doctor? If you buy a house, will it automatically become a home? Marriage is a social institution. Medicine is a scientific system. A house is a physical structure following a floor plan. The missing ingredients that enliven and animate these systems and structures are relationship, spirit and heart.

Attending church and following a system of religious beliefs will not necessarily develop your relationship with God, even with faithful attendance and involvement in programs and committees. The way you experience church must extend beyond your presence in the pew and your memorization of the teachings. Religious beliefs and rituals are like the husk that carries the grain; they hold a valuable, life-giving essence, but you must break through the husk to find that essence. One of the ways I think about religion is as a structure, a system. I believe this system is important because it carries and contains centuries of teachings and traditions, but don't confuse the husk for the grain, or you will receive no nourishment. Love is the power that pierces this husk to unleash its raw power and heal us.

"LOVE THE LORD YOUR GOD WITH ALL YOUR HEART, WITH ALL YOUR SOUL AND WITH ALL YOUR MIND." Matthew 22: 36

CHAPTER 3

HEALING PRAYER

Pythagoras said that the most divine art was that of healing. And if the healing art is most divine, it must occupy itself with the soul as well as with the body; for no creature can be sound so long as the higher part in it is sickly.

Apollonius of Tyana

I believe prayer is an important element of the healing journey. In my services, prayer is the focus. I ask the participants to examine their lives and open themselves to God, then everyone is invited to say prayers of healing together. After the service, people who want healing prayer directly from me stand in line and I pray with each one individually. Frequently, this process takes many hours.

I often hear questions about how I pray and what is happening, physically and spiritually, when I meet with people. I can offer descriptions about the heat in my hands, the dramatic healings some people receive through these prayers, and the beautiful changes some people describe in phone calls and letters. However, the phenomenon cannot easily be explained in words.

I believe the most profound thing you can do to bring the power of healing prayer into your life is not only to go to people like myself, but to develop a daily prayer life. You will be greatly blessed if you develop your own prayer life, so you can enlarge your capacity to embrace the transforming, healing power of God -- for special needs, in crisis, and in your everyday life.

DOES PRAYER WORK?

Does prayer work? The alleged apparitions of Medjugorje address this point quite frequently. One of the strongest messages Christ's Mother gives is about prayer. She says prayer is more powerful than we can imagine, and can affect natural catastrophes and even wars. We hear that message, but do we believe it?

The world was given a tremendous example of the power of prayer in recent years. The entire world watched intently as events unfolded on January 16, 1991. Do you remember what happened on that date? The United States became involved in a war with Saudi Arabia. Where were you at 7:00 p.m. on that day? Most of the people in the United States were glued to their televisions. We watched as members of the Army Reserves were called into active duty and the war became real to everyone.

Why am I telling you this? I am using this example to illustrate the power of prayer. Americans were frightened. Everyone prayed. Members of all faiths held prayer services for the quick resolution of this war. You could drive down streets in every city and town and see signs outside churches and even businesses saying "Pray for Peace." Everyone was afraid; everyone knew someone who had a relative or friend who was going to fight in Operation Desert Storm.

The unity among groups of people was amazing. That war not only unified us for a military cause, it unified us spiritually. I saw beautiful things happen during that time. Everywhere I went, people were praying for the troops and for a peaceful end to the war. Churches built gigantic displays in their sanctuaries showing the names of men and women from their congregations fighting in the war. My church had 10 minutes of prayer at the end of every Mass on

Sunday, and many Catholic churches said Masses every Monday night for Peace.

Do you remember what happened? Sudam Hussein failed terribly in his attempt to seize territory in the Middle East. The war ended after about 100 days with the Allied Forces' casualties reaching only 150 people. This number is remarkable considering the potential loss of life. That, quick, successful conclusion was a wonderful, concrete example of the power of prayer.

THE MANY FACETS OF PRAYER

Prayer is multi-faceted. The word "prayer" is similar to the word "love," because the expressions of each offer so much variety. Think about it. You can love your spouse differently from the way you love your work. You can say you love chocolate or football or your grandmother and still have many nuances left for the feeling and expression of that emotion. Prayer also has great variety in its expression. When I looked up "prayer" in the dictionary, I noticed some interesting differences in the definitions.

prayer n. 1. a devout request or petition to a deity. 2. The act of praying, esp. to God. 3. A set form of words used for a devout request, petition, etc. 4. Spiritual and wordless communion with God. 5. A religious service. 6. Something prayed for. 7. Any earnest request.

Notice the above definition says prayer can be a "set form of words" or it can be wordless. It can be done by an individual or it can be done as a religious service. Prayer can be a petition we set up to ask for something or it can be a spiritual communion with God. That's a lot of diversity!

Lay people, religious educators and clergy say prayer has many methods of expression. There is petition, thanksgiving, praise, contrition, adoration and meditation. Books specifically on this subject list prayers for you to try or they suggest you simply talk to God and pray with your heart. If prayer comes easily to you, you probably don't need advice about how to do it -- if it's not broken, don't fix it! However, many people tell me that they have difficulty in one way or another with prayer.

Some people tell me they don't know what to say when they try to pray with the heart, so they use only rote prayers (prayers said repetitiously or mechanically). Sometimes rote prayer is all you've got. So, people can find themselves in such a state of anguish that the most comforting thing for them to do might be, simply, to whisper a prayer they have known for a long time. I say the Rosary, daily, sometimes I enjoy it, and sometimes I do not, but I say it.

Sometimes repetitious prayer yields deep spiritual fruit, as if praying this way busies the conscious mind and frees the spirit to have deep union with God. For example, I know people who pray the Rosary every day for long periods of time and they say this discipline brings them much spiritual satisfaction and joy. Others say they find rote prayer too confining and get bored with it, so they usually talk to God in their own words. As long as you are praying, I have very few suggestions about how you should or shouldn't do it. The issue with me isn't how you do it, but that you do. If the door is open, God will make a way to come in.

No, I am not going to bother you with advice about how you should pray. This is your journey, remember? You and God will find the way. The most common problem I hear isn't that people don't know how to pray, but that they don't find the time to pray, in spite of their good intentions. Prayer seems to end up in the basket with diet, exercise and all the other things we know are good for us, but frequently don't discipline ourselves to do.

The other thing I hear is that people reach a point in their prayer life when it doesn't feel good to pray. It becomes a chore. When you feel that way, you may need discernment to determine whether something has gone haywire, or if you are really experiencing a deepening of your spirituality. How so? If your prayer life is full and meaningful and has some maturity, you could probably tell me about periods of time when prayer came with difficulty. You could tell me about times when you felt spiritually dry, even though you prayed faithfully. If you have ever done any historical study on the subject of prayer, you find this spiritual condition has occurred with many people over the ages, common people and saints alike. We are told the spirit is often being fed at that time, and the flesh resists. We are told God leads us to spiritual fullness and maturity through detaching our prayer from our own desire for delightful results, even if the result we yearn for is simply delight in God!

I have experienced this phenomenon myself. I have felt frustrated and even disheartened when I have prayed fervently and not felt the spiritual high I would like nor seen the results my conscious mind desired. At other times, I have been low and tired and received an unexpected lift that gave me tremendous joy. Yes, the path of prayer is fraught with passages into the desert as well as beautiful walks beside streams of living water. With practice, I learned to approach prayer as a way of life, rather than a chore or a means of getting what I want.

If you are praying regularly, you are likely to experience both joy and frustration with the quality of the experience. Along with the quality of our prayer time, most of us struggle with a more insidious problem: Unfortunately, we have times when the prayers just don't get said.

WHY DON'T WE PRAY MORE?

What blocks our way to praying? The obstacles are often the same ones that, as I have already said, prevent us from doing other activities that are beneficial and even enjoyable to us. We have all had the experience of making a decision to do something like exercise more, eat less, or read the Bible more, only to have it get away from us somehow. Procrastination? Lack of self-discipline? Busy with other things? Working long hours?

We Americans can get a little flabby when it comes to our spiritual life also. We haven't had much adversity directed toward our religious values and practices; so many of us take our religious freedom for granted. Although we may have some restrictions on our religious freedom, such as those regarding prayer in public schools, true persecution due to religion is not common in this country. Many of us Americans have ancestors who braved dangers to come here because they wanted, among other things, freedom to practice their religion. Can we muster some enthusiasm about our manner of worshipping? Can we find a way to incorporate something like prayer into our lives so we value and cherish it? If we can't, prayer will be merely another thing we do that fills up the day. If we check it off the list to get it out of the way, we relegate it to a slot in our appointment book. If praying feels "good for you," like eating your spinach or brushing your teeth, it will only get added to the list of tasks of the day. Prayer will become one of the "must-do's" that fill up our hours yet make them feel empty and boring. Cramming your prayer time into a busy schedule can be like eating a beautiful meal when you're already late for an important meeting -- not enjoyable, and probably indigestible.

IT'S ABOUT TIME

Most Americans have a good bit of leisure time, but we tend to fill it up with activities, hobbies, or work that seems important but may not be. Yard work is a good example of this latter time-stealer. If you like yard work and find it an enjoyable form of exercise, that's fine. However, if you find yourself looking forward to the weekend and then catch yourself dreading the lawn mowing, weeding, spraying, planting, pruning, or whatever is on your "to do" list, stop in your tracks and ask yourself if there is a better way. Can you find places to simplify? When you die, do you think anyone will say, "He sure did keep his lawn beautiful?"

I am always surprised to talk with people who can afford to hire someone to take care of their house and yard, but who still manage to find themselves in the same predicament as the rest of us. I know people who buy time for themselves by hiring household help, then run their kids ragged going to soccer, ballet and gymnastics. Then they drive themselves crazy with volunteer work and social engagements. Similarly, many people who win the lottery have said it doesn't bring them what they expected. They're not cleaning their own toilets anymore, but they haven't achieved any peace either. It's not enough to say "Put God First." You've got to strip away some of the busy, panicked activity that saps the spirit. If God is constantly vying for first place against a jam-packed schedule, you're only adding another contestant to your rat race!

"Can't do it," you say? "Impossible." "I've already tried that." "You can't possibly understand how complicated my schedule is." Well, pick something. Consider this example. How many hours do you spend in a week watering houseplants? Is it worth it? Mary got rid of hers. She gave them to a friend, and she said it was a tremendous relief not to have to pick off the dead leaves, dust, mist, water and fuss over the occasional spills, bugs or diseases that turned up.

Now, don't get me wrong. Maybe you love your houseplants and find the time you spend caring for them therapeutic and relaxing. Maybe it gives you joy to see them flourish. Some folks even talk to their plants, and that's wonderful! Such activities can even be healing, but that was not the case for Mary. Her plants got to be like little silent naggers sitting around her house. I am not suggesting you give up all the things that give you pleasure, but simply think about where your time goes and contemplate how much of what you do is necessary or enjoyable. We talk a great deal about creating inner peace. Sometimes you can create peace by clearing away the SHOULDS and MUSTS that torment you.

THE TASK OF QUIETING THE MIND

Have you ever sat down to pray and found yourself doing a silent litany of your own SHOULDS and MUSTS? You could even be sitting in church where you might expect to be free from such distractions. You try to clear your mind and think spiritual thoughts. You try to feel close to God. Then it begins. "SHOULD I invite the Smith's over for dinner? They've had us over twice in the last two months." Never mind that you don't enjoy the Smith's company, you've gotten it into your head that you aren't being hospitable and living up to your social obligations, and that little thought gives you a momentary nag. Here comes another one: "I spent $500 on that exercise equipment in the basement. I MUST start using it. I MUST figure out a way to make more money. How can I add another $50 a week to my income?...That's not a lot to ask. If I had the extra cash, I wouldn't have to worry about money anymore. I MUST get my son to get his hair cut. He's looking like a Neanderthal. What do people think? I SHOULD have new siding put on the house. It will need painting soon, and I can put the money I'd spend on the painting toward the siding, and then I'll never have to paint again. I really MUST go on that diet starting tomorrow! I SHOULD check out that sale today. I MUST be sure to stop at the store on the way home and get a giant-sized box of thank-you notes so I can spend the rest of the day writing them." Am I exaggerating? Pay attention to your thoughts next time you try to pray. It would probably surprise you to see the list you could write!

A sage once said these thoughts are like birds flying through your mind. You can observe them and let them fly by, or you can invite them to make nests in your hair. In other words, those thoughts are the static of your conscious mind, your ego, trying to get you focused on extraneous details and funnel your anxiety into acceptable containers. If we take them seriously, those thoughts will consume our attention and distract us from our prayer. If we try to prevent them from entering our minds, the effort will be as useless as trying to chase birds from the sky and will have the same effect of distracting us from our prayerful, peaceful state. The best way to deal with those thoughts is to observe them quietly and let them float by. "Oh, there's that thought about cleaning my house when I get home. That's Okay. Let it go. I'm praying right now. Oh, there's that thought about how much I hate my boss. That's Okay. I know I shouldn't hate him but I do. I'm going to let that thought go right now. I want to pray." Even thoughts that might seem terrible to us are simply examples of that phenomenon. Have you ever thought, "I can't believe I just had that thought while I was praying." When that occurs, calmly observe those thoughts and let them float out of your head. If you let those things drift out of your mind, eventually your mind will become clear and you can focus on your prayer.

The deeper anxieties within all of us, our fears, conflicts, and emotional pain, are normally repressed by the conscious mind. Why? Because the thoughts are painful, and the ego's job is to organize and interpret life experiences in such a way that survival is optimized. By the way, I am using the term "ego" to mean that part of the mind that serves as a mediator between the reality of the external world and our intangible inner conflicts, feelings, drives, expectations and anxieties. The ego helps us defend against the pain of life and function in the world. This is the definition of "ego" as it is used in psychoanalytic psychology. This meaning is different from the common usage that connotes self-love or selfishness, as in "What a huge ego he has!" Protection from too much pain is part of the ego's task. When we attempt an activity such as prayer or meditation, we begin to open ourselves, to relax and invite the unconscious thoughts and impulses to take form and percolate up into our consciousness. This process can be uncomfortable, and we might feel "antsy" and not know why. It's just the ego trying to get you off the hot seat -- "Come on, here, this is a waste of time! You've got things to do!" Your conscious mind is trying to get you focused on external, physical reality to avoid the awakening of your deeper Self.

Some people give Satan all the credit for these distractions, but I think he gets more credit for human troubles than he deserves. If you want to get yourself all troubled and busy rebuking Satan during your prayer time, that can become yet another distraction! Tell God you want help if you really believe spiritual warfare is going on, but try to let go of those thoughts, too. Above all, be patient and gentle with yourself and stick with the prayer.

Remember, if those things happen to you, they are all quite normal! They happen to both Mary and me. Many people we know who are deeply spiritual still experience ego intrusions. We also have plenty of evidence that it has happened to people throughout the ages, including Saints!

Is it really important to pray? YES. Even Jesus separated

Himself from the crowds and His own disciples regularly to make time for prayer and union with the Father. (Luke 5:15, Mark 1: 35) Doesn't that tell you something?

MAKE ROOM FOR TRANSFORMING PRAYER

Are there any activities you wish you could give up but have some "SHOULD" floating around in your head keeping you bound and resentful? If you develop an attitude of looking for things to strip away, you carve out a space for Spirit to slip in and transform your life. Prayer time can become a natural part of this transformation.

I have heard people say, "My work is my prayer" and "This talk we've been having is our prayer." Sometimes that's true; I've already said at the beginning of this chapter that prayer can be many things. If you find you have NO quiet time alone with God your prayer life is probably lacking something. Examine it closely. Do you only pray when you are driving in the car or waiting in line, and then a quick "Our Father" before you go to sleep? Only on Sunday? If so, you need to clean out the clutter of things and activities in your life and make room for your spirit in prayer. The trick is to do it in such a way that you don't make prayer another one of your "shoulds." The idea is to have less anxiety, not more.

Look what Mary did. "I begun to get rid of things in my house as they break, wear out or stand in the way of my peace. I look at things I own and ask myself, "Do I own this or does it own me? How much of my time is required to maintain or clean this thing? How much do I really use this thing and enjoy it?" Slowly, my life is being transformed. I'm not saying everyone should do this, but I can tell you it has been very freeing for me to let go of nonessentials and to have more time for the important things. Like what? Like my kids. They don't care if the meal I prepared is on a lovely silver platter I spent a half hour polishing. They enjoy good, simple food and seem to appreciate a less frazzled mother who has time for them and has the energy to have fun! Who was I trying to impress? Who made the rule that I had to have a perfect house and a hot, three-course meal on the table every night? Thank God I let go of some of those chains!"

God doesn't want to pry the things of this world out of your hands so you will be miserable, and He doesn't want you to spend all your time on your knees grinding out an internal battle of the world against the spirit. He wants you to shed the things of this world like an old, heavy coat that doesn't fit anymore. It doesn't always have to be a big battle with overtones of spiritual warfare -- sometimes it can be a gentle letting go. I am not saying it's always easy, but it might be easier than you think. When you start veering away from worldly concerns, you may wonder why you ever allowed them to have a hold on you.

Why have I included this lecture about where we put our time? What does this have to do with prayer? Everything. Prayer can enhance your ability to simplify your life and strip away unnecessary activities and extraneous material things. As you shed these hindrances, you have more time to pray and more peace. I am not trying to push an ascetic lifestyle on anyone, but if you feel busy and stressed, you might consider Simplicity as an option. I'm not necessarily talking about self-denial where the desires of the flesh are forced aside in favor of the spiritual. That discipline is right for some people, but that is not what I am talking about here. My recommendation is for a gentle letting go, rather than another internal wrestling match. I am talking about freeing yourself of unimportant things so you have time for essentials, such as prayer.

I'M JUST TOO LAZY

So, you don't really have a problem finding the time to pray? You simply don't do it? (Glad you're being so honest!) Well, something made you pick up this book. Maybe you're supposed to take a look at your life and make a change. Maybe you're in need of healing, and that need is drawing you into the spiritual sphere. Whatever is tugging at you, pay attention to it!

I have another chapter titled "Patterns" that I encourage you to read and see if you find a pattern that fits you. Sometimes we can learn a great deal from our patterns of resistance. Why are you resisting prayer? Maybe you just don't want to do it. That's simple enough. If you are saying you want this, but you don't do it, I want you to delve into the possible reasons why. Maybe you are a procrastinator, a television addict, a shop-till-you-drop expert, or have some other time and energy drainer such as too much preoccupation with food, alcohol or sex? Whatever it is, your resistance tells you a great deal about yourself and may reveal an area where healing is needed. Professional counseling can be helpful when we need a place to unpack all the stuff that's bogging us down. If you can't get yourself out of a stall, or if you feel you are constantly spinning your wheels, consider talking to a professional who can help you get unstuck.

A Twelve-Step program might be in order if your obstacles to a spiritual life are in the form of addictions and compulsions like alcoholism, substance abuse, compulsive overeating, gambling, compulsive overworking, shoplifting, pornography or some other sexual addiction. You are a candidate for the offshoot program, Alanon, if a family member or loved one has that type of problem and his or her behavior has affected you. Obsessive thoughts and compulsive activities can consume our time, ruin our health, relationships and finances, and keep us distracted from spiritual growth.

What does all this talk about how we spend our time and energy have to do with healing? Why am I talking about "shoulds" and "musts" and anxieties? Well, I believe these concerns have a great deal to do with healing. The things I have discussed in this chapter are symptoms of your spiritual condition. This spiritual condition is crucial to prayer, and I believe prayer is crucial to healing.

Spiritual symptoms, such as ongoing fear, anger, depression and anxiety, are important and should not be ignored, the same as you would not continually ignore physical symptoms and pain. When you go to the doctor and tell him your stomach hurts, he will need to cover a number of things to assist you with your healing. If he simply gives you a pain killer, he may be masking an important symptom. Is your stomach pain related to your diet? Are you worried about something? Grieving? Did you do 500 sit-ups the night before? What medications are you taking? He might decide to do X-rays or take blood tests, etc.

Similarly, if your prayer life is not functioning, it may be a symptom of your spiritual condition, and I am attempting to lead you along a path that will help you explore where the real problem is.

Occasionally the "Just Do It" philosophy works, and I can tell somebody "Just Pray," and it's that simple. More often, though, it helps to examine our spiritual lives so the discipline of prayer isn't merely layered over a tormented spirit.

BUT...YOU DON'T UNDERSTAND

Okay. Now I am going to get into some of the nitty gritty I hear when I get into life transformation talks with people. All the resistance starts kicking up when I suggest to people that they control and are responsible for their own lives in how they spend their time.

"My job is too stressful." "I'm working 60 hours a week, and quitting is absolutely not an option." "My parents are aging and call me every day to run over and make a household repair, bring something from the store or drive them someplace." "I have no time for myself!" "I'm a single parent trying to raise two kids and go to college at night." "Because of my financial situation, I'm holding down two jobs." "I have no free time for myself." I hear it all.

Anyone can get in a bind. Life can really beat us up, and that's no exaggeration. If you imagine what the people in the above examples might be like, you could easily picture well-intentioned, goodhearted folks trying to do the right thing. Our circumstances can make us feel as if tight fists are wound around our necks. We can hardly breathe. We are spiritually constricted.

Periods of severe trauma, tragedy or prolonged stress can lead us toward prayer or, ironically, away from it. During those periods, we can feel abandoned by others, abandoned even by God. We have all sat in church during a difficult time of our lives, hearing the "Good News" and thinking to ourselves, "If God is so great, why is my life such a mess?" "What is He doing about it?" This is a fair question and one we ought to ask -- and answer fairly.

Most of you know the little story "Footprints," about how God carries us through troubled times when we aren't even aware of His presence. For those of you who don't know the story, here it is:

FOOTPRINTS

One night a man had a dream. He dreamed he was walking along the beach with the Lord. Across the sky flashed scenes from his life. For each scene, he noticed two sets of footprints in the sand; one belonging to him, and the other to the Lord.

When the last scene of his life flashed before him, he looked back at the footprints in the sand. He noticed that many times along the path of his life there was only one set of footprints. He also noticed that it happened at the very lowest times in his life.

This really bothered him, and he questioned the Lord about it. "Lord, you said that once I decided to follow you, you'd walk with me all the way. But I have noticed that during the most troublesome times in my life, there is only one set of footprints. I don't understand why, when I needed you the most, you would leave me."

The Lord replied, "My precious, precious child. I love you and I would never leave you. During your times of trial and suffering, when you see only one set of footprints, it was then that I carried you."

Living through difficult times is always trying, and when things get worse instead of better, we can be tempted to believe God is either not present, not interested or angry with us. Even this experience of spiritual desolation can be an opportunity for spiritual growth! Read the Psalms for examples of beautiful prayers full of torment and anguish.

Mary had a terrible experience when her youngest son was five years old. One day he was the picture of health, the next day he had a slight fever and the day after that, he was hospitalized with severe abdominal pain. The diagnosis was cancer. Listen to her tell you what happened. "I sat by his bed and prayed and could not understand what was happening. I entered a world I believed happened to other people. His condition was deteriorating rapidly. He had surgery and started chemotherapy that made him sicker. I busied myself with taking care of him. I only slept a little because he woke me up many times in the night. When he was sleeping, I often couldn't fall asleep.

One night I felt so sad, angry and pent up that I couldn't bear it anymore. I was standing in the bathroom of my home, and I cried. I began to scream at God and beg him not to let this happen to my baby. I lay on the floor and sobbed and hit the floor with my fists. Finally, I did not have the energy to keep crying. I was relaxed and went to bed and slept well.

I know if I had tried to do this at the hospital, security would probably have been called and I might have been offered a sedative. Even though the crying and wailing was painful, I believe that it was good for me. It was a release and a letting go, which opened me up so God could touch me more deeply. I was so tired of bearing up, so tired of people telling me how well I was doing when I felt completely broken inside. God knew where I was and how I was, and how difficult it was for me to surrender. The weight of my circumstances broke me, and until I was broken, God could not enter. When I finally said, "I can't do this anymore!", I felt the Holy Spirit saying "Good!" and that Spirit rushed in. I believe my letting go and sobbing was a deep and honest prayer."

PRAYER IS A MYSTERY

Prayer is an important ingredient of healing, but it is perhaps the most mysterious element of the process. Prayer is active and passive, dynamic and still. It is full of paradox that confuses us if we use our intellect to try to unravel its meaning or value. Fiery orators raise their voices about the healing power of Jesus Christ and yell, "Claim your healing!" Clergy of a gentler persuasion petition God for healing but quietly ask for patience to endure our cross if we are not healed. Confusing, isn't it?

We have all visited people in the hospital who have said, "I know there are no accidents and this is all part of God's plan. If only I could understand it, I could handle this better. Why does God want me to be here? I've prayed for Him to heal me, but I'm still here. Why?"

LOOK WITH THE EYES OF THE SPIRIT...LIKE A CHILD

When things of the spiritual dimension, such as prayer or faith, confuse us, we are usually looking at them with the eyes of the world. We are using our rational mind and ego to analyze the spiritual, and the result is confusion. Things of the spirit are always mysterious. Jesus told us to become as little children to help us avoid this spiritual pitfall. (Matt. 18: 3-4, Matt. 19: 13-14, Mark 10: 14-15, Luke 18: 16-17) How do we do that?

Your rational mind can muddle your spiritual thoughts, but your rational mind is not your enemy. It is a useful tool. It analyzes information daily that allows your survival. "The light is green for the traffic, therefore, that approaching car is not likely to stop. I will wait until the light turns red and then, cautiously, step out from the curb." This simple little example illustrates the constant processing our brains must do for us to function in this world. Think of the myriad of tasks you must complete each day, and you will surely appreciate the value of this tool.

Little children don't have to do this. Young children do not have the capability for analytical thought, and they have adults to protect them from harm as they explore their environments. They look, touch, pick up, shake, taste, and throw things without thinking about consequences. Intellectually, they can't begin to match us adults, but spiritually they are pure and uncontaminated by rational, analytical thinking. If you put a spoonful of something up to a hungry baby girl's mouth, the baby will usually open its mouth and taste whatever it is. She can't ask you what it is or if she'll like it. She won't care if the container it came in was tamper-proof or what the expiration date was on the package. She won't wonder about how many calories it has, if it's low in sodium, high in fiber or contains essential vitamins. She won't think about starving children in the world who don't have enough to eat. If she likes it, she won't plan to buy it in the future or give it up when Lent comes. She'll trust, but she won't even have to tell herself it's Okay to trust. Trust is natural. The spoon could hold ice cream, spinach or bitter poison, but the child will open her mouth to taste until she learns to do otherwise. This childlike trust delighted Jesus, because God flows through this portal with ease.

In time, the child learns, through experience, to think analytically. We adults don't have to worry about teaching children to think through their daily decisions. We don't set them down and say, "Today I'm going to teach you how to use your rational mind to decide whether to wear a sweater or a coat." Yes, we teach these things to children, but in an unconscious way. At this level, the use of the rational mind is caught, not taught. Slowly, through experience and with the guidance of parents and other adults, children learn how to analyze data in their environments that allows them to predict consequences and control many outcomes in their range of choices. Thank Goodness! This process is normal and healthy.

So how can we maintain a sense of mastery and control over what happens to us and still have the trusting nature of a little child? We can't! The rational mind resists naive trust. So why would Jesus tell us to have the faith of a child?

Take a look at what Jesus said in Matthew 18, verses 1-4:

At that time the disciples came to Jesus, asking, "Who is greatest in the Kingdom of Heaven?" So Jesus called a child, had him stand in front of them, and said, "I assure you that unless you change and become like children, you will never enter the Kingdom of Heaven. The greatest in the Kingdom of Heaven is the one who humbles himself and becomes like this child."

What did Jesus say? He said to humble ourselves and become like children. We don't think He meant to stop using our rational faculties altogether, but spiritually we should be like children. Analytical thinking leads us to compare and contrast. Who is the greatest in the Kingdom of Heaven? In the spiritual realm, this is a ridiculous question. If we are humble and childlike we don't analyze in this way. Analytical thinking leads us to do cause-and-effect problem solving that is fine for figuring out how much to spend on a new car. If we make $19,000 a year, then we really can't afford that new Mercedes. If we use it in the spiritual realm, we can't appreciate things like God's grace. "Wait a minute, God loves me and blesses me, and I don't have to do anything to earn it? Must be a catch in here somewhere!" The spiritual realm, the Kingdom of Heaven, doesn't follow the laws of cause-and-effect.

Nicodemus struggled to understand the spiritual realm with his worldly thinking when he sincerely questioned Jesus about the teaching of being born again. Jesus was teaching of a spiritual rebirth. Nicodemus was confused about what this could mean, because he knew a person "certainly cannot enter his mother's womb and be born a second time!" See what Jesus says in John 3: 6-12:

"A person is born physically of human parents, but he is born spiritually of the Spirit. Do not be surprised because I tell you that you must all be born again. The wind blows wherever it wishes; you hear the sound it makes, but you do not know where it comes from or where it is going. It is like that with everyone who is born of the Spirit."

"How can this be?" asked Nicodemus. Jesus answered, "You are a great teacher in Israel, and you don't know this? I am telling you the truth: we speak of what we know and report what we have seen, yet none of you is willing to accept our message. You do not believe me when I tell you about the things of the world; how will you ever believe me, then, when I tell you about the things of heaven?"

So if you're trying to figure out why you're lying in the hospital sick or what God wants you to learn from any other problem you have, give yourself a break. You may have a worldly lesson to learn. You may need to stop smoking, lose weight, change your negative thinking, etc., to assist your body in its healing. You may need to slow down, and your body has made you sick to get you to rest. However, if you are searching for a spiritual answer, you need to get off the cause-and-effect wagon. If you are in need of healing and you go to the spiritual realm, stop thinking about how you can get God to give you what you want or what you have to do to earn your blessing, or what lesson you're supposed to learn. Think about that child I was describing earlier, wide-eyed, leaning forward with her mouth open, anticipating the spoonful of food coming toward her. Enter the presence of God with this childlike wonder and expectancy.

St. Therese of Lisieux (1873-1897) exemplified this childlike approach to God. This book is dedicated to her because I have learned from her and have been touched by her. If you read about her life, you will discover her way to reach God, which she called the "Little Way," was to envision herself as a little girl reaching for her father's hand. Trusting and open, she reached out expecting God to care for her and provide for her. When we come to God this way, we can be free of anxiety. Therese did not ask God to explain His ways to her, she trusted. This "Little Way" is not the only way to God, but I can recommend it as a wonderful and effective way to healing, especially if you are looking for reasons, signs and causes. Let go. Jesus would be delighted:

"Consider the lilies how they grow: they toil not, they spin not: and yet I say unto you, that Solomon in all his glory was not arrayed like one of these. If then God so clothes the grass, which is today in the field, and tomorrow is cast into the oven: how much more will he clothe you, O ye of little faith? Fear not, little flock, for it is your father's good pleasure to give you the kingdom." (Luke 12: 27-28, 32)

PRAYER IS ACTIVE

Prayer implies that we do something. Obviously, if we kneel and recite prayers, pray specifically for others, lay out petitions to God, we are actively doing something. However, even if we are calming the mind to receive spiritual communion with God, we are still actively involved. If you have ever sincerely tried to meditate, you know it can be a rigorous discipline to find the time, make a quiet place and do the work of quieting the mind. Sound easy? No one who has ever meditated on a regular basis would say it is easy. Relaxing, yes. A beautiful experience, yes. But easy, NO. St. Therese used to meditate on the "Our Father" for three hours, one word at a time. This meditative, reflective prayer brought her deep communion with God and appreciation of his graces and mercies.

PRAYER HAS AN IMPACT -- IN THE WORLD AND WITHIN US

I thought of many stories I could tell you about people who received fantastic results from their meditative, quiet prayer. Scientists who received insights that led to remarkable discoveries, saints who received messages that prevented the suffering of many people, and ordinary persons who received understanding through meditative prayer that if they changed jobs or made a certain business deal or volunteered their help in a certain way, they would be doing God's will and their prayer petition would be granted.

As I considered these stories, I had one concern. I do not want you to get the idea that prayer is a device to get you what you want in "this world," in the physical realm. Prayer may lead you away from your desires and for things of this world, even if they are "good" things. Deep, contemplative prayer may lead you to indifference about the things you originally thought you wanted, because God may show you in the spiritual realm these things are not important.

Mahatma Gandi looked at prayer this way. He said: "God answers prayer in His own way, not in our way. His ways are different from those of mortals. They are therefore inscrutable. Prayer presupposes faith. No Prayer is offered up in vain. Prayer is like any other action. Prayer bears fruit, whether we realize it or not, and the fruit of sincere prayer is very much more powerful than the so-called action."

We must approach meditative prayer as purposeful and meaningful for its own sake, not as means to an end. Yes, meditative prayer will bear fruits of peace and deeper communion with God. Yes, we frequently do benefit from it by receiving more of what we want in the physical realm, such as healing of our bodies, emotions, relationships and finances. If we allow God to direct our petitions, if we concentrate on adoring and glorifying God, if we abandon our lives and fly to Him, it will be His good pleasure to give us everything we need! "Seek ye first the kingdom of God, and all these things will be added unto you." (Matthew 6: 33).

TYPES OF PRAYER

By now, I hope you realize I do not believe there is one right way to pray. Prayer is your own dialogue with God. Develop it. Nurture it. Cherish it. Be careful not to fall into the idea that because it works for you, because it was the way your family or your culture always did it, your way is the only way. I believe we should not ever condemn or belittle the way others pray or worship. I want to respect the right of others to worship God as their spirit leads them.

With that in mind, I want to say something about the way I experience prayer in my Catholic religion. I do not believe the Catholic religion is the only way to know God, but it's my way, and many of those reading this book will probably be Catholics, so bear with me, if you happen to be of another persuasion.

In the Catholic tradition, the strongest form of prayer is the Mass. I always had difficulty thinking of Mass as a form of prayer. The Mass is the time when we Catholics believe we are receiving Jesus Christ in the form of the Eucharist. This experience is a powerful way to be in Communion with Christ. It is our chance to draw quite close to God. In that context, it is powerful prayer.

PRAYER FOR OTHERS

I typically have my healing services at the conclusion of a Mass. A type of prayer I do during these services involves a favorite hymn of mine. The song is "Battle Hymn of the Republic," and before I play it, I ask everyone to think of someone they know who might be in need of healing. Then I ask them to use their index finger, of one hand, to write the name of that person (or persons) into the palm of their other hand. I invite everyone to sing the chorus of the hymn and, if they would like, to hold that palm up in the air, pointed towards heaven. I tell them they do not have to get highly emotional during the song, to close their eyes or sway, but they are welcome to let the spirit lead. (I am not personally expressive of my spirituality in this way, but I am open to it and welcome sincere spiritual expression for everybody.)

If a name does not come to mind right away, I suggest they consider family members they might be worried about, names of persons with whom they are angry or persons from whom they need forgiveness. Frequently, when people come through the prayer line that night, they mention the name of the person whose name was written on their palm. This is one of my favorite parts of the service.

In the prayer line, I see people with a variety of obvious afflictions. They stand in front of me with walkers. They might be wearing hearing aids. Some have a noticeable vision problem or they could be sitting in a wheel chair. Some stand there with no visible affliction, but if I look closely, I notice they have the furrowed brow or clenched teeth of one who lives in chronic pain. If you could hear their prayer petitions as I do, you might be surprised to hear how often the prayer that comes from their lips is not for themselves. Do you know what they say to me? After waiting in line for hours, they tell me: "I don't want anything for myself. I just want my children to come back to church. I want my grandchildren to be baptized. I'm just praying for my kids."

Do I pray with them? Of course I do. Do I empathize with their emotional pain that cuts deeper than their physical ailments? Certainly. Do I feel concern for the sense of failure they might have because they are afraid they didn't have the proper influence on their children's spirituality? Surely. Could I sympathize with the anger they might feel because they believe someone adversely influenced their child and caused them to pull away from church? Absolutely. Yes, I pray with these people and encourage them to pray for the spiritual welfare of their children. You can never go wrong when you pray for God to touch people, to heal them toward their spiritual good. Nonetheless, I want to remind you that whenever you pray against the will of another, you must be careful. Do you want people to do something against their will or do you want God to enter into their lives? Pray, dear reader, that those whom you love and have petitions for are touched by God for their highest good. God may have a better plan than yours. Tell him what you want, "I sure do want my kids to go back to the Catholic Church, Lord," but tell Him you will accept His will for them. "Lord, since you know best what their deep spiritual needs are, please heal them and guide them and help me. Do not let my opinions and comments get in the way of your work. Help me to trust You to work in their best interest." You can't go wrong with that prayer.

What about people who ask me to pray for them? I believe when someone asks me for prayer, the request is sacred. I will even try to write the person's name down on my prayer list and do my best to live up to the responsibility I have committed by saying I will intercede for them. I try to remember to tell people when I am praying for them. I even try to check with people who have asked for prayer to see how they are doing. Sometimes I go through the individual names in my prayers. Sometimes I pray for the intentions of those on the prayer list. The point here is that I take the commitment to pray for others seriously. If someone asks you for prayer and you think you might forget, say a little prayer for them as soon as you get the chance. Take your prayers seriously; they can be powerful.

THE COUPLE THAT PRAYS TOGETHER...

In the talk I give during my services, I strongly suggest husbands pray with their wives. You should see the nervous reactions I observe as people squirm in their seats. I ask the men, "When was the last time you prayed with your wife, and I don't mean only sitting in church or muttering grace over Sunday dinner?" I ask them to think about the last time they prayed with their wives before they went to bed or before they got up in the morning. I stand in the pulpit of the church and watch as the wives' elbows go flying into the sides of their men. I watch as some nervously turn to each other and give a knowing smile. I watch all this, and I wonder why couples don't pray together.

I tell husband's sitting in the pews that when they go home that evening and crawl into bed, that they should say one "Our Father," one "Hail Mary," and one "Glory Be" in thanksgiving for the woman lying next to them, even if they hate her! I usually get laughter at this point. I tell them to do it again the next night, and again the third. Then I tell them to petition Jesus for something they want in their relationship, and I tell them to watch what happens. I tell the women to do the same thing. I encourage the couples to say these three simple prayers together. How much time does that take? Anyone can do it!

I have received numerous letters and phone calls from people telling me that when they spoke those prayers with their spouse, they got results. Men and women who were married many years ago admit to me that the last time they prayed together was at the altar. They prayed that God would bless their marriage and be part of their relationship, but left the thought behind as they left the church on their wedding day. Bringing spirituality into the marriage can help revitalize and heal the relationship.

Of course, my suggestion to say three simple prayers each night is only a start. A couple could develop their prayer life together in ways that could draw them closer. They might try spontaneous prayer that could deepen their understanding of one another. Speaking aloud, in prayer, in front of another person, voicing your needs, fears, and joys, can be an intimate experience. Wouldn't it be moving to hear your spouse pray sincerely before God, just for you?

For couples with children, consider the spiritual dimension prayer can bring to your family. Praying together is a beautiful way to deepen your love and commitment to each other. Today we rarely hear of family prayer unless we count going to church and saying grace, at meals, together. If prayer is not part of your family life, you might try slipping a petition in during grace at meals or bringing your children together to pray for something special. Don't expect children to sit down and pray an entire Rosary with you, especially if they aren't used to saying long prayers. You'll lose them if you force them to pray this way. The main thing is to invite them to prayer, to show them by participating with them that we can take our fears, concerns and thanks to God. Discuss with them the way you experience God in your life. Show them by your example that you believe God loves and touches us with healing. Once they understand this to some degree, you can then ask them to pray with you for longer periods of time. You may be surprised: you might get them to pray the Rosary with you.

MEMORIZED PRAYER

Memorized prayer has a bad reputation with some people, because it can become mechanical. These prayers can be monotonous, boring and meaningless. They can also be comforting, soothing and transcendent. I am going to use the Rosary as an example to illustrate my point. Non-Catholics could substitute any form of prayer that is memorized or read rather than spontaneously expressed.

I know people who grew up saying the Rosary and disliked being forced to pray this way. They left this prayer behind, considered it old fashioned and prayed spontaneously. Yet, I know converts who are introduced to the Rosary as adults and love it. How do you explain that?

I strongly favor developing a prayer life that is full and meaningful according to the style of praying that resonates within you. I cannot tell you what words to pray. I must respect your spirit when it comes to these specifics.

I have produced a tape called the "Healing Rosary" in which each prayer is preceded by a healing petition. You may have heard of scriptural Rosaries that use Bible verses after each Hail Mary. When I pray this way, I open my heart more to my prayer and stay focused on what I am saying. However, the Rosary can also be said as a meditation focused explicitly on the Joyful, Sorrowful and Glorious Mysteries of the life of Christ. This meditation can be done so completely and intensely that the devotee experiences spiritual rapture through the repetitious prayer. If you have never disciplined your mind to pray from memory or from a prayer book, you might want to try it sometime. To discover your way, let the Holy Spirit lead you.

CONTEMPLATION

To clarify, the type of contemplation I am presenting here is a state of mystical awareness of God's being. Eastern religions have a rich tradition in this discipline. Christianity has a lesser known tradition of mysticism, but you can read many beautiful accounts of personal, mystical Christian experiences of God written by saints from the present time all the way back through the centuries. Contemplative prayer is a quiet discipline that empties us and opens us to be touched deeply by God.

I have to admit I have a difficult time with contemplative prayer. Mary finds it easier to do, and she loves it. Still, I attempt it regularly. For those of you who, like me, grew up Catholic and never learned anything about meditation or contemplation, I am going to tell you how I experience this type of prayer. I admit I am a novice. If you are more sophisticated in your prayer and meditation, you may wish to skip my story.

I usually do this exercise in church, sitting in front of the Tabernacle. There I am less distracted and more aware of the presence of Christ. I say nothing. I simply sit. I try to empty my mind, which is the point where the exercise becomes difficult for me. I allow my esoteric thoughts to float through my head, and I try to focus only on the presence of Christ, in the room. After the busy thoughts subside, I become relaxed.

When my mind is clear, I close my eyes and tell Jesus I want to sit with Him and be quiet. I do not tell Him anything else. I do not ask Him questions or seek answers. I do not even give praise or thanksgiving. I let Him know I am only His, and I only want to be with Him. Sometimes I can sit for long periods of time. Sometimes it is only a few minutes; the length of time is not important. I try to empty myself and experience being with God.

Sometimes I get so relaxed I feel as though I'm sleeping, but I know I am awake. I can hear everything going on around me. If people happen to start whispering, I can hear them. If some noise occurs outside the church, I can hear it. The main difference in my state of awareness is that I feel glued to my seat. I feel totally at peace. Some call this state a form of "resting in the spirit." Once I have quieted myself enough to reach this point, I feel blissful. When I get my conscious self out of the way, God speaks to me at a spiritual level and brings me deep healing.

You may try variations on this type of prayer, such as unspoken prayer for healing. Instead of verbally petitioning God for healing, you may enter this state and imagine God's holy, healing power soaking into your body. You may do this and imagine a loved one receiving the healing. Other examples could be to calm your frayed nerves, to rest in God's love and mercy, to release negativity, or to absorb forgiveness into your Self.

The common denominator is to allow your conscious mind to rest. Put aside your questions, petitions, irritations and stresses. Forget time. Rest. Listen. Be.

SPIRITUAL COMMUNION

Perhaps you are already aware of this lovely experience of God. I only became aware of it a few years ago. While reading about the lives of saints, I discovered many of them practiced what they called "spiritual communion" with God many times during the day.

Before this discovery, I thought of Communion only in terms of going to church and receiving the Holy Eucharist. However, you can also pray to have a spiritual communion with Christ even though you cannot be at church. Spiritual communion does not replace Holy Communion, it is just a way to ask Christ to be especially close to you.

The following prayer could be a guideline for entering into Spiritual Communion:

Dear Jesus, I mentally turn my eyes towards you in Heaven where you stand waiting for me to come to you. I love you, oh my God,

and even though I cannot receive you in Holy Communion right now, come nevertheless and visit me with your grace. Come into my heart spiritually. Purify it. Sanctify it. Render it like unto your own. Lord, I am not worthy that you should enter under my roof, but only say the word and my soul will be healed.

PETITIONS

Petitions are the stated objects of our prayer. We are bringing to God the laundry list of things we believe should occur in the world -- what we want, don't want, wish for or hope for; we bring our prayers for others, the Church, nations, and the world. We pray for the sick, hungry, and infirmed. We pray for victims of natural disasters and wars. We pray for our neighbors. We pray for the needs of relatives and church members. Children pray they perform well on tests at school and that the bully will stop pestering them on the playground. Adults pray they will have enough money to pay bills, that their boss will stop belittling them or their spouse will be more affectionate.

Mary had a serious bout with depression in her life. Listen to her tell about it. "I was self-destructing. I seriously considered committing suicide. Imagine the sadness of the people who cared about me, if I had been able to fulfill my wish! Now that I am a mother, I shudder to think about how I would feel if one of my children committed suicide, yet that is almost what I did to my family. I just didn't think about how it might affect others, because I was too overwhelmed by my own pain. I mention this here only to encourage those of you who are praying for someone you love. Take heart. My mother and grandmother prayed for me for many years. I know their prayers allowed me to reach beyond my despair and let God touch me. I know today that I received many graces and mercies by their continued prayer."

Petition prayers contain the seeds of our discontent, and some would say we should pray less in this vein and more for the will of God to prevail -- in our hearts and in the world. That advice sounds selfless and holy, doesn't it? The prayer for the will of God is a tricky one, though, and can be a path down a blind alley, a dishonest prayer away from Self. If you are sincerely able to pray in this way, resting in God's will can be supremely peaceful. The trouble is, most of us do not rest there easily. If you are wrestling with something, don't deny your pain and grit your teeth to accept God's will. Open your heart to Him and pour out your petition.

Consider the account in Genesis of Jacob's night of wrestling with the angel:

And Jacob was left alone, and there wrestled a man with him until the breaking of the day. And when he saw that he prevailed not against him, he touched the bottom of his thigh, and the hollow of Jacob's thigh was out of joint as he wrestled with him....and Jacob called...the place Peniel, "for I have seen God face to face, and my life is preserved." Genesis 32: 24-30.

This story has been cited many times to illustrate the spirit in turmoil as he wrestles with "the angel" -- the agent of God's will. Sometimes the human spirit wrestles to receive God's blessing. Sometimes we must petition our pain and torment in torrents of words to tell God the depths of our feelings.

Have you ever spent a sleepless night in physical pain? Have you ever tossed and turned with worry? The poet John Keats said, "Do you not see how necessary a world of pain and trouble is to school an intelligence and make it a soul?" Go ahead and wrestle with it! Toss and turn and cry out to God the petition from the depth of your soul!

The prayer of honest petition may be the first step toward the will of God. As you pray your petition, imagine putting your concern into God's hands. Imagine God having form and reaching out to you as you place your concern into His hands. Include in your petitions a request to have peace about your problem. Do not imagine God only wants you to pray for His will to be done. Yes, that is a perfect prayer, but we are not perfect! Be honest with Him. He promises He will open His hand and provide for you.

Catholics sometimes pray for "the intentions of Our Lady," another way to pray for the good of the world. We believe She intercedes for us, from a position of vast understanding and closeness to God. If we pray for the petitions of Her heart, we are saying we know Her desire is for our good, beyond what we even know to ask for.

Finally, if you pray a prayer of petition, I suggest you not "hedge your bets" by throwing in a disclaimer that if your petition is not granted you will "offer up your suffering" for some good cause. Catholics have a long history with redemptive suffering. If you feel called to endure suffering for another, I suggest you receive spiritual direction regarding the clarity of your purpose. Don't sit on the fence with this one!

I regularly see people who tell me they want freedom from pain. Several times I have prayed with people who told me they wanted easing of their pain, but after the prayer told me they were "redemptive sufferers." I quickly say to these people, "Then why are you praying to end your pain?" They look dismayed that I would say that to them, but I am genuinely surprised they don't think through the choice they have made when they state they are suffering redemptively. We all have three choices when it comes to prayer petitions:

a. **We may choose to suffer redemptively and offer up our suffering for the good of others**
b. **We may choose to petition God for what we want and be specific for our wants, needs and requests.**
c. **We may choose to pray for God's will and for the highest good in the situation, accepting whatever outcome God ordains.**

God knows what is in your heart. (Matt. 6: 6) You may need clarity about what you want, but you do not have to enhance God's understanding of what you are asking. Be honest with God and with yourself, and He will lead you to the peace you seek.

PRAISE AND ADORATION

Prayers of praise and adoration are among the most beautiful and memorable we can imagine. Reflect on Handel's "Messiah" or Psalm 23, or on Mary's Prayer of Praise, beloved by most Catholics, known as the "Magnificat," found in Luke 1: 46-55:

My soul doth magnify the Lord, and my spirit has rejoiced in God, my Savior. For He has regarded the low estate of his handmaiden: for behold, from henceforth all generations shall call me blessed. For He that is mighty has done to me great things; and holy is His name. And His mercy is on them that fear Him from generation to generation. He has showed strength with His arm; He has scattered the proud in the imagination of their hearts. He has put down the mighty from their seats, and exalted them of low degree. He has filled the hungry with good

things; and the rich he has sent empty away. He has helped His servant Israel, in remembrance of His mercy; As he spoke to our fathers, to Abraham and to his seed forever.

When our hearts are overflowing with praise and adoration, we feel wonder and awe before God. Our entire being resonates with joy. We can cultivate this desired state by speaking, crying, singing, and shouting prayers of praise at any time.

MEDITATION

Sources disagree about the exact way the term "meditation" is used. Some use the term interchangeably with my definition of "contemplation," already covered in this chapter. The differences in definitions do not diminish the beauty and value of these two spiritual pathways.

I use the term "meditation" to describe prayerful concentration on some aspect of God or the life and passion of Christ. In this state of reflection, we can gain a deeper understanding of God. Sometimes we gain new insights that deepen our faith, compassion and understanding.

Catholics meditate in this way when they recite the Rosary. Each decade (a section of beads representing certain prayers) is devoted to one of the 15 "mysteries" of the Life of Christ. They are the five Joyful Mysteries, the five Sorrowful Mysteries and the five Glorious Mysteries. However, we can also meditate on a verse of scripture, a favorite painting with a spiritual theme, or a scene of nature -- anything that inspires us to spiritual insight and peace.

THE TECHNIQUE IS ONLY A VEHICLE

When you discover the techniques of prayer and meditation that work for you, you will know. My only advice: allow the meditative technique to be the vehicle -- the means to an end, not the end in itself. Let the technique enhance your spiritual growth; if the technique ceases to serve you, try another method.

I will not elaborate on specific types of prayer and meditation because I would have to write an extremely long book to cover the subject. My purpose in drawing techniques of prayer and meditation into the mystery of healing is to address the importance of your personal prayer life in that mystery.

He spoke a parable unto them to this end, that men ought to always pray.... Luke 18: 1.

....Be constant in prayer. Romans 12: 12.

Pray without ceasing. 1 Thessalonians 5: 17.

CHAPTER 4

CONFIRMATION
PRAYING FOR SIGNS FROM GOD

How do we know when our prayers are answered? Sometimes it's obvious, of course, but sometimes we're not so sure. Sometimes we pray for signs, and then interpret their meaning and alter our lives accordingly. A sign is a remarkable event or symbol that reveals the will of God. Asking for signs and interpreting their meaning can be a risky business. When are we tempting God and when are we asking for His guidance? What is the difference between a desire to receive a sign from God to help us spiritually and merely wanting an easier way through our difficulties? Sometimes we might just be saying, "God, show me what to do, so I don't have to think about it or do the work of understanding and painful self-discovery."

I hear stories all the time from people who tell me they have received some sort of sign from God. I know the interpretations aren't always correct, because some of these signs contradict each other. Sometimes these signs lead people to do things they later regret. I hesitate to include this section in the book because I am talking about something that, to some people, is essential and not open to question. Some people are protective of their "words of knowledge" or other signs they believe they have received from God, and they should be. I do not intend to judge whether the signs people receive are authentic; instead I want to invite you to think about the topic because sometimes I see it cause confusion among sincere believers.

If you think you would like to have a sign from God about something, ask yourself why you want this sign. Do you want a sign to prove you are loved or special? Asking for what you really need to feel a special awareness of God's love, doesn't always have to have a sign.

If you want to be able to tell a fantastic supernatural story about receiving a vision, tell God about that. Ask Him to give you understanding of your need. Try not to ask for a sign. Is your faith weak and you want, like Thomas, a sign from above to assure you God is there? Well, go ahead and admit that in your prayer. It is really Okay. Pray foremost that your faith be strengthened.

PONDER YOUR SIGNS TO RECEIVE GOD'S MESSAGE

If you do believe you have received a sign from God, I suggest you wait and watch for the meaning of the sign to unfold. Mary had an experience before her son fell ill with cancer. She tells it this way, "I was at a healing service Paul was conducting at my church. I was a member of the healing ministry there and was helping with the service. I prayed the Rosary along with everyone else that night. The next day I saw a friend who had been at the service, and she excitedly told me that the Rosary she had been praying with had turned to gold.

I am much more open to such things now than I was then, but at the time I thought to myself, "Why would such a thing happen? Maybe she was mistaken. Maybe the links of the Rosary were gold before the healing service."

She showed me her Rosary and said, "Have you looked at yours since last night?"

I said, "No." I gave no consideration to the possibility that my Rosary would change color. I knew they were just simple wooden beads with silver links.

Later that night when I arrived home, the thought came to my mind that if it could happen to my friend, it could happen to me, too. I picked up my Rosary case off the end table next to my couch and spilled the Rosary into my hands. I couldn't believe what I saw. I sat there for a moment handling the beads and looking at the links that were inexplicably GOLD. The crucifix remained silver; the beads were still wooden; but the links that had been silver had turned a dark amber color.

I thought, "This has to be a sign from God, but what in the world could it mean?" I called Paul, whom I barely knew then, and asked him what he thought it meant.

He said, "What do you think it means?"

I told him that I was stumped. Was God trying to tell me something? Did the Blessed Mother want me to do something for her? Was I going to have an apparition? I didn't know then that this phenomenon happens fairly frequently, especially to people who go on pilgrimages. I began to feel a little bit special and my pride started working and suggesting that I might be chosen for something.

Little did I know that only a couple of weeks later, I would be sitting in a hospital with my child, holding on to that Rosary with all my strength. The experience of my son's tragic illness and the pain of watching him suffer terribly was extremely difficult for me, as it would be for any parent. I began to understand the meaning the sign had for me. It was simple. "I am here. Don't lose your faith. I was a mother, too. I watched my son suffer, and it pierced my heart with sorrow. I understand. I am with both of you. Pray." God gave me a sign not because I was chosen for something special. We are all chosen. He gave me a sign as a lifeboat over dark waters. I had to live out the meaning of the sign.

After several years, I am still deepening my understanding of this event in my life and realizing that my sign was a blessing for my difficult journey. Someone with stronger faith might not have needed such a sign, an anchor to help them hang on. I went from a slight feeling of being special to a humbling gratefulness for the gift of my sign."

HOW WILL YOU RESPOND?

Mary could have said "no" to her sign. In the depths of her pain, she could have fired the Rosary across the room and angrily rejected God for what was happening to her son. "How could a merciful God allow a child to suffer like this? He is either a cruel and merciless God who does not care, or He simply does not exist, she said. I heard those words occasionally from people I met in the hospital who did not believe in God or who had abandoned their faith. I, too, could have left my faith and gone forward with my life in another way. So, I did have something I was called to do with the sign; I had a choice to make in how I responded."

On a much higher level, the Blessed Mother did this when She was given a sign, a visit from the Angel Gabriel. Her response was, "Be it done to me as you say." (Luke 1: 38) She accepted her path and trusted God, even through extremely difficult times. Mary deepened her appreciation of Our Lady's experience as she prayed her Rosary in the hospital and reflected on her joy and suffering. When she received Her sign, the Virgin Mary did not have immediate, full understanding of the meaning of the angel's message, and she did not go around telling people about it. The first chapter of Luke says She was "deeply troubled" (Luke 1: 29) by the angel's message. In the second chapter of Luke, it is written that even after the birth of Jesus, the visits of the angels, shepherds and wise men, Mary still wondered about these events and pondered them in her heart. (Luke 2: 19) The meaning of all of this was not fully revealed to Her. She had to watch and wait and live through everything that was happening. She did not have an easy life. She still had to act on faith and trust.

WHAT DOES IT MEAN WHEN WE LONG FOR SIGNS?

Do you want a sign? Do you need a sign? What for? The Pharisees asked Jesus for a sign because they did not have faith in Him. They did not ask for healing or understanding or faith to believe as others did. They didn't think they needed changing or healing. Those who came to Him, childlike, to touch His cloak, to be healed in their time of need, received the better portion.

Then some teachers of the Law and some Pharisees spoke up. "Teacher," they said, "we want to see you perform a miracle."

"How evil and godless are the people of this day!" Jesus exclaimed. "You ask me for a miracle? No! The only miracle you will be given is the miracle of the prophet Jonah. In the same way that Jonah spent three days and nights in the big fish, so will the Son of Man spend three days and nights in the depths of the earth. On the Judgement Day the people of Nineveh will stand up and accuse you, because they turned from their sins when they heard Jonah preach; and I tell you that there is something here greater than Jonah!" Matt. 12: 38-41.

SIGNS OF THE TIMES
GOD'S SIGNS FOR THE WORLD

I want to tread into this area very carefully. First, I want to say that I firmly believe it is possible for people to receive guidance, even signs, from God. These events can be significant and I do not want to appear to be minimizing or questioning the way God works. I have the opportunity, in my work, to talk with many people all over the North American Continent. I am concerned, because I hear many stories that cause me to wonder and question what is happening.

When I travel to cities all over North America, one of the stories I hear over and over is that someone in the town, I am in, is receiving apparitions or locutions. Usually the story goes that he or she is being scrutinized to see if the messages are authentically from God, but in the meantime, the person is receiving a great deal of attention from those who want to hear what God is revealing. Sometimes these events become widely known, and many books have been written documenting these messages. If you are unfamiliar with this phenomenon, visit any Catholic bookstore and ask to see the volumes on apparitions, visions and locutions that have supposedly occurred in the past five or ten years. You may be surprised to see what a common occurrence this is.

The Catholic tradition is rich with such events, such as the appearance of the Blessed Virgin Mary at Lourdes, Fatima and Guadeloupe. These three apparition sites are probably the most well known to the general public, but most Catholics are aware that many other apparitions have been documented all over the world. The Catholic Church chooses to deal with these supernatural events by stating that such things may occur, but declares them miraculous only after much study and deliberation of the individual event is done. Some of these instances are not verified by the Catholic Church; sometimes they are declared a hoax; and sometimes the Church states that, from the evidence, it could not make a decision whether the event was a miracle. In the latter cases, the Church leaves it up to each individual's discretion to believe in the validity of the event or not. In all cases of apparitions, the Church does not declare all Catholics must accept them as true.

The Protestant Church does not lean toward such signs and apparitions as much as the Catholic Church. It tends to take prophecy and revelation directly from scripture. Even so, some Protestant denominations permit and encourage charismatic gifts such as speaking in tongues, interpretation of tongues and prophecy. Christians of both persuasions can get themselves into trouble over signs, wonders and other supernatural events. If you want to believe in such things as visions and signs, I believe it is a matter of taste, and not a must.

WHEN SIGNS CAUSE CONFUSION

There have been many times when I have heard people tell me of specific signs they received that they interpreted as messages from God. I have heard about roses given to people as signs, lights in the sky, telephone calls, voices coming out of thin air, apparitions, angels and many other phenomena. I am sure many of these people did receive these signs. However, in some of these cases, the outcome is not always what the person had hoped for. As I continue to hear from these people over months and years, I sometimes hear tales of distress and confusion.

I have friends and acquaintances who have a pat answer to this dilemma. They wrap it up in one quick sentence: "The sign was really not from God, it was from Satan." Possible? I suppose. However, giving the devil the credit may be the easy way out, and I'd like to explore the possible meanings further.

I think that if you receive some sort of sign you believe came from God, you cannot assume you understand its meaning right away. Remember the Virgin Mary "pondered these things in her heart." (Luke 2: 19) You might be wise, also to pay attention to the sign yet watch and wait as God unfolds its meaning for you. Also, remember you are not necessarily called to respond to your sign. Signs are "bread for the journey," not a first-class ticket, so you can sit back and let it all happen. If you receive a sign or what appears to be a strong answer to a prayer, maybe God is telling you He is blessing your endeavor or request but you are going to have to work at maintaining it or even making it happen. Merely receiving a sign does not mean your problems are over...they may only be starting!

I cannot overemphasize the number of times I have been told of specific signs people received, and then something went wrong. I have heard so many stories from people who tell me they received a sign from God, Jesus or Mary or one of the saints whose intercession they have requested. When I talk to them days, weeks or months later, I am surprised to hear these people say that what they believed they had received in answer to a prayer was not really what they wanted. On top of that, they question the sign they received and begin to wonder if it really was from, you guessed it, Satan.

Many people have the tendency to dismiss the power of evil and the reality of Satanic activity. I want to state for the record that I am as concerned as anyone about the presence of evil in the world today. However, I do NOT believe we serve God or ourselves well if we jump to conclusions about what Satan is up to. He is a deceiver and the author of confusion. The Bible says so. (John 1: 7, 2 Thess. 2: 9, Rev. 12: 9) Isn't confusion also a state of mind that occurs naturally when things "don't add up?" Sometimes our confusion has something to teach us, to show us we have taken a wrong turn. So don't wallow around in your confusion or spend too much time wringing your hands because something evil seems afoot. The answer is simple. Turn toward God! You can never go wrong when you do that.

Regarding the authenticity of miracles, the Bible says, in Matthew 24: 23-26 that signs and wonders are not to be trusted in and of themselves. Jesus said:

"Then, if anyone says to you, 'Look here is the Messiah!' or 'There he is! - do not believe him. For false Messiahs and false prophets will appear; they will perform great miracles and wonders in order to deceive even God's chosen people, if possible. Listen! I have told you this ahead of time."

Many other scriptures tell us supernatural events occur and that God works miracles for our welfare, so we can safely conclude the purpose of this particular scripture is to promote caution. It is not wise to attribute, automatically, any event in our lives as a direct message from God, or as the work of Satan. Stay close to God; keep your eyes focused on Him. It is not our job to take on Satan and figure out what he is doing. Christ does that for us. Don't forget human good and evil are a reality, too, and we must take responsibility for it. That's what the story of Adam and Eve is about, right? Like Adam and Eve, we don't want to take responsibility for our own choices but would rather say, "The devil caused it."

GIVE ME MY HEART'S DESIRE...AND A SIGN

I have talked to many people, men and women alike, who ask me to pray for a companion to share their lives. They long to be loved and to give their love to someone, and my heart always goes out to them. I will pray for this petition any time I am asked. However, I have heard so many stories about the winding paths of romance that I am no longer a very enthusiastic "matchmaker for God." I believe that when we fall in love or want to fall in love, we can't pin down exactly what the outcome will be, and we can't expect God to do it for us, either. Pray, but don't expect God to smooth out all the details for you.

Sometimes when I pray with people about their heart's desire, I hear from them later and they tell me they believe they received a sign. They might have been asking for the intercession of St. Therese or the Blessed Mother and they received a rose. Perhaps they were praying to Jesus and they believe they heard his voice, or they were sitting in church praying for God's help and had an overwhelming sense of peace come over them. Then they tell me they recognize this as a true sign for them to understand they will receive what they desire.

Then the BOMB is dropped. I have received further calls from many of these people. Sometimes they sob uncontrollably to the point that I cannot understand their speech. They tell me how the person that God drew into their life is the worst person who ever walked the face of the earth. I have heard people say the person who seemed to be "the one and only" for whom they had been waiting all their lives is really a low-life jerk they now hate with a passion! "He is too controlling!" "She is an unbearable nag!" "He's a total slob!" "She doesn't understand me!" Then they ask those BIG questions: "How could this have happened?" "Why did God give me a sign that has made my situation worse?" "Why do I feel as if I was better off when I was alone?"

THE MATCH MADE IN HEAVEN

A woman whom I know very well and believe to be a highly spiritual person had such an experience. I will call her "Sue."

After many years of living alone, Sue believed that she was destined to live out her life without a mate. She was 45 years old. She had been married at age 22, but that relationship ended, and she was divorced at age 29. For the next 16 years, she dated many times. She did not have any serious love relationships. Then she met Tom.

Sue was swept off her feet. She and Tom became inseparable and completely in love, but Sue was scared. She was afraid of marriage and wanted to know with some certainty that he was the man she was supposed to be with, so she wouldn't make another mistake. She decided to take the matter up with God.

Sue and Tom decided to make a retreat together. Both of them were Catholic, and they chose a small monastery in Southern California. As the retreat was ending, Sue decided to take Tom and their relationship directly to God. They were sitting together in the chapel at the monastery, basking in spiritual ecstasy. They were happy just to be together. Occasionally Tom would place his hand on Sue's and they would look lovingly into each other's eyes. It all seemed so perfect and blessed!

Sue wanted confirmation from heaven, so she looked at a statue of St. Therese about ten feet away from them and thought, "St. Therese, if God wants Tom to be with me, please let me have a sign." At that moment, Tom got up as if he had heard her prayer. He took a rose from a vase of flowers sitting in front of the statue and handed it to her. He said, "I want you to know I love you, and here is a rose to prove it."

"Hmm, prayer really works," thought Sue.

Sue turned her attention to a statue of the Blessed Mother, on a pedestal, across the aisle from where they were sitting. She decided to invoke her blessing on this situation. She silently said, "Dear Lady, if Tom is to be with me, please let me have a sign to show you approve of this relationship." Again, almost immediately after she said the prayer, Tom reached in his pocket and took out a Rosary. As he placed it in her hand, he told Sue, "This Rosary belonged to my mother. I want you to have it. I know the Blessed Mother wants this, too." Sue almost fainted! Those signs were beyond coincidence and she had to take them seriously. She almost disturbed the church service by grabbing Tom and kissing him. She had received not one but TWO signs from heaven!

A third sign came later. As she walked out of the church, Sue decided to ask for one more sign so she would have three and she would interpret that as a confirmation. For some Catholics, three is the number of signs they perceive as a definitive confirmation because this is the number of the Holy Trinity. Sue decided to wait for the opportune time to receive her third request.

Sue and Tom decided to go out to dinner and have a romantic evening. They chose a quiet restaurant on a waterfront. They were able to enjoy the sunset from their table. Everything was working out beautifully. Sue was engrossed in Tom's conversation and looked at him lovingly. She thought to herself, "God if you're listening, bless this relationship. If Tom and I are to be together, let Tom ask me to marry him." Tom looked at Sue that exact moment and said, "Sue, will you marry me?" She was delirious. All she could think of was living happily ever after. Sue left that restaurant higher than a kite.

As I listened to Sue, I became very excited for her. It seemed to me, too, she had received answers to prayer. She was finally getting something she had wanted for a long time, a person to share her life in marriage. We prayed prayers of thanksgiving together over the phone. Several weeks later, I received a wedding invitation in the mail to attend the happy union of Sue and Tom in Holy Matrimony. I attended the ceremony. It was beautiful. Both Sue and Tom looked extremely happy, and I was delighted for them.

About six months later, I received a call from Sue telling me all the horrendous things Tom was doing to her. The list was quite long. After almost an hour of conversation, I suggested we pray. I told her to keep in touch with me, and we hung up. A few weeks later, I got a call from Tom who told me his side of the story. He told me Sue had changed and was not the woman he married eight months before. An hour later, he stopped talking and we prayed. I told him if he needed to talk, he could call me again. The next time I heard from Sue, she said divorce was imminent. Six months later, the marriage officially ended.

What happened? Sue got her signs. Everything looked so good. Why did the union fall apart?

Tom and Sue blamed each other's lack of consideration as one of the main downfalls of the marriage. Sue went further by saying Satan caused it all to happen. I have heard experts in the counseling field say marriage is work, and when the honeymoon is over, the real marriage begins. It doesn't mean the relationship becomes work and drudgery, but the relationship must be lovingly cultivated and cared for. Sacrifices must be made. Communication must be developed. Experts would say Tom and Sue put unrealistic and immature expectations on their marriage. Perhaps they expected their marriage always to be as exciting as their courtship.

Let's look at the marriage of Tom and Sue, what they experienced in their relationship and what they believed about each other and their signs. How were they led to believe they should be together forever? Tom and Sue were committed to each other and wanted to be married. They claimed they experienced confirmation about their marriage from God. They were in love. What went wrong?

Without being too hard on Tom and Sue, I want to say I believe that God may give us direction, guidance and even signs, but because we are human, we sometimes mess things up. I DO NOT want to blame Tom or Sue. We are all human and capable of falling into troubles, especially in relationships. Perhaps the divine message was not indicating Tom and Sue would go off and live happily ever after, but that if they took advantage of the opportunities provided in a marriage, they might have important work to do in relationship to each other. They might have missed an opportunity to receive some important learning and develop parts of themselves that could only be developed and tested in relationship with another, including the day-to-day battle of wills that occur in jockeying wants, needs, schedules and chores. Perhaps that potential was seen with the Divine Eye, and God said, "Go ahead." Of course, the possibility also exists that they misinterpreted a series of coincidences as signs from God. After all, nothing supernatural occurred, and the events they called signs could have been rationally explained away.

In the case of Sue and Tom, I found out that Tom wanted children. Sue didn't. She felt she was past her childbearing years. Sue said she never saw Tom's temper until they lived together. Tom didn't like the way Sue accused him of being under the influence of Satan because he didn't do what she wanted him to do. Sue thought Tom's work was dumb and boring; Tom never understood how Sue could be so devoted to her work and resented the amount of time she gave to her career. They never talked about these subjects before marriage. Disagreement led to disillusionment and resentment.

I don't believe heavenly guidance is always toward the sweet and easy road, although it is always toward our highest good. Although my interpretation is not the only one possible, perhaps the potential of Tom and Sue's union was for their highest spiritual good, and they each mistakenly thought the other person was supposed to gratify them and to fill their needs. Some powerful and strong marriages have been between people who argue with passion and love with passion. Sparks fly. (I'm not talking about abusive relationships, but impassioned ones.) I don't know what exactly went wrong for Tom and Sue because I wasn't there with them to see for myself. I heard everything second hand. However, I can be sure in saying that if this couple thought receiving a sign was a way to avoid the pain, risk and work of being in a marriage, they had the wrong idea. Maybe you have another interpretation. What do you think?

BY WHAT SIGNS DO YOU CHART YOUR OWN COURSE?

What are your signs? Do you believe in them or consider them superstition? Have they been reliable and helpful? How do your beliefs fit in with your signs? By what stars do you chart the course of your life? Have they led you toward courage, inspiration, and healing?

I tend to be slightly wary of signs and wonders, and I don't ever use such symbols or events as the only means of knowing the will of God. If I think I might have had a sign from God that I have difficulty understanding, I always ponder and pray about it before I act. Then I measure it against scripture, time-tested teachings, common sense and previous life experience. Frequently, we humans know what we should do, but run around looking for signs or seeking advice because we don't want to accept what we already know. Sometimes we want to have our confusion cleared up without putting forth any effort. Sometimes we're bored and want a spiritual "kick."

I started going to Medjugorge in the 1980s. I was struck by the simplicity of the Blessed Mother's messages. I realized these messages were nothing new. I began to see we already had the knowledge of how to live in God's will. She was only making this point more evident.

For a long time I was spiritually stimulated by the sensational events going on in Medjugorge. I was amazed by the visionaries' stories, the descriptions of the beautiful Blessed Lady and the many reports of miraculous events occurring there. I read everything I could find on the subject, and I finally made eight pilgrimages to Yugoslavia.

Eventually, I had to get down to the business of living out the messages apart from the heightened intensity of the Medjugorge experience. On what basis would I continue to chase after more miraculous signs? Would making any more pilgrimages improve the way I applied the teachings of Christ to my life? Was I running after more signs to avoid the real challenges of my life with Christ, those being love, prayer, forgiveness and service to others? I already knew about those challenges, and I knew I fell short. Talking about the latest "message" of the Virgin Mary was more fun than putting it into practice. Consider this irony: Her messages were usually about how important it was to live out your Christian faith!

If you believe you want or need a sign, go to the source of your need. Ask God to provide for your need and heal you, then watch for His signs as they present themselves. Do not expect God to send you signs to remove your responsibility to think, trust and act. Use signs from God as you would use signs along a roadway. They will direct your ways and light your path. Remember you are on a journey.

CHAPTER 5

FAITH, GUILT AND FORGIVENESS

"Daughter, your faith has made you well." Mark 5:3

I could write an entire book on faith, because it is so important to the subject of healing. It was also important to Jesus in the days when He walked on the earth and prayed with people to heal them. If you read those stories in the Bible about Jesus healing, a common theme comes through. Over and over, He tells people their own faith healed them. Why do you think He does that? Probably because healing is effective when the person receiving the healing is involved in the process through their faith.

WHY DO SOME PEOPLE CALL IT FAITH HEALING?

Faith is important, a significant part of the healing process, but it is not the only ingredient of healing. To concentrate only on faith is a mistake. I have heard many stories from people who describe their experiences with a "faith healer" or a prayer group where they prayed for healing for themselves or another and did not receive what they requested. When they asked why not, they were told they didn't have enough faith.

I am always sad to hear this. I wholeheartedly disagree with the practice of telling hurting people that their prayers aren't working because they lack faith. It only leads to frustration and pain for the people seeking healing. Yet, having faith is undoubtedly important. Where is the balance?

A better question to ask the sick person is, "What do you have faith in?" If we can stop and listen to the person who is ill, we might find out they have plenty of faith, we just don't know what their belief system is. Understanding the belief system of the person who is ill is helpful in aiding their healing.

FAITH IS BELIEF IN THINGS NOT SEEN BUT HOPED FOR

Faith can be closely associated with another word, and that word is TRUST. Sometimes they mean the same thing. Ideally, we seek to be in relationships with others who will abide by what they say. As the relationship progresses, we find out how truthful they really are and how capable they are of holding our trust. In relationships that are enduring, TRUST is a key factor. St. Paul says faith is "belief in things not seen but hoped for" (Hebrews 11:1). If your experience of others is based on trust, then you can believe in them and have reason to expect them to come through as you hope they will. Before they act, you trust they will be true to what they have said. You have faith in them.

That's what happens with Christ. He tells us to trust Him, and if we do He will give us all we seek. He will open every door and all we ask for shall be given to us. (Matt. 7: 7-8) Once you learn to trust God, you will develop faith.

HOW DO WE LEARN TO TRUST?

How do we develop the capacity to trust? Why do some of us never possess it, and why do some of us develop trust but later lose it? If our early experiences in life were not nurturing, if our parents or caretakers were unable or unwilling to provide love and proper care, we may not have learned to trust the world to provide for us. In that case, we were hampered and may have to make a giant leap to perceive God as loving and trustworthy. For some of us, the leap is too great. We can benefit from asking God to grant us the grace of faith and trust, the grace to look at our lives in a new way. If our parents or caretakers were cruel and punishing, we may have even learned we could depend on the fact that we would be mistreated. Small infractions of rules or normal trouble children get into became, for some of us, an occasion for severe punishment. We could trust in a negative way that those things would happen. "Oh, no, I broke the dish, my parents are going to kill me!" Is it surprising, then, that some of us developed the picture of God not as a nurturing provider, but as an impatient parent standing ready to punish us for our sins?

WHAT GOOD IS GUILT?

If you believe God is standing by, waiting to punish you, you probably have some trouble with guilt. Guilt can be a useful emotion if it leads you away from behaviors that are bad for you or others. If you have mistreated your friend in anger and feel guilty about it, and that guilt leads you to say you are sorry and reconcile with your friend, that can be wonderful, as long as you can let go of the guilt afterwards. Once guilt has done its job, let it go!

What if you do not feel guilt when you hurt another? If you rationalize your anger by reminding yourself what a jerk your friend can be at times, both you and your friend may then suffer the loss of the relationship or suffer unnecessary pain until those difficulties are mended. A little guilt isn't a bad thing. Consider it to be a jab in your side to get you moving in the best direction.

Your reconciliation with God should be similar. You fall short, confess to God, and come back into reconciliation with Him. Wonderful! The Bible says God does not even remember our sins when we do that. (Hebrews 8: 12) What about the kind of guilt that sits and festers or chews us up inside, even after we have tried to confess and be released from it?

SOMETIMES GUILT IS UNNECESSARY AND UNHEALTHY

Extreme guilt over small infractions is unhealthy and unnecessary. Guilt can be damaging to our self esteem, our attitudes toward others, our relationships, our health, our work and our spirituality. If you suffer from this type of guilt or preoccupation with the things you do that are "wrong," please get help. Find a spiritual director, priest, minister, counselor or other mental health professional who can help you develop healthy ways of perceiving and responding to your guilt feelings. Do not gravitate toward people who are themselves guilt-ridden or who seem to be feeding off your problem or promoting the continuation of your guilt. Search until you find the source of help that can bring you healing so you can return to abundant life which Christ came to give us. (John 10: 10)

A woman I will call "Sally" felt guilty because she hated her mother-in-law. She responded to her hatred and guilt feelings by acting the opposite of the way she felt. She was ingratiatingly kind and helpful, offered to take the woman to the doctor and bring her things from the store, had her to dinner weekly and included her in most family activities. She prayed to be released from her extreme dislike, and she felt guilty and mean-spirited because she couldn't seem to effect the change she desired.

Sally tried taking her problem to confession. Perhaps it didn't come across as a serious problem, and the priest wanted to console her and ease her concern. She was told she must be a good daughter-in-law for all the things she was doing and she should not worry about it. If God forgave her and the priest smilingly told her not to worry, why did she feel she still had a problem? That consolation didn't help her get rid of the hatred and guilt. When she hesitantly tried to suggest to her husband that sometimes his mother bothered her, his response was she must be having a bad day, because everyone loved his mother. He then said, "I know how close the two of you are."

Sally finally went to counseling and discovered she really did like her mother-in-law, but she felt resentful about how much of her own life was spent taking care of her mother-in-law's needs. At first, she felt guilty about pulling back on her care-taking, but she began to assert herself and learn how to manage her life and her feelings in a new way. She began to give herself permission to have a wider range of feelings. She started to express herself. She stopped thinking that a good Christian doesn't have feelings like resentment and anger. She stopped believing she should never get tired of taking care of others. She started setting some limits on the amount of time she spent with her mother-in-law, and began enjoying the time they spent together much more. She surprised her husband one day by saying, "No, Saturday night I don't want your mother here, and if you invite her I'm going bowling!" She said this without feeling guilty.

GUILT FOR SERIOUS SINS

Guilt that impairs us and holds us back from life has to be faced. What if our infractions are serious? What if we have done something so terrible that we cannot ever forget it? What if others have been affected by us and suffered greatly at our hands? Did you kill or injure someone through drunken driving or some other irresponsible act? Did you have an abortion, and you feel guilty about it? Have you participated in incest or some other sexual misconduct? Did you steal from someone? Have you beaten your children? Were you unfaithful to your spouse? Did you neglect your aging parent? Do you see how you sinned or fell short, and have you tried to confess and make amends? Do you still believe God is standing by, ready to punish you, or He is in some way disgusted by your behavior? If you are nodding your head yes, as you read this, then part of your healing journey involves the process of healing of guilt and possibly making restitution for what you have done.

God's forgiveness and grace are free. That means all you have to do is repent and receive His forgiveness and love. However, it might be helpful to you and others if you make restitution. Penance is another way to help us feel cleansed of our sins.

Penance is some act, or sacrifice, we offer when we sin, because we are sorry and feel bad. Sometimes it helps us experience more deeply our reconciliation with God. Restitution is an act we do for those we have wronged, to try to make up for what we have done to hurt them. Penance might be in the form of a prayer, an act of charity or abstinence from something we enjoy. Restitution might come in the form of money, if our sin has affected another financially. It could involve making a repair to someone's property, admitting our guilt if someone took the blame for us, or simply making an apology. Penance should be between us and God only. Restitution also involves the person or persons to whom you have caused harm.

I believe that penance and restitution for our sins may be redemptive and healing for all involved, even though these acts do not "earn" forgiveness from God. God's forgiveness is immediate and free, but human forgiveness usually is not nearly so pure or as easily available. So, restitution can help us accept God's love and forgiveness and one hopes it leads to reconciliation with other people. God doesn't need us to persuade Him to forgive us, but sometimes we need to do something to help us feel the forgiveness deep down.

By way of example, have you ever seen the movie "The Mission" with actors Robert DeNiro and Jeremy Irons? In this film, DeNiro plays the part of a man who cruelly exploits natives in South America, selling them into slavery and killing many in the process. He experiences a conversion, but he cannot forgive himself for what he has done. He becomes a priest and devotes his life to the same people he had persecuted, in part to make restitution for what he has done to them. Still he cannot feel free of his past sins.

As a self-inflicted penance, he carries around his old armor in a large net. It is heavy and tiring to carry this load, but he does it as penance for his past life. He joins a group of priests going to minister to a village of natives who have converted to Christianity. Together, they set out into the tropical forest, for the long journey to the settlement.

He carries his heavy net of armor on the trip and struggles greatly. He will not let go of it. His companions try to persuade him that God has forgiven his sins and his penance is unnecessary. Finally, he reaches the settlement and sees several natives approaching. They all know who he is and remember his past cruelty to their people. An understanding develops between him and the natives as they realize what he is doing with his armor. The natives gently release him from the heavy net and set it aside. He collapses in sobs and tears of remorse for what he did and he is finally able to accept forgiveness and abandon his penance.

Do you feel the need for such a release from guilt? Part of the program of Alcoholics Anonymous, and all other 12-Step Programs, involves making restitution to all we have wronged, provided others will not be hurt by our doing that.

Many people in AA describe this step as most painful, because they must face people they have deceived, cheated or otherwise mistreated. If you are suffering from this type of guilt, a 12-Step Program might be in order for you. Keep searching. Keep praying. Keep connecting with others. Healing of this type of guilt is a process that takes time and patience. It doesn't happen overnight.

THE PROBLEM OF TIME

The healing of most emotional problems, guilt included, usually occurs over time. I do not mean to limit God, for surely He can heal as He pleases, but my observation has been that many profound healings occur gradually. I have observed many people who jump up and down in front of me immediately after healing prayer, saying their pain is gone or some other affliction they had has disappeared. I see an equal number of people who are disappointed initially because they experience little or no change in their condition.

Many times I will pray with people for physical problems like poor vision, loss of hearing or migraine headaches, and nothing happens right away. Several weeks or months later I might get a letter from them saying their vision had slowly improved, or their hearing continued to get better and they now hear perfectly, or they had one or two headaches afterwards, but no more after that. Why does this happen? I'm not sure, and I have decided it is not my job to figure this out. God has His ways of doing things, and I shouldn't try to interfere. I believe the timing of healing is a private matter between the individual and God.

SOMETIMES THE ANSWER TO THE PRAYER IS IN THE JOURNEY, NOT THE DESTINATION

Have you ever pleaded with God to give you something you really wanted? Have you ever knelt praying so long that your knees hurt? Have you ever sat in church for long periods of time, staring into space, imploring God's help? Have you ever cried yourself to sleep praying for something to happen?

Did this pleading prayer go for naught? No, it didn't. God listened to your petitions, saw perfectly what your need was and stayed with you through that time. He decided when and how to respond. Sometimes His timing doesn't coincide with our schedules. If you wait for Him, you'll not only receive, you will receive in abundance. Doesn't Christ tell us that when He says, "I have come that they might have life, and have it abundantly?" (John 10: 10) Just wait for Him. He knows best.

Many times I advise people not to push the process. I have to remember to take this advice myself. Can a child understand why he cannot have Christmas tomorrow or why she can't cross the street alone for a few more years? Waiting is hard. Sometimes the things we learn in the process of waiting are important, and in these cases, the answer to the prayer is in the journey, not the destination.

If you would like to read a moving story that exemplifies this point, get a copy of the book Showing Up for Life by Heidi Waldrop. Her story about many years of compulsive overeating may be difficult to understand on the surface, especially for those of us who have never had this problem. However, as you read along, you will see the story of a life unfold in all its beauty and complexity. You can see how she came to know and understand God and herself through the painful years of growth that led her to health in mind, body and spirit. A "zap" healing from God or a magic weight-loss pill would have cheated her of the beautiful understanding she acquired on the journey. Eventually, she did lose weight, but only after she accepted her problem, surrendered it to God, and learned to love herself, whether she was fat or thin. She accomplished this through faith in God and His grace, psychotherapy, a 12-Step Program and her own determination. (If you are obese or use food to comfort yourself and avoid facing life's problems, don't miss this book!)

If Heidi Waldrop had been granted an easy way out, she would have been like a butterfly removed from a cocoon to spare it the struggle of breaking through and coming out into the world. Do you know what happens if you remove a butterfly from its cocoon? It dies. Some struggles are good and bear beautiful fruit. Granted, determining which struggles we must endure and which ones we can skip over can be tricky. The wisdom to know the difference comes from God.

Consider also the story of a man who was addicted to pornography. He spent hours looking at pornographic videos and masturbating. He felt guilty about it. He believed it wasn't right, and he wasted so much time during the day that it was adversely affecting his life. He couldn't stop his actions for more than a few days. In time, with prayer and spiritual counseling, he arrived at a healthier understanding of his sexuality and began to see what he was doing was an addiction.

Even when he gained this insight, the behavior did not cease on its own. He had to pray and make a strong effort at first to break the power of the addiction. Today, he says that he believes it is better that he did not get over this problem easily. He says that the struggle gave him humility about the limitations of his will-power. He had to learn to surrender his problem to God first. He now realizes his need for God, and he has more empathy for other people with addictions. He says:

"If I had simply prayed for God to end my problem and He had responded right away, I never would have gained the understanding I have today. I would have remained an egotistical person, and I would have had an arrogant attitude about God giving me everything I asked for immediately. I would not have learned patience. I am a better person now. God did help me with my problem, just not the way I wanted Him to. God's way was better."

WHAT IF WE DO NOT GET WHAT WE PRAY FOR?

Early in my ministry, I had to taste a bitter pill. I took it personally when someone did not receive healing the way they asked for it. I couldn't understand why some people received physical healing and some did not. I had no explanation for the couple whose three-year-old child died of a malignant brain tumor two days after I prayed with them, and why a drunken man who stormed into the church where I was conducting a healing service received instantaneous, dramatic healing.

I started to get confused. What did faith have to do with those two instances? Eventually, I learned faith has a lot to do with these inexplicable occurrences, because these kinds of cases challenge my faith. I have learned not to question too much. This is God's plan, not mine. When I see puzzling cases like those I try to get myself out of the way and let God do His work. My human mind will never understand the mind of God. My best answer seems to be to tell God in prayer what we want, but also pray for the highest good to be done. This is another way of saying we surrender to His will, but at the same time we open our hearts to Him and are precise about what we want.

SOMETIMES FAITH IS CONTAGIOUS

A beautiful example of faith was shown to me. From time to time, I am invited to conduct my healing services at Protestant churches, and this story took place in a Baptist church in North Carolina.

Months before, the pastor of the church had called me and asked if I would pray with one of his parishioners who had cancer. I agreed, and the two of them made the long drive to my home. We visited awhile, I prayed with the man, and the two of them left. Several weeks later, I got a call from the same pastor saying his friend went into remission and was doing fine. He was even driving his motorcycle again; something he had been unable to do for some time, because he was in too much pain from the cancer.

In our telephone conversation, the pastor asked if I would be willing to do my healing service at his church. I was surprised by his invitation because he knew I was Catholic, but apparently it didn't matter to him. I admired the man for being willing to take a somewhat controversial stand by inviting a Catholic "healer" to his church, imagining what some members of his congregation might think of the idea. My curiosity began building up that day, and I couldn't wait to see how the service would go, what the people would be like, and how I would be received.

The time came, and I stood in a Baptist church one Sunday afternoon in front of a crowd of about 600 people. The talk went fine and when I finished I asked, as I always do, if anyone would like me to pray with them. Nobody moved. "Is there anyone here who wants prayer? If no one does, I'm going home," I said in a humorous tone. However, I was indeed worried nobody would come forward.

After a minute, one old man came up, then a woman. I thought, "This is going to be a quick service." Then a woman in her sixties approached me. I asked her to tell me her name and what she wanted Jesus to do for her. She lifted the hair over her right ear and pointed to a tumor about the size of a baseball.

She told me her name was Myrtle and that the tumor had been removed twice but came back. The doctors said it was malignant and they thought she would be dead in a matter of weeks. The tumor was creating pressure inside her head and causing excruciating pain. She was taking morphine for the pain, but even that strong medication wasn't helping much.

When I tried to ask her if she believed Jesus could take care of the tumor, she put her hand over my mouth. "That's what I'm here for," she said. I put my hands on her head. My left hand was over the tumor. It felt just like a baseball in my hand. I bowed my head, closed my eyes, and started praying.

I want to interject here that sometimes when I pray with people I can feel heat in my hands. When I prayed with Myrtle, I felt tremendous heat shoot through my hands. I have had this phenomenon explained to me by several people, both Catholic and Protestant, but I cannot tell you exactly what the heat means. I imagine it is the power of the Holy Spirit. Sometimes I feel it, and sometimes I don't. Sometimes the people with whom I pray feel it, and sometimes they don't. Sometimes I do not feel it, and still I see Jesus heal people. The only thing I can tell you is that when I do feel it, the person with whom I am praying usually feels the effects through some form of healing.

As I prayed over Myrtle and felt my hands getting hot, I simply said, "Jesus, you heard what Myrtle said. Please help her." Much to my surprise, as soon as I said those words, the tumor disappeared. I could not believe it. My hands were on this woman's head. Where I had felt a large tumor only seconds before, I now felt a normally shaped head. I pulled my hands away and said, "Myrtle, I don't want you to get too excited, but I want you to put your hand on your head and tell me what you feel." The entire church watched in rapt attention as Myrtle stood there praying with me. When she realized the tumor was gone, she started yelling at the top of her voice, "Jesus! Jesus! Jesus! Thank you. Oh, thank you!" She even fell to her knees, right there in the sanctuary of that Baptist church.

When she finally composed herself, she stood up and started to walk away. I grabbed her by her elbow and said, "Myrtle, unless it will embarrass you, will you tell these people what just happened?" Well, she wheeled around and in her best North Carolinian accent said:

> "Y'all know me, I've been coming to
> this church for thirty years. Y'all know my
> condition. Y'all know I have a tumor that
> is malignant on my head, and the doctors
> told me that I only have two months to live.
> But look! It's gone!"

She said this while pointing to where the tumor had been minutes before. Everyone in the church stared at her.

Those 600 people watched Myrtle walk down that aisle and out the back door of that church that afternoon. When I asked again, "Is there anyone else here who wants me to pray with them?" they came out of those pews like I was giving away hundred-dollar bills!

Does this story have humor in it? Yes! Am I making fun of the people in that church? Absolutely not! Some of my Protestant friends have a better knowledge and understanding of Christ than we Catholics do. The fact that we are Catholic, does NOT give us the corner on Jesus Christ. What is the point of this story? The thing God responded to was Myrtle's faith, as she stepped forward that day and asked for prayer.

She received a beautiful healing, and her experience fired the faith of 600 other people in that church.

ARE THERE CONDITIONS FOR FAITH AND HEALING?

I am sure there are ways we can prepare ourselves for the conditions of faith and healing. "Readiness" is a word we sometimes use to describe the attitude of people toward their healing, when it occurs. I am not going to talk about this too much, because some people jump right into faith and others take a long path; some people resist, others surrender easily. I try not to be judgmental with those who struggle to have faith. I encourage them to continue to allow God to draw them closer to Him, and remind them to be gentle with themselves. Remember the story about the butterfly?

What were the necessary conditions in Myrtle's story? Do you think Christ cared for one minute that I was a Catholic from Pittsburgh who wasn't even sure what he was doing, praying with a staunch Baptist from North Carolina? No, He did not. He didn't care about the religion or race of the people with whom He prayed during His time on earth. He looked into their hearts and responded to their faith and sincerity. Jesus responded to Myrtle's faith, and to her sincerity.

Jesus even says in the Bible that you do not need to have enormous faith to pray and receive. He talks about having faith the size of a tiny seed in Luke 17: 5-6:

The apostles said to the Lord, "Make our faith greater." The Lord answered, "If you had faith as big as a mustard seed, you could say to this mulberry tree, 'Pull yourself up by the roots and plant yourself in the sea!' and it would obey you."

SEED FAITH

A tiny seed holds great power. If you don't believe this, look out your window at a large tree. Reflect on the growth of tiny seeds as they turn into huge trees. Trees that provide oxygen for life on the earth. Trees that give food and make homes for animals.

All life comes from small seeds. "Seed Faith" is the recognition of the powerful potential we all have. Seeds of doubt can also be planted and have equal power to grow and develop into powerful influences. You decide which you want to plant.

One night I was doing a healing service in a Knights of Columbus hall in St. Louis. A special little boy named Bobby was there. Bobby, a quadriplegic, was in a elaborate electric wheelchair. He had almost no movement below his neck, but he had enough movement in one hand to operate hand controls on the chair. I was struck by the fact that Bobby was virtually trapped in that chair, dependent on others to transfer him on the occasions when he needed to be moved.

Bobby wheeled the chair up to me with his mother following close behind him. I knelt down in front of the ten-year-old boy and immediately was greeted with a big smile. When I asked him what he wanted to pray about, he quickly said, "I want Jesus to make me walk."

Some of you may think I shouldn't encourage false hope in anyone, especially a child, with an injury as severe as a damaged spinal cord. I think about this sometimes, and I understand the criticism, but I don't believe praying with someone for healing is giving false hope. I have watched God and the resilience of the human spirit prevail in the face of gloom and doom predictions. I admit I sometimes advise people to be careful about their wild expectations, to continue to see their doctor, to act prudently, but I never turn away a request for prayer unless I can see it will hurt someone or go against the free will of another person. In Bobby's case, the truth was he wanted very much to walk again. Why should I tell him not to want that anymore? I won't step on the seeds of anyone's faith. Jesus didn't either.

I placed my hands on Bobby's knees and started praying. I could feel the heat going through my hands intensely. When we finished praying, I stood up. Bobby looked disappointed. He tried to move, but he could not. He swung his chair around and moved off, and I felt a twinge of disappointment, too.

Several days later, I got a call from an extremely excited boy. It was Bobby. He told me he had experienced some movement in his body. I was ecstatic. We talked for a while, and I enjoyed the child's enthusiasm. I didn't think much about his call again until about six months later, when I returned to St. Louis.

I was doing my healing service and I noticed a young boy sitting to my left in the front pew. When I announced it was time for those who wanted healing prayer to come forward and form a line, the boy moved from the pew onto the floor. He had to drag himself to the front of the church and up the four steps to the altar. I looked at him, as everyone else did, and sat down beside him on the floor. I asked his name and he replied, "You know me, I'm Bobby!" I couldn't believe my eyes. He had full mobility of his upper body. He looked at me and said, "I want Jesus to make me walk." I said, "Okay, let's pray."

I put my hands on his knees and prayed, and I could feel extreme heat moving through my hands to his legs. Bobby said he could feel it, too. We finished and he made his way out of the church with his mother's help. Several weeks later, I received a call from Bobby's mother saying he could then walk with the help of braces and crutches. Again, I felt emotional and moved by the faith and determination of this boy.

About one year later, I received another call from Bobby's mother, this one telling me he was walking with braces and could manage without the crutches. I was pleased to hear that, and we prayed thanksgiving prayers together on the phone.

That story only spanned a few short paragraphs, but the time that it covers was about two years. Bobby never gave up during all the times I prayed or spoke with him. He always told me he believed Jesus would make him walk one day. His faith was like that of the Centurion's in the Bible, the one whose servant was healed by Christ. Jesus said He had not seen faith as great as his in all of Israel. (Matt 8: 10) I know Jesus thought the same of Bobby.

Would it have been wrong for Bobby to pray for strength to accept his life as it was? It may surprise you that I believe prayers for acceptance also require faith and are equally fine. If Bobby had wanted me to pray with him to accept his life in a wheelchair, I would have. If Bobby had wanted God to show him how to live a full, meaningful life as a quadriplegic, I would have gladly prayed for that, also. His dream was to walk again. I was happy to pray for that dream, and to hear that it came true.

FIRM FAITH

I met another interesting young man on a trip to Canada who had unwavering faith. He also had a spinal injury, but he was not using a wheelchair. He came to the service in a full body cast.

The church was full that evening, and towards the end of the prayer line, a woman came up to me to ask for prayers for her son. She explained she had been holding his place in line and she would like to go to the back of the church and get him. I watched her walk to him and saw him standing in the back leaning against a wall. I waited a long time for the two of them to walk back to me. His mother introduced him. He was a handsome, well-built young man I will call "John."

John told me his story. About two months before that evening, he had gone swimming and jumped in the shallow end of a pool, mistakenly believing it to be the deep end. The impact of his head hitting the cement at the bottom broke his back in three places. He was going to have to be in the body cast for several more months, and the doctors' prognosis was that he would never be able to walk normally again.

I asked him what he wanted to pray for. He probably thought that was a stupid question; it should be obvious, but I always ask people to state out loud what they want, so I am clear and we are both praying for the same thing. He was clear about wanting a total healing and a return to vigorous health. I realized this would be a dramatic healing if it occurred.

I looked at the young man with a big smile on his face. As I placed my hands on the cast covering his chest and back, he said confidently, "I know I'm going to be healed." I was amazed at his faith. I started praying, and John started to squirm. I asked him if he was all right, but he looked at me and did not answer. After about thirty more seconds of prayer, he told me he could feel the heat from my hands going right through the cast. Even I was surprised at that, because the cast was thick. I prayed a bit more, then stepped back. He said he was sure he was healed and wanted to remove the cast, but his mother and I persuaded him to wait until he saw his doctor.

The young man, with the help of his mother, slowly made his way down the aisle of the church. He was walking as you might imagine a robot would walk, swaying from side to side and making small, slow steps. The sight tugged at my heart, and I hoped the boy would indeed receive a physical healing. He was only 15 or 16 years old, and I felt regret at the thought of him being so impaired for the rest of his life.

John had assured me he would call me after his visit with the doctor, and about two weeks later, I got his phone call. In an excited voice, he said he had terrific news. The cast was off! He told me that he went back to the doctor a little early, and after several X-rays were taken and examined, the doctors could find no breaks in his spine.

I thoroughly enjoyed listening to the rest of that phone call, as he continued to talk and happily express thanks to God. Although I have not seen the young man again, several newspaper articles have been written about him and me, and a testimonial video was made about his healing. He is now in his twenties and is working with his local church, ministering to young people and testifying to them about the power of our Lord.

FAITH BRINGS HEALING, BUT SOMETIMES HEALING BRINGS FAITH

I have given you three stories of three people who were from various parts of the country. They differed in age and physical problems, but each one of them was healed because his or her faith was strong. One of them had to wait two years, but finally his prayer was answered. Faith that strong is wonderful, but let me tell you a story of how this can work in reverse.

I once conducted a healing service at a small church in the Midwest. Next to the church was a convent and a large infirmary that housed about 150 retired nuns with various ailments. Most of the women there were in their eighties.

After the service, the Mother Superior of the convent came to me to thank me for coming. During our conversation, I asked her about the nuns in the infirmary and told her I would like to visit them. I told her I would pray with any of them who were interested. She was delighted and walked with me over to the building.

I thought I would be there a short time, but I was surprised at the enthusiastic reception that awaited me. I spent several hours with those nuns, and that visit turned out to be one of the most wonderful experiences of my ministry.

The Mother Superior ushered me through the entire five floors of the infirmary. I must have prayed with 75 nuns that afternoon, and I saw Jesus perform some beautiful healings with those religious women. Several women stuck out in my mind as humorous and heart-warming.

Most of these nuns had trouble hearing. As the Mother Superior introduced me, she yelled at the top of her voice and tried to explain who I was and that I was there to pray with them. They looked up at me and said, "Hello, Father" and the Mother Superior looked exasperated. Their confusion might be explained by the fact that I was dressed in black, and might easily have been mistaken for a priest who had temporarily removed his collar.

The Mother Superior said, "He's not a priest, sister, he's a layman." She said it so many times she finally said to me, "Didn't you tell me you had a daughter?"

I didn't know what she was getting at, but I said, "Yes."

She answered, "Well, we'll just let them call you Father because you are one. We won't mention you're a parent, not a priest. I'm getting tired of having to explain every time. They'll never know."

I just chuckled and went off following her from room to room.

In one of the rooms sat a nun with an afghan draped over her legs. She did not look our way when we entered the room, and the Mother Superior explained she had been blind for about ten years. She was almost 78 years old.

I walked over and knelt down beside her as the Mother Superior introduced me. Her name was Sr. Mary. When I asked her how I could pray for her that day, tears welled up in her eyes. She told me she would be happy if she could see the bird that sat outside her window and sang to her each day. I told her to close her eyes, and I made the sign of the cross on each eyelid with blessed oil. I placed my thumbs very lightly on her eyes as I held her head in my hands. All I said was, "Jesus, please help Sr. Mary see again." I added a short prayer and stood up.

I was about to leave the room when I saw the nun getting out of her chair. She uttered no words, but simply stood up and turned around, faced the window and walked towards it. The Mother Superior and I were in the doorway, and we noticed Sr. Mary was crying softly. The Mother Superior walked over to her to see if she was all right and noticed Sr. Mary was smiling. Sr. Mary turned to her and said, "Jesus is wonderful, I can see the little bird that's been singing so beautifully." The Mother Superior and Sr. Mary grabbed each other and embraced. I enjoyed that beautiful moment and the quiet faith of Sr. Mary.

Later that afternoon, I met a very different nun named Sr. Rita. She was in her nineties and had been in the religious life since she was a teenager. When I first saw her, she was standing in the hallway leaning against the wall. She held on to a walker and had a scowl on her face.

I have to admit that I passed by her twice as I walked in and out of the rooms to pray with the other nuns. She looked as if she could chew me up and spit me out, and even the Mother Superior said it might be best if we left her alone. Out of curiosity, though, I finally walked over to Sr. Rita, even as the Mother Superior said, "I wouldn't do that if I were you."

Sr. Rita did not look pleased to see me approaching. The Mother Superior said, "Sister, this is Paul, and he would like to know if you want him to pray with you?"

I stepped up to her quickly. I did not want to give her the opportunity to refuse. I said, "Sister, what would you like Jesus to do for you today?"

The beautiful nun looked at me and said, "I wish He would make my DAMN legs quit hurting."

I broke into laughter. The Mother Superior put her hands to her head, shook it and said, "Rita, Rita, Rita." She then looked at me and tried feverishly to apologize for Sr. Rita, but I continued to laugh.

I turned towards Rita. I said, "Sister, you stand there and don't move." I then knelt down in front of her and placed my hands on each of her knees. She maintained an unimpressed look on her face. I said, "Sister, if you're ready, I'm going to ask Jesus to heal your DAMN legs." I said this to break the tension, and it seemed to work, because she gave me a half-hearted smile. I lowered my head and said, quietly, "Jesus, take Sister's pain away from her, and do it permanently."

I felt the heat rush through my hands, and I asked, "Sister can you feel the heat?" She looked surprised as she nodded her head and told me she could. Then she quickly added, "...but that doesn't mean anything, cause it really only hurts when I walk."

I said, "Well, let's walk."

I stood up and even moved the walker away from her. She said, "Don't do that; I can't walk without it." I assured her I would hold on to her, and I stood close to her as we walked down the hallway. I said, "Do you feel any pain?" and right away, she began to cry. The pain had left her.

We continued walking, slowly at first and then a little faster. With each step I released my hold on her a little more until she was walking by herself. I finally stopped walking and let her continue on her own. The joy within that woman became apparent as she moved with ease up and down the hallway. She went into every room on that floor and showed the other sisters what had happened. The more she moved around, the louder she got. The Mother Superior and I stood in the middle of the hall and watched as Sr. Rita darted everywhere.

As I got ready to leave, I was in the reception area of the infirmary saying my good-byes when I remembered there was a little chapel there in the infirmary. I excused myself and said I wanted to make a brief visit to the chapel and would be right back. My intention was to go in and take a moment to thank God for what He had done that day for those women.

As I opened the door to the chapel, I hesitated and stopped. There, kneeling in front of the Tabernacle, was Sr. Rita. She had placed her walker on the altar and was bent over in prayer. I could hear small sobs of delight coming from her, and the words I could hear were all words of praise and thanksgiving.

Sr. Rita didn't realize I was standing there, and before she could notice me, I slipped out of the chapel. I felt so much happiness for her. I found the Mother Superior and asked her to come with me. I took her to the chapel door and opened it enough for her to peek in. Rita was still there, kneeling and praying. We closed the door respectfully and stood quietly a few moments, looking at each other. Finally, the Mother Superior broke the silence and said, "Isn't God wonderful?" All I could do was smile.

Look at how Christ worked in reverse of what most people would call "faith healing" to heal Rita's faith! That nun appeared to have lost some of her faith, or perhaps it had gone a little sour. Her only concern was with her "DAMN legs," as she put it. They must have hurt her terribly. Christ used the dryness and pain in Rita to show her His power and rejuvenated her faith.

LEAVE ROOM IN YOUR FAITH FOR SURPRISE AND DREAMING

I believe God likes to work in ways that surprise us. My evidence for this opinion is partly from observation and partly from personal experience. If we leave the door open for God's surprises, He has shown me many times He will enter that door with party hats and balloons! How do we keep that door open? We have to be willing to risk, and we have to be patient. We have to abandon our expectations and keep life and love flowing in our hearts. And we have to remember how to dream!

Do you remember when you were young and you felt that your whole life was before you? You would lie in the grass and look up at the sky and feel alive and full of hope. You wondered about what the future might bring, and because you didn't know any better, you dreamed it would be

WONDERFUL. If you're like most adults, you can look back and see a gradual fading of those dreams. Maybe you say, "Well, I had to grow up and be an adult sometime," and you shrug it off. Maybe you had an abrupt experience that ended all your dreaming, such as the death of a parent. Maybe you had to go to work to help support your family. Maybe your sweetheart broke up with you and the pain of that rejection hurt so much you never got the energy back for another dream. Maybe you flunked out of college and forgot your dream. Whatever happened, most adults look at young people and think their dreaming is something they'll outgrow. Can you not close your eyes and remember how it felt to believe in dreams?

What does that have to do with faith? Remember what St. Paul said? "Faith is belief in things not seen but hoped for." (Hebrews 11: 1) Hmm...sounds like a dream to me! I can hear the cynics and all the responsible adults saying, "Now wait a minute...that sounds childish and selfish." Some dreams I suppose we should outgrow, but many, many dreams are good and full of delight and Healing! What happens to these dreams?

I would like to suggest to you that if you can remember any of your dreams, you probably can trace the paths that led you to sacrifice the dream and call it a "silly fantasy." What happened? Was it only about growing out of a phase? If you threw away your dreams, I believe the reason is not because you grew up and became responsible, but because you were afraid. That's right. Afraid you would never get what you wanted. Afraid you would never "measure up." Afraid people would laugh at you. Afraid you wouldn't be able to put food on the table unless you conformed to what others thought you should do. If you would like to see a lovely little movie about what happens when people lose their dreams, check out "One Magic Christmas" with Mary Steenburgen. Maybe you'll start dreaming again, too!

SOMETIMES GOD'S SURPRISES ARE HARD TO BELIEVE!

When I began my healing ministry, I attended many other healing services. I wanted to see what they were like, almost like checking out the competition. I went to a service in Chattanooga, Tennessee. The service was given by Evangelical Pentecostals. It was very much alive with music and jumping up and down, and there was plenty of praising going on. I took all of this in and became particularly attentive when it came time to call forward those who wanted the healing prayer and laying on of hands.

I noticed several times a petition for relief of back pain was requested, and the preacher made the petitioners sit in a chair and lift their legs so they could rest them in his hands. He placed his hands behind their heels and asked them to relax. He showed the audience that one foot was shorter than the other. With their legs resting in his hands, he prayed that the power of the Holy Spirit heal the person's legs. After the prayer was finished, it seemed the shorter leg grew. During that evening, I saw that happen several times. Even though I was a strong believer in healing through prayer and laying on of hands, I must admit I was skeptical of the authenticity of that technique. I even thought those people were fakes planted in the audience to make the service more believable. Shame on me.

About a year later, I was doing my service at a church in Canada. The people in attendance at the church that day numbered about 700. I had been praying for about three hours when a woman stepped in front of me. She was wearing an expensive business suit, and the pants of the suit hid her problem. When I asked the woman what she wanted Jesus to do for her, she told me she had polio when she was young. As a result, her left leg was several inches shorter than the right one. When she lifted the left pant leg I could see the shoe on that foot had been built up with a thick heel and sole.

I remembered the healing service I had attended in Chattanooga, and looked around the altar area until I found a chair. I brought it down to the woman and had her sit down. I told her to relax and to place both feet into the palms of my hands, as I had seen the preacher do in Tennessee. I said, "Jesus, I saw you do this in Chattanooga; please do it now." I cannot explain my surprise as I felt her left leg growing in my hand. I watched in total amazement for more than a minute, as the leg grew to the same length as the right one. Does this sound too sensational to you? It really happened.

The woman sat with her eyes closed in deep prayer. I prayed silently until it seemed the process was finished. Then I asked her to open her eyes, and when she realized what had happened, she started to yell. She kept saying, "Oh, my GOD. . . Oh, my GOD. . . Oh, my GOD!" She sat and stared at her leg. After a few moments she stood up and started to run around, testing her newfound freedom. She could walk without the use of a cane and without the use of her built-up shoe. She looked like a child being chased by a playmate, trying to get away in a game of tag. She kept running back and forth in the front of the church, praising God, and waving her orthopedic shoe in the air.

I finally got her to stop and reminded her that she should keep praising Jesus for the healing she got that day. She promised she would, and she walked away from the altar with tears still streaming down her face. She probably thought I was used to that type of occurrence, but I was as surprised as she was. In fact, I don't think I have ever been as surprised as I was that day in the Canadian church. My own faith was strengthened, and I became solidly aware of the meaning of the scripture that says, "With God, nothing is impossible." (Luke 1: 37)

CHAPTER 6

ANGER

"It's not the anger, it's what you do with it."

What do you think might be the biggest obstacle to your healing? Lack of faith? As I discussed in the last chapter, lack of faith can be a real problem, but I believe an even bigger problem is ANGER. Perhaps you have heard this opinion expressed before. Perhaps you realize how destructive this emotion can be to your physical and spiritual health. Anger will not only obstruct healing, it can cause ill health. However, the problem isn't really your anger, but what you do with it.

Do you let your anger rule you? Do you spout off at people whenever you feel like it? Are you the type to squelch your anger and hold it inside? Do you tie yourself up in knots with suppressed rage? Do you deny you ever even feel anger? These approaches will definitely cause you difficulty. They are unnatural and harmful.

Let's be honest and expand on this subject a little. Stop and think for a moment. Imagine you are standing at the front of a prayer line, in a church, getting ready to ask for healing prayer. Instead of, "What kind of healing are you looking for tonight?" you hear, "Who are you angry at?" What would you say?

Is it your brother? He calls you on the telephone, and as soon as you hear his voice, you want to rip his ears off. Is it your sister? Mom never made her do half the work you had to do. She got all the dates. She's thin. You're fat. You hate her. Is it that priest or clergyman who said something to you

20 years ago and made you furious? Not only is that minister doomed, but so are all religious leaders of all persuasions, including the hypocrite deacons, council members and ushers. If you attended Catholic school, you may have a special place, in the blackest part of your heart, for that "little old nun" who disciplined you. She's dead now, and you happily imagine her in purgatory being beaten by little ruler-toting demons. Does any of this sound familiar?

FORGIVE OTHERS...AND RECEIVE YOUR HEALING

I met a woman at a healing service in New Orleans who had a perforated left eardrum. The cause of her injury was rather unusual. She and her brother had been teasing each other like they did when they were children. He grabbed her, and the two of them fell on the floor. As they wrestled like two little kids, a pencil in his shirt pocket accidentally pushed into her ear. She was deaf from that day on.

I stepped towards her to place my hands on her head near her left ear. She stepped back and said, "I don't think this is going to work."

I said, "Why did you come up here?"

She replied, "I came here to go to Mass. I didn't know there was going to be a Healing Service here tonight. All I wanted was to come to church and be quiet. I sat through the service anyway, and I even prayed all the prayers afterwards. I haven't prayed the Rosary in years." She continued, "I wanted to leave, but something made me stay. I watched as the people came to you, and I saw how some of them were being healed. I thought maybe Jesus could help me."

She stopped for a moment and tears came to her eyes. She told me she was scared because she listened to what I said in my talk about anger. She said she had an overwhelming amount of anger toward her father. I told her to try to tell me about it quickly, because the prayer line was long. Her story deserved a much longer consultation, but she did her best to explain how years of abuse had built a solid wall of anger around her heart. She told me that from the time that she was five until the time she was 11, her father sexually abused her regularly.

I said, "I can understand why you're angry."

She said, "Wait, it gets better. When I was 30 years old, that fool found Jesus." She was speaking of her father. "He would come to me and beg me to forgive him, but I couldn't bring myself to do it." At that point she became extremely tense and clenched her fists. "I told him I hated him, and I hoped he rotted in Hell for what he did to me."

The woman had endured much pain, and she was still angry and suffering. I told her it was Okay to feel angry; it was completely understandable.

She brushed me off and said, "Wait. That's not all." She told me that after many years passed, her father became elderly and she thought she might at least try to reconcile with him before he died. She didn't know how she would do it, but she decided she would call him and arrange to see him. She lived only a few miles away, and she hadn't seen him in eight years.

Her father was happy to hear from her, and they made plans to meet the next day. However, he had an unexpected heart attack that night and died. She never saw him alive again. The anger she felt all those years was tangled with her bitterness over not being able to reconcile with him. She felt angry and defeated.

I thought the woman was genuinely tired of holding her anger and wanted to let it go. Her father's death took away the opportunity to forgive him face to face, and she seemed to feel cheated and overwhelmed by the unfairness of her situation. I decided to offer her another place to put her pain, if she was willing. I asked her if she could give her suffering to Christ, but with an additional twist. I suggested she also offer up her suffering to help someone else in her predicament who didn't have anybody to pray for them. I meant for her to do that quietly in her mind, but to my surprise, she started into a self-proclaimed confession out loud.

A large Crucifix was hanging on the back wall of the church. The body of Christ was about two times the size of an average man and created a strong presence in the room. As this woman started talking, she fixed her gaze on the body of Jesus, and her eyes never left it during her entire prayer. It went something like this:

> "Jesus, You know that I'm not very good at this, but I'm going to try anyway. You know how much I hate my father for what he did to me. But I don't want to hate him anymore.
>
> I offer my suffering to You right now. If there is a little girl who is screaming this very minute because her father is hurting her, please go to her and help her. Jesus, I give You all the pain that I endured. I give You all my tears that I shed. I give You all the hurt that I received. I give it all to You.
>
> I want You to do one thing for me. Even though my dad is dead, You know where he is. Go to him right now and tell him that I forgive him."

At this point, a miracle occurred. The woman's hearing was completely restored. I didn't even lay my hands on her or touch her at all. Christ simply touched her. She opened the door to her hurts, and Jesus healed them. I was astounded.

The woman's deafness had nothing to do with the anger she had harbored. The ear had been damaged for only nine years, whereas the pain she had carried from child abuse had been with her for 50 years. Think about what happened there. That woman was tired of carrying her anger and made a sincere effort to give it to God. She let her anger go out, and Christ walked in. The response was beautiful to observe.

If anger, rage, revenge and hatred are consuming you, think about the story you just read. Are you ready to give it up? If reconciliation is possible, think about how you could go to the other person. If reconciliation is not possible because the person is dead or if contacting them would cause more pain, reconcile your differences with God as the woman in the story did. Then, let it be.

ANGER AS A PATTERN

Anger is a genuine, normal emotion, and you can feel it flare up within you. Many times it will happen in response to events and people in your life. Anger can also be a habit. You can feed it as a habit by dwelling on it, and it can become a destructive pattern.

Let's look at an example of normal, appropriate anger. You have a young child who needs some encouragement. She is crying because she has fallen down and bruised her knee, and you are giving her a hug and consoling her. Someone wants your attention and says, "Would you quit, already? Leave that kid alone and get over here."

You would probably feel some anger, and it would be normal and healthy to assert yourself. You might say, "Look, my child is important to me, and you'll have to wait a minute." You might be even more colorful in your response. Anyway, I don't think there would be anything wrong with asserting what you feel in that situation. After all, even Jesus expressed anger with the moneylenders in the temple. (John 2: 14-16)

The anger that I am concerned about is the anger that sits and festers. If you were the parent in the previous example, what would you do after you asserted yourself to that rude, impatient person? Would you let it go and get over it, or would you pull it back up throughout the day, relive it and dwell on it for the next week? You could tell several people the story, with an attitude of "can you believe the nerve of that guy?" and embellish the story with details that cause consternation in the listener. You could find yourself thinking about it during the day, coming up with clever things you should have said to let him have it. Most of us have that tendency to some extent, and it is the habit of anger I am talking about. The experience of anger is normal, but hanging on to it puts you on Satan's playground. He will use it to destroy you. Don't believe his lies!

If you are into the habit of bringing up past offenses like a cow chewing its cud, I hope you'll admit it is not really enjoyable. It doesn't feel good. When I do it, I often feel irritation and tension. Sometimes we get stomach problems or headaches. So why do we do it? It's a habit. It destroys our peace, but at some level whether or not we admit it, we get some enjoyment out of it. It occupies our minds and gives us a chance to see how we have been wronged by others. Perhaps it feeds our feelings of low self-esteem. Our thoughts could go something like this: "Gee, what a jerk I am that people are always taking advantage of me and trying to push me around." "People don't like me." "The only time I get attention is when somebody wants something from me."

"Poor little ol' me." We might count the ways we have been mistreated and either get angry or get depressed because life is so hurtful for us. The habit is sadly intensified when individuals have had some trauma or abuse that can make their anger or depression habits feel like dark clouds that will forever hang over their lives. They really have been hurt by others and can't escape the thoughts and emotions that come with those memories. They wish they could.

HOLDING ON TO ANGER IS UNHEALTHY

The last paragraph illustrates the two paths that anger can take when we don't let it flow, and let it go. We can churn and grind with anger and refuse to let it go, or we can stuff it inside and bury it so deep we believe we don't even feel it anymore. These two patterns are very different, but they have one thing in common. They don't work at getting rid of our anger.

In the first case, we can choose to hold on to our anger and churn it around like a big, mean emotional washing machine. As that anger churns around inside us, making us angrier by the minute, we can take little handfuls out and throw it at other people. We can invite others to churn with us and get their washing machines going, too.

What happens when we stuff our anger inside? "I'm just not an angry person. I never seem to get angry."...(Sigh). That choice is no better. People who handle their anger by denying or repressing it are candidates for depression and other illnesses.

LET IT FLOW AND LET IT GO

Regardless of the circumstances that started the anger pattern, how justified your anger is or how certain you are that you were the wronged party, one thing is clear: The anger is inside you, and you can affect its control over you more than you think. First, anger is not a bad thing! It is not a sin and it is not unhealthy. People who resolve "not to get so angry anymore" are probably headed for trouble because never allowing yourself to get angry could be like trying to stop up a naturally flowing stream. What would happen? The water would build up and go somewhere else, possibly causing damage. It can take a tremendous amount of energy to hold back that flow of anger. It usually ends up going somewhere else, like when we kick the dog because we're really angry at our neighbors. The energy and creativity we put into our justifications for our anger show that sometimes we are trying to prove we deserve to be allowed to be angry. Think about the men and women who have lived in abusive environments. Whether this was spousal or child abuse, sexual or verbal, the anger is real, but most times it is hidden, and most times it is displaced. Displaced anger can be destructive.

Maybe our parents or teachers or some other authority told us years ago that we just shouldn't get angry. "Turn the other cheek," they said, "That's what good Christians do." Well, I can't deny that for some saintly folks, there seems to be a point where they are able to react this way to their anger. Maybe you're at that point in your spiritual development, but if you think you are, be careful. I strongly recommend you have a spiritual director or counselor who can advise you on the fine points of this particular path. In fact, I am working on not denying my anger, but rather being honest with myself and others at times when I feel angry. Asserting anger in a healthy way frees us to let it go. It prevents a buildup that leads to festering emotions that can cause serious health problems.

Where do we get the idea that anger is bad? Little children cry and scream when they are angry, and seem to get over it quickly. However, children have to be taught they cannot throw tantrums, scream and hit people when they get angry. They must be taught constructive ways to assert their feelings, express what they want or need and accept that they can't always get things their way. But what about the times when children get the idea that anger is bad?

When our parents or other adults tell us feeling and expressing anger is bad, what happens? We might deny it for so long we eventually don't feel it anymore. Emotions give us nudges, taps or jolts from time to time, but if we don't acknowledge them, they can do all sorts of strange things. One of the things that can happen is we become emotionally numb, and anger is the prime emotion that causes this syndrome.

When Mary was in psychotherapy years ago, her therapist sat back in her chair one day, sighed and said, "OK, now what are we going to do about your anger?" Listen to Mary tell it.

"I stared at her in disbelief." "What are you talking about? I'm not an angry person." I believed this. I felt it. Anger was not what had brought me into therapy. I went for help because I was depressed. Well, many professionals in the field of psychology describe depression as "anger turned inward." After many months of work, I could finally tap into the anger I felt - the anger that had been completely available to me as a child, but that I had learned to repress. When it started to percolate again after years of being denied, it scared me. I didn't like it. I didn't want to feel it, but I eventually learned to befriend it and learn from it. My anger had a great deal to teach me, and it continues to teach me today.

My anger helps me to stand up for what is right, for what I believe in and to get what I need to live my life. It helps me be a better parent when I can say, "When you don't do your chores, I get angry!" rather than stuffing the anger and ending up being critical and judgmental with my sons. It helps me in relationships to be able to say that I'm angry, express the reason for the anger and tell the other person what I need from them. I might not get my way, but I honor my emotions by admitting my feelings and articulating my needs. I will feel better, whether the problem gets resolved to my satisfaction or not. I'm not always right when I get angry. Sometimes I'm selfish or I have misunderstood what someone else said or did, but dealing with my anger as best I can when it presents itself, or soon after, keeps my emotional stream flowing. It prevents the difficulties that come from emotional repression."

JUSTIFYING OUR ANGER

If parents and other authority figures told us when we were growing up that we shouldn't feel or express our anger, we might have learned they would relent if the reason for our anger was good enough. We might, as adults, look for reasons why we should be allowed to be angry. "Wait a minute," we might say, "when you hear my story, you'll be upset, too! Mother Theresa would be angry if this happened to her!" We interject into a story things that justify the simple emotion we felt.

Wouldn't it be better if we could express our anger? "Hey, I get angry when you turn the TV up loud because I can't concentrate!" instead of "You inconsiderate jerk, can't you see I'm trying to work the crossword puzzle and improve my mind while you're watching that stupid boob tube?" If we didn't need reasons to justify being angry, maybe we could deal with conflict better, before it turns into war.

ANGER WITHOUT BLAME

Can we change our thinking about our anger and see it as just another emotion that pops up in our lives? Can we allow ourselves to feel it and allow others to do the same? Maybe then we won't need to blame other people for our feelings of anger. "You made me angry" could become "I'm feeling angry." It seems like a little change, but shifting the pronoun from "You" to "I" can also shift the focus and take the attention off assigning blame. Give yourself permission to feel your anger, and you won't need to blame others for it as much.

Of course, when some person or event has caused you significant harm, there is a natural tendency to blame the offender. Christ taught us, In the Lord's Prayer, we are supposed to forgive those people (Matt. 6: 12), but it's hard, isn't it? Our society isn't set up to be forgiving. For example, our court system is set up to find out the truth. The judge wants to know who is to blame, so they can be punished. However, even if the offending party is found guilty and punished, the victim often continues to feel anger. Blaming and punishing are only part of the solution in cases where significant harm has been done. We all need to face the anger we feel, express it and let it go.

WE USUALLY AREN'T FIGHTING ABOUT WHAT WE'RE FIGHTING ABOUT

When we become angry and we try to hold it back, it frequently pops up somewhere else. The husband and wife arguing about finances might really be angry about something else and are afraid to address the real issues. They want to fight because they are angry, but they don't want to express their true feelings. They argue about something else to vent their emotions, but they do not share the true source of their pain with each other, and they do not resolve the problem. They simply develop a hurtful pattern for themselves to fall into whenever they want to vent their frustrations.

I suppressed and repressed many of my feelings as a child. When I became an adult, I developed some unhealthy emotional patterns. Underneath it all was a seething anger. Until a few years ago, I didn't see how these patterns had developed, but now I understand that I wasn't born angry. I don't blame my parents, or the other adults in my life, for I believe they were trying to do their best to raise me. I simply see the way my life unfolded and the way I reacted led me to become destructive and full of rage.

My parents were married July 20, 1941. They were both Ukrainians, and they lived in a Ukrainian section of Pittsburgh. Everyone had definite ideas about how things should be done. They had rules about conduct, religion, social events, and even what kind of foods we should eat on certain holidays.

If you grew up in any strong ethnic section of a large city, you know how powerful those influences can be. I might also add that some aspects of my heritage have added great richness to my life. It definitely wasn't all bad. I still make Ukrainian Easter eggs every year. I reminisce about my father teaching me how to make them, exactly as his father taught him. I still enjoy Ukrainian food, polka music, and have many warm and funny memories of my passionate, opinionated, crazy relatives.

December 8, 1941, my father was drafted into World War II. I was born July 15, 1942, into a house of women, my mother, my aunts and my maternal grandmother. Can you imagine how spoiled I was as the only child for these women to dote upon? I still have fond memories of my grandmother holding her "Pavlo," which is Ukrainian for Paul, and rocking me to sleep singing Ukrainian songs. I lived like a little prince.

In 1946, my father came home from the war. He returned to a wife he barely knew and a son he had only seen twice. He returned with emotional scars, as all men do, when they experience the horrors of war. He returned to responsibilities and family expectations.

I had no understanding of my father, then. All I knew was that some guy moved in and took my mother away. In 1948 my brother was born and I was dethroned as the prince of the castle. I had another contender for my mother's attention and affection. That year my grandmother died, and I was devastated.

As a young boy, I became very overweight. I was teased by classmates about it and, being a sensitive child, their taunts bothered me considerably. I was hurt and angry. My mother was a large woman, so I came by the weight problem honestly. She commiserated with me and tried to help me feel better by giving me goodies, which only made my problem worse.

My family didn't remain in Pittsburgh. During most of my school years, we moved around the country, and I attended schools and mixed with children whose families were quite different from mine. When I was in the eighth grade, we moved to Georgia. At that time, few Catholics lived in the South. I was different. I was a Yankee. I was fat. I was Catholic. I didn't fit in. I entered adolescence completely miserable.

In the ninth grade, I started working out and losing weight. I was getting interested in girls, but my mother was very strict about that. I wasn't allowed to date during my entire four years of high school. I couldn't even go to the school dances and proms. The situation made me angry and frustrated, and to this day I don't know why my mother was so strict with me.

I always worked and played sports to give me something to do to get out of the house. When I was able to drive, I contributed money I had earned for half the cost of a family car. My father bought the car, then decided I would be only allowed to drive it to pick him up after work or to be the family chauffeur. I was not permitted ever to use it to go out with my friends. I was furious!

I was NOT an abused child, but I was angry and frustrated and had no healthy outlets for my feelings. My parents were not terrible people. In fact, I was extremely close to my mother, even though she was strict with me. I am not attempting to show how tough Paul Rymniak had it growing up. I am trying to show how the way was paved for me to develop low self-esteem, experience emotional frustration and suffer from underdeveloped social skills.

My mother decided I was going to be a doctor. Her first choice was a priest, but she knew I wasn't going to agree to that, so she settled for a doctor. I graduated from high school and went off to college with no idea about how to socialize with mixed groups of my peers. I fumbled my way through and was doing okay with school when my mother called and told me she was in trouble and I had to come home.

When I saw her, I knew she was very sick. We discovered she had terminal cancer, and she died when I was 20 years old. Not long after that, my father also died of cancer. I was in my twenties, on my own, and had no restrictions on me anymore. I felt all alone with no roots. I was unprepared to take on the world, but that was what I wanted to do. I didn't want to be a doctor; my mother had wanted it, but now she was gone. I didn't finish my medical schooling. I went wild, and I got into trouble.

I had a terrible attitude about women and had no healthy relationships. I stole and cheated in my business dealings. I am still amazed I never got caught doing some of the horrible things I did. I used people and never thought about their feelings. I allowed greed, envy and jealousy to fill my thoughts. I developed obsessions, addictions and compulsive behaviors that ruled my life.

I was full of rage. When people mistreated me in the littlest way, I wanted revenge. I felt my life had been one long series of frustrations, and I acted like an animal backed into a corner. Many of the people I interacted with had the same emotional make-up, so it was easy to carry on the destruction. I was driven to force people to feel my WRATH, to feel the pain and anguish I felt. I became enraged and wanted to torture people emotionally and break them. I went to extraordinary lengths to get them. In one case, I waited five years to get revenge on someone. When I got my revenge, it was empty. I felt absolutely no satisfaction. Anger was running my life and ruining my life. My "eye for an eye" way of thinking was killing me.

I take a risk in telling about this part of my life. Some readers may think ill of me or wonder how someone like me could be working with a healing ministry. My purpose is to convey to you that if God can forgive and heal someone like me, He can surely do the same for YOU! If I go back twenty years and think about the kind of person I was, I would have to say that one of the biggest miracles in this book is the conversion of my angry heart. The loving, merciful heart of Jesus Christ made that healing possible.

St. Paul and St Theresa had a burning desire to convey to people the message in Romans 8: 38-39:

"For I am convinced that nothing can ever separate us from his Love. Death can't, and life can't. The angels won't, and all the powers of hell itself cannot keep God's

love away. Our fears for today, our worries about tomorrow, or where we are, high above the sky, or in the deepest ocean, nothing will ever be able to separate us from the love of God demonstrated by Our Lord Jesus Christ when he died for us."

The assurance of this message helped bring me through my terrible problem with anger. I wasn't cured of rage overnight, and my own healing isn't over yet. God is still working on me. I am starting to understand I am human and I make mistakes. I have to allow myself to do that and admit it, and I have to make allowances for other people to make mistakes, too. I am giving up the angers and resentments I carried for many, many years. Slowly, day by day, I continue to change and grow.

Are you in the same kind of situation I found myself in years ago? Do you have some problem with anger? Are there people you no longer talk to because anger has caused estrangement between you and them? Friends? Family members? Co-workers? Is it possible for you to go to them and try to patch things up? Call them. Write to them. You don't have to go to an extreme, simply tell them you would like to reconcile. Remember, though, if you believe more harm than good will come from contacting that person, make the reconciliation in your own heart and with God. In any case, pray about it first. Let Christ go before you and smooth the way toward the one with whom you intend to make peace. Make peace in your heart and let your anger go. You will feel exhilaration. You will feel joy. You will feel love. You will feel the power of Jesus Christ fill you. You will feel Jesus Himself. Try it. IT WORKS.

CHAPTER 7

WHAT IS YOUR PROBLEM?

What is your problem? How would you answer that question? The question is presented as an aid for you to reflect on. Often discovering the meaning of the problem is the key to the beginning of the healing process.

Jesus's healings, as documented in the Bible, are numerous. We can reflect on those healings many ways. One way is to see the meaning the problem may have had to the person or the interpretation other people gave the problem.

What do I mean by this? Consider the following examples and see if you agree Jesus was concerned about the meanings behind problems.

When Jesus prepared to heal the man who had been blind from birth, his disciples asked, "Master, who did sin, this man or his parents, that he was born blind?" Jesus answered neither was the case, but the key to his healing was only that the works of God should be manifested in the man. (John 9: 1-3) He was saying, "Hey, guys, you don't get it. This man isn't blind because of anything anybody did! This just happened. Forget about looking for someone to blame right now. Just watch how beautifully God can heal!"

Another time Jesus was speaking to Martha and dealt with her anxiety. She didn't ask for a healing, she blamed someone else for a problem she had. If you recall, she was full of anxiety, because there was so much work to do and Mary, her sister, wasn't helping her. She was busy, busy, busy. She had the best of intentions, and she wanted everything to be beautiful and hospitable for Jesus's visit. When Martha told

Jesus to get Mary to help her, he could have easily told Mary or the others present to help Martha. He might have even shocked everyone by getting up himself to help, as He did when He took the role of the servant and washed the feet of his disciples. (John 13: 5) Instead, he correctly saw and interpreted the core of the problem, Martha's anxiety. He said, "Martha, you are anxious about many things." He probably saw that even if everyone got up and helped Martha, she still would have been anxious and displeased. He invited her to come to the feet of the master and relax. (Luke 10: 38-42)

Perhaps this is an occasion for you to take a close look at your problem and begin to unravel what it might mean for you. Why do you think you have your problem? What does it mean to you? How does it shape and define your life?

Victor Frankl in his book Man's Search for Meaning writes about his experience in Auschwitz and other concentration camps during World War II. One of the points he makes is that people's acceptance of a situation and their survival can depend on what it means to them. He writes of hunger, malnutrition, sickness, humiliation, fear and anger at the injustice of inhumane treatment. All this is rendered bearable by cherished images of beloved persons, by religion and by a grim sense of humor. Even glimpses of the healing beauties of nature, such as a tree or a sunset, comforted him. Frankl was fond of quoting the philosopher Nietsche: "He who has a 'why' to live can bear with almost any 'how.' " Frankl believed those who gave up on the meaning of life, those who lost hope, and those who despaired became apathetic and were not as likely to survive. He wrote, "...the sort of person the prisoner became was the result of an inner decision, and not the result of camp influences alone." He believed any person could, even under such horrible circumstances, decide what his mental and spiritual path would be. The key for Frankl was the meaning one made of suffering and death. No one can give that meaning to another. It is a "way" each person must find with his inner being.

Thomas Moore, a psychotherapist and author of Care of the Soul, says people come to him every day eager to be rid of one problem or another. Instead of helping his clients get what they "think" they want, he asks them to pay attention to the problem they are presenting. Instead of giving them help to run away from the problem, he invites them to use their problem as a teacher. Before you try to cast off your problem, ask yourself what you can learn from it.

UNDERSTANDING YOUR PROBLEM

"I don't want the cheese, I just want to get out of the trap."
Spanish Proverb

How does your illness or problem affect your life? Do you miss work or are you unable to work altogether? Does it affect your relationships or social life? Your self-worth? Does it affect your mood or energy level, your feelings about God and the way He operates in your life? Does it cause you financial stress, or does it perhaps provide you with financial gain through worker's compensation or other benefits? Do you have litigation pending due to some injury to you? Is your problem causing depression? Does it get you attention from others? Is your problem mental, physical, or spiritual? Is it primarily one thing or a combination of many? I want to introduce a concept that is at the core of any change....SECONDARY GAIN.

SECONDARY GAIN

Secondary gain is a benefit, sometimes obvious and sometimes hidden, in staying stuck where you are. Don't get angry and start seething or wringing your hands. Don't ask, "How can he possibly be so cruel as to suggest I want to stay in this awful situation?" Merely sit back for a moment and take in this concept for whatever it might be worth to you. Bear with me.

A great deal of research has been done that shows that people who are motivated to make a behavior change are much more likely to make that change and stick to it. Think about the success of Alcoholics Anonymous as a good example. Why is that program so effective? You might say because members offer support to each other in a group. That's true. You probably also are aware that Alcoholics Anonymous doesn't force anybody into treatment or force them to come to their meetings. Members confront the alcoholic. They are not wishy-washy and they don't tell the person it doesn't matter whether they drink or not. They make it perfectly clear that they are not going to play games with them. They never force their ways on anyone. They try to make the person understand they need to stop abusing alcohol and come voluntarily to the meetings. Newcomers are made aware that they must take control of their lives while surrendering their lives to God, or a Higher Power, as AA puts it sometimes. Most alcoholics will admit that many people tried to tell them they were drinking too much but they wouldn't listen. They made excuses. They hid the truth from others and from themselves before the day came when they saw the truth. When this finally happened, they were able to change.

Whenever we make any change, we engage a process. That process involves movement away from something to something else. That process can be inner change or outer change. It can be dramatic or subtle, but it will surely be connected to other things in your life.

For example, if you are receiving worker's compensation benefits because of an injury you received on the job, you will receive payments as long as you are unable to return to work. If you didn't like your job or your boss, staying stuck with your injury would have advantages for you. In exchange for being hurt and in pain, you receive money and are released from the job and boss you dislike. If you begin a process of change away from the injury and toward healing, other's might think that was a good thing. However, it will cause you at least a little stress, because you might have less money, at least for a little while, and you might not have a successful return to work. What if I'm not ready? What if I re-injure myself? What if I get fed-up with my boss? A person in that situation must make a conscious decision that the potential outcome is worth the risk. In other words, giving up the Secondary Gain, staying at home and collecting money for not working, is worth the potential good that can come from having the injury healed.

WHAT'S THE PAYOFF?

Sometimes secondary gain is an obstacle to healing. When I pray with people, sometimes I see they are not ready for their problem to be removed because the "payoff" is too important to them.

Early in my ministry, I prayed with a man who had severe neck pain. He had endured the problem for several years. Doctors had not been able to help him much. His healing was one of those instantaneous ones where the pain completely disappeared after brief prayer. He jumped up and started running around the room, swinging his arms in all directions, assuring himself he could move without pain. I frequently observe people doing this when they have suffered with orthopedic problems. When they realize that their pain has subsided, they begin rolling their necks, making circles with their arms, touching their toes, or whatever movement caused them difficulty before. These rituals always amuse me, but I understand their surprise that the pain is gone and their desire to test their pain free bodies.

When he had satisfied himself that he could move freely without pain, he smiled. He asked if I would wait while he went to get his wife. I said I would, and he left the room. He came back a few minutes later, dragging his spouse with him. She was protesting and telling him to stop pulling her, looking around in bewilderment.

When I looked into the woman's face, I saw she was quite annoyed. She looked irritated as her husband described the nature of her physical problem. He told me she had severe lower back pain. He wanted me to pray with her.

I spoke with the woman briefly, then placed my hand on her lower back. As I prayed, I felt the heat shooting through my hand. The woman said she felt it, too, and she also said her pain was going away. Then a strange thing happened. She **complained**, because she had received a healing!

I asked her what the problem was, and she told me that she had been collecting worker's compensation for more than a year, because the back problem was related to her work. She was concerned she would have to return to work, and the thought caused her great turmoil. She was accustomed to being at home and receiving benefits. She didn't want to go back to work. Her husband looked dejected. She ran out of the room. He didn't know what to say. He lowered his head and left the room disappointed.

REINFORCEMENT

Here is another scenario. Perhaps you receive attention from friends or loved ones because of a sickness you are experiencing. It gives you a topic of conversation. It gives others a reason to approach you and ask how you are. If this is so, you are getting reinforcement to remain ill. If you hate your job or your boss and an illness allows you to stay home where you can enjoy leisure activities, you do not have strong reinforcement to get well. If you have headaches that allow you to get out of social engagements you hate but your spouse enjoys, you get strong benefits from having headaches.

Please understand, I am not talking here about faking illness. I am not talking about anyone consciously willing themselves to be sick or otherwise remain stuck in a bad situation. I am talking about illness caused, or influenced or prolonged by the mind, but the illness itself is quite real. These illnesses may be termed psychosomatic, but nevertheless, they can even cause death. Don't fall into the trap of believing an illness that is "just in your head" is minor or easy to get rid of. I invite you to think about the way your reinforcements might be blocking your process of healing. The goodies that come from the illness or problem may be blocking your healing path.

Secondary gain operates through a form of conditioning with which you might already be familiar. If you recall Pavlov's dogs, you already know about the psychological principle of conditioning. The dogs were conditioned to respond with salivation; when someone rang a bell. Dogs do not naturally salivate when they hear bells, but those hungry dogs were conditioned by hearing ringing bells at the same time they were given food. In time, they salivated without the stimulus of food. The conditioned stimulus of the ringing bell was enough. Over the years, psychologists have revealed a great deal about conditioning and reinforcement, and we know the principles also apply to human beings.

People usually feel resentful when anyone suggests that secondary gain might be operating in their lives. They think they aren't being understood, and that is a valid feeling. I do not want to go around accusing people of being at fault for all his or her sicknesses, financial problems, or relationship difficulties. Even if it were true, it doesn't help the person alleviate their difficulty. Blame is like a loose cannon; it can be very powerful, but it can explode at the wrong target. What is helpful is for people with problems to look at themselves only, and consider how secondary gain might be operating in their lives. The goal is clearer understanding that will release the person to move toward change and healing, not to assess blame or hand out punishment. However, changing is most difficult if you aren't aware of the ways in which you are rewarded for not changing. It's hard to ask God wholeheartedly for anything, if even a small part of you isn't completely sure that change is a good idea.

Of course, secondary gain doesn't apply to everyone. Some people are completely sure about wanting healing and appear to have no rewards for their illnesses or problems. However, look for secondary gain, use it as a screening device for your psychological readiness for healing. Could there be any way in which your problem is giving you some benefit? Not that you want the problem, but is there a little part of you that enjoys the complaining and the hand-wringing? Before you say, "No, don't be ridiculous," think about it another way. Is there a little part of you that enjoys the attention from others? Is there a bigger part of you that cannot ask for help, love and care from others? Is your problem giving you something to hide behind? Something to talk about? Remember: Let your problem be your teacher.

PRAYER TO UNDERSTAND YOUR PROBLEM

Dear Jesus, help me to understand if there is anything blocking the path of my healing. Help me to learn from this problem. Show me if there is any place where I am wanting to hold on to this problem, or if I am afraid of the way my life might change if the problem went away. If any such barriers are there, Dear Lord, please melt them away so that I might be open and ready for you to come in and give me abundant life.

Amen.

CHAPTER 8

PATTERNS

What are the patterns of our lives? What are the familiar ways we have of doing things? What are the rituals, methods, and habits we use to organize and simplify our activities of life? How do we organize our experiences so they are understandable, manageable or meaningful?

Think about it. We have a myriad of ways in which we make sense of the world and how we function in it effectively using what we might call "life patterns". If you go to bed every night at 11:30 after watching the news on TV, you have an established pattern. If you get a new job that requires you to rise at five a.m., you might decide you need to get to bed a little earlier. You might miss your evening ritual of watching the news and going to bed, rising at seven, enjoying breakfast and a leisurely cup of coffee before leaving for work. Now you have to be at work at six a.m., and you find it hard to adjust to the early rising. You now have to grab a quick bite to eat and rush off while it's still dark. However, in a few weeks you realize you like the job better than your old one and you enjoy the free time you have at the end of the day. You now arrive home early enough to have a relaxing dinner with your family, and you watch the seven o'clock news, which is better than the 11:30 news, anyway. You have made a successful adjustment. This change is made easier by the fact that there's a payoff. You like the effects you get as a result of the change in your pattern.

But what if you like staying up late? You insist on continuing to go to bed at 11:30. Your body needs more than five and a half hours of sleep, and you find you feel worse. You're irritable. You're not effective at work, and you snap at your co-workers. You decide the new job is no good, and you quit. You either didn't see the need to make a change and adjust, or you weren't willing to make the effort to begin with.

This example is a bit simplistic, but I am trying to illustrate how we all fall into patterns that can help or hinder us. We may find that a certain pattern works for us, or works for a while. Sometimes we find it necessary to change old patterns and the way we negotiate them, because ultimately the changes effect our satisfaction with life.

Patterns are everywhere. We depend on them. They save time and help us feel secure. If we change too many of our patterns too quickly, we feel stress. Culture shock occurs when we try to function in another culture and don't have our old familiar patterns. New language, new signs, foods, customs, music...these changes can be interesting and fun when we travel, but they can wear thin when we must try to adjust for any length of time.

Experiences make us acutely aware of patterns in our lives we never even noticed before. We become aware of them only in their absence. Consider the familiar daily and weekly things you do. Consider the seasonal patterns and rituals you follow. What would your life be like without them?

Our patterns bring us comfort because they reduce decisions we must make and bring predictability to our existence. Take church liturgy, for example. What do you think would happen if several hundred people arrived at your church each week to worship, and everyone had to decide first how the service would go? The result would be a mess. The liturgical pattern provides a structure for worship. In addition it provides predictability and comfort in knowing it will not change dramatically from week to week. When changes do occur, some of us have tremendous difficulty accepting them.

Remember Vatican II? Regardless of what you believe about it theologically, some of the negative feelings about the post-Vatican II liturgies were simply people's reactions to being disrupted from their beloved rituals and patterns. We are creatures of habit, and we resist change.

Now, maybe you find liturgical changes exciting. Can you think of another pattern in your life that you want to remain unchanged? What if everybody decided not to have Christmas trees? What if we decided there should be no turkey at Thanksgiving? What if we decided never to ring in the New Year on Dec. 31? Would it bother you? Would you miss it?

SOME PATTERNS ARE NOT HEALTHY

As I have mentioned before, I have many obsessions, compulsions and addictions. Some of them I have been able to alleviate completely, some of them I have been able to modify, and some of them still hold me in the grip of panic.

Have you ever stopped to think about the obsessions, compulsions and addictions in your life? Should we call them by a less ominous name? Maybe we should refer to them as patterns, because we all have them.

We drive to work by the same route every day, and then someone suggests a different way. We try the new road, and before the ride becomes only a few minutes old, we find a multitude of reasons to explain why this is not the way we should be going. We tell ourselves the new way has more traffic. There are more stop signs or traffic lights to slow us down. More cops patrol in the area, and we all know they have a quota to fill on traffic tickets, so we're probably going to get one. Then all the people we pass on the road, seem less friendly. We get to work though, and see we arrived 20 minutes earlier than usual. So the following week we try the new route again, and the same thing happens. We get to work 25 minutes earlier, that time. After the third try, we see for ourselves that the new way is the better way to go, because it not only saves us time, it's easier and safer. Why do we go back to traveling the old road again? It seems strange that we would continue to fall prey to that kind of trap, but It happens all the time.

We have other patterns. Take these examples. We walk into church and always sit on the same side, in the same pew. We always go to the 7:00 a.m. Mass on Sunday, because we have the rest of the day to do something, or we go on Saturday, because we can then have the whole day on Sunday to kill ourselves doing a multitude of things. God forbid, someone would be sitting in our seat, in our pew, in our designated area, when we arrived at church. This would make the Mass invalid. Then there are those ritualistic things we do. Some start praying the Rosary. Some pick up the missals and follow the service, reading every word. Some sit silently. Some run out of church after communion, because the big sports event is on TV, and they have to get home to get ready. Some have to be ushers and count the money, or else the rest of the week will be bad if they don't have some idea how much money the church took in that week. It doesn't matter that they can read the exact amount in the bulletin the next week; they still have to know immediately. Some of us have to be at the exact Mass Father so-and-so is conducting, or else sacrilege will be committed. Some of us have to be lectors or commentators, because if the word of God isn't spoken by us, then the whole congregation will go home empty. Then there are those who must hand out the doughnuts and coffee after Mass or else the community spirit of the church will fall into complete disarray. Then there are those who have the duty of condemning everything everybody is doing within the confines of the parish. Nothing seems to be done right with those people, no matter who's in charge. Those people usually see themselves as the true Messiah of the church, but that's as far as it goes. They condemn and give advice, but never get involved. All these things are done in The Name of God.

Please realize I am looking at the above scenarios as observations, and I am not trying to be judgmental. I am poking fun at all of it. Do you see how all of those actions become patterns in our lives, that even if we moved to another town, those manifestations would still occur, and we would probably do it all again. It all becomes relative, because we are all conditioned by our actions.

Why do we get ourselves locked into patterns and refuse to change? Why do we, immediately, try to throw up every obstacle we can think of to sabotage any kind of change? We are all guilty of this kind of behavior. It is taught to us at an early age. We are conditioned to go through the day with the same routine, and sometimes these routines are inflicted on us. We were told we would have to say our prayers or we would rot in Hell. It was made apparent to us that if we didn't do our chores, we would be punished. If we said something that parents didn't like, we probably got a swat across the face. All those things set patterns in our lives, and we do the same things to our children when we raise them.

Sometimes we're conditioned so well that the patterns in our lives become compulsive, addictive or obsessive, and then they become habits we cannot break. The behaviors we act out are ways we found to manage anxiety. It's that simple. Almost anything we do can be turned into something bad, if we become totally fixed upon it or when we lack moderation. Some people are addicted to their negative thoughts and the feelings those thoughts produce. Some minimize their behaviors by saying, "It's just a bad habit I have, and I can't break it."

I see many people with those patterns in their lives. I see how those patterns can be destructive and can even block healing. They can even stop the graces and mercies that flow from God to us, but not because God wants it, but because we, in essence, want that.

People come to me asking for prayer about a specific emotional problem, and they truly want it taken away. They tell me they have confessed it numerous times, but the guilt is still there. People even tell me they realize the problem and understand it. People admit they can tell when their emotions are going to get them into trouble, because they can see it coming. They can sometimes even pinpoint the exact moment when depression or anxiety will hit, and they realize how helpless they will be.

A woman in Chicago told me she was afraid to be in the house all alone. She went through a ritual of locking all the doors and then went back several times during the day to make sure they were still locked. At night, when she went to bed, she especially made sure her bedroom door was locked. She even had two other locks installed on that door for additional security. Then she would lie, petrified, on the bed all night, only half sleeping, because she was scared. I must add here that the woman was married and had children, and when her husband was home, that pattern of hers did not occur.

I found out her brother sexually molested her four to five times a week for almost four years. I also found out her parents would not allow the doors in the house to be locked. Not only the doors inside the house, like the bedroom and bathroom, but even the front and back doors remained unlocked. Although they could be shut, they were not allowed to be locked. Consequently, anyone could come and go out of anyone's room, or in and out of the house, unchecked. That gave open access for the brother to come and go as he pleased, even into his sister's bedroom. So, late at night, he went into her room, did what he wanted to, and then left. He also threatened her with physical harm if she told their parents what he was doing. So, it wasn't surprising that she would have a compulsive behavior pattern.

We prayed to lift the situation from her several times, but nothing happened. I suggested she confront her brother about her memories, and talk about them. At first she was resistant, but we continued to pray that she would not only have relief from her torment, but she would have the courage to call her brother and talk with him.

Finally, the day came. She mustered enough nerve and called him. He was shocked she would call and confront him after 25 years. He thought she had forgotten all about the incident. He vehemently denied everything at first. As she kept talking, he finally broke down and started crying. He asked her to forgive him for what he had done. She did, and as you probably have guessed, she never locked her bedroom door again.

In this situation, many deep-rooted psychological problems existed. But because the woman came to grips with what had happened, she is now free of the pattern she went through, night after night, when she was alone.

TOTAL AWARENESS

I have come to realize that my life had been filled with many unwanted patterns. As I mentioned earlier, some I have eliminated, some I have modified, and some still drive me crazy.

Through my constant prayer and nurturing from God, I have become healthier. I have been resurrected from most of these patterns. I am not saying I am completely out of the woods, but I have a different outlook on life. The changes have been slow in coming, but they are apparent, not only to me but to others.

For a long time, I kept praying Jesus would take those problems away with a snap of His finger. Maybe if He had done that, I would not have been healed emotionally, and somewhere down the line all of this could have surfaced again, and caused me greater harm.

I have found that once a pattern has been broken, a sense of accomplishment occurs, and you feel great. I once lost a hundred pounds and quit a four pack-a-day smoking habit at the same time. I cannot tell you how I felt. Not only was I healthier for the whole experience, but mentally, my life had changed. My self- confidence and esteem rose to a level beyond imagination. Thank God I never smoked again, and I have kept most of the weight off, after all these years.

So after having gained knowledge about my ability to perform under pressure, why do I still have unhealthy patterns? I still can't answer that totally, but I have learned one thing: Christ is still by my side. He still loves me, and he keeps revealing this to me in many ways. He does it through my prayer partner and through a host of other people. He is constantly affirming that I am a good person, even when I forget that, and I still do that often. He lets me know I am important to Him. He lets me know I can trust Him, unequivocally. He has truly taught me that He is my best friend, and I love Him.

He has given me a spiritual friend and prayer partner who prays with me about anything. This prayer partner has lifted me up many times out of the depths of depression. Many times she has made me re-focus my views and turn them back to Christ. She has become a friend I can depend on, and what makes this more fascinating is that I never ever see her. My friendship with her is strictly over the phone, because she lives in another state. I will always thank Jesus for my friend Lynn.

Next is my prayer life. I have come to know Christ the best through this method. He has shown me His true colors, often. He has never failed me, and I believe deep in my heart that He never will. I know this, because I still wander away from Him, and when I fall, He still takes me back every time. This is called unconditional love. He lets me be like the prodigal son again and again (Luke 15: 11-32). He watches me when I stumble. Sometimes when I stumble he waits for me to get up and come to Him, but that's because there is a lesson he wants me to learn.

So, can deep-seated patterns be changed or altered? Can obsessions be alleviated? Can compulsions be overcome? Can addictions be stopped? The answer is YES. I say that with conviction. I say that because I have overcome obsessions, addictions and compulsive behaviors. It isn't easy but it can be done.

Pay attention to what Jesus Christ is doing in your life, especially if you are praying to Him to help you. Pay closer attention to the people He puts in your life, whether they are friends, companions or acquaintances. Pay attention to the fact that you can receive professional help from a variety of sources. Don't let the words psychologist or counselors scare you. Pay attention to your ability to be compassionate with others. Not only does misery love company, it can provide growth in your life, if you use it correctly.

Pay attention to what your own conscience is telling you. Even Pinocchio learned to let his conscience be his guide, and he became a real boy. But most of all, pay attention to what your heart is telling you, especially when you pray. Why do you think the visionaries, past and present, get divine messages that tell us unequivocally to PRAY WITH THE HEART. It could be your salvation. It could be the thing that makes you stop being compulsive, addictive and obsessive. What's more, it could make you break a PATTERN.

CHAPTER 9

FATIGUE AND CONFUSION

The Byproducts of any Chronic Problem

"I'm sick and tired of being sick and tired." "I've tried everything, you're my last hope!" "My friend tells me to do one thing, my priest tells me to do another, my husband tells me to do something else, I'm so confused." How often those of us in the so-called "helping professions" have heard those words! Have you found yourself thinking or saying these things?

Let's say that you had a problem and you were able in a short time either to solve it yourself or find a professional, such as a doctor or a counselor, who could assist you. You would probably feel satisfied and relieved. You would also feel confident in your ability to face your problem, look for a solution and follow through to completion. I would say, "Bravo! Good for you!" You have gotten rid of something you didn't want, you got rid of your problem. You exercised your abilities in areas such as assertiveness, perseverance, and self-discipline, and no doubt bolstered your self-esteem in the process. You may have even received praise from others for your efforts. You learned some important life lessons that could be useful in the future when you face your next problem. If you prayed for help, you would probably feel grateful to God for helping you, and you would feel confident He would help again the next time you asked.

In the above example, what would you have learned about Life? That you would be able to persevere in life's hardships later on? That by not giving up, you could eventually get past future problems? Maybe you learned God is loving, available and helpful to you, and you have competent abilities to meet life's challenges. I could make the list longer, but the point I am trying to make is that if your problem is solved within a reasonably short time, the likelihood is greater that you will deal with it positively and have a sense of mastery when it is over.

On the contrary, if you have a problem going on for a long time and you have tried several solutions that have not worked, how do you suppose you would feel? You would probably feel defeated and frustrated. Your energy level for coming up with a new solution would probably be lower, your emotional reserves might be depleted and possibly, depending on the problem, your financial resources could be affected or they might be running low. You might be doubting your self-worth and your ability to meet life's challenges. You might even be questioning, "Where is God when I need Him? Why is He allowing this suffering to go on?" You might feel He is punishing you or trying to teach you something. You might get so exhausted that you want to give up. You might surrender to God your problem and let it go, or you might despair and go into a deep depression.

Let's say that in the above example you finally did get a resolution to the problem. Let's say the problem had lasted several years, and it finally went away. What do you think you would have learned about life? You might have learned you could endure pain beyond what you thought you could. You might have learned that even when you gave up on God, He didn't give up on you. You might have learned patience and the ability to be charitable to others. You might have found out who your real friends were during that time. You might have learned you are human and you have limits.

You can learn something from any kind of problem, even those that never go away. I want to talk about the symptoms of fatigue and confusion that often accompany chronic problems. When a problem hangs on and on, we sometimes get so enmeshed in it that it becomes a life focus. It drains us, and our mental and emotional state might make us feel like we are living in a fog. Depression is common to people at such times. A book called Praying with Theresa of Lisieux, by Joseph F. Schmidt, exemplifies this point.

Theresa of Lisieux, for those of you who don't know, is St. Theresa, the Little Flower. For years I have had a slanted view of this Saint. After reading all the books about her I thought she was a woman who had it all together. Everything pointed to her saintliness. Everything I read told me about her beauty and free spirit. Everything convinced me she was humble, and living in a convent gave her so much peace and joy that nothing could possibly have disturbed or upset her.

After reading Schmidt's book, I learned she was quite human and many things troubled her. She spent many days struggling with a multitude of things that caused her great torment. She fought constantly to maintain her sanity, and for all the wonderful things I have learned from her, I still saw a fresh and rewarding new side of her.

St. Theresa struggled with bouts of depression and she had thoughts of suicide. She even felt many times as if she had lost her faith. I couldn't believe that when I read it, but it was true. I don't want to over simplify this example and paint a picture of a beautiful saint that might be contrary to what you have read or that you believe. I'm only saying that even the people we hold in the highest of esteem, saintly or otherwise, have the same problems as we all do.

A few of the annoyances in Theresa's life never went away. She lived with those problems all her life. How she dealt with them was interesting. One nun in her convent annoyed her greatly. Theresa went out of her way to be kind to her, but the more she tried to be gracious, the bigger the problem got for her. This went on for a long time, and the consternation it caused Theresa was always present. Even when the nun in question confronted her with things, Theresa always smiled and was loving, to the best of her ability. What gives this story a twist of irony is Theresa's two sisters, in real life, were also nuns in the same convent. They thought the troublesome nun and Theresa were the best of friends, because Theresa and she appeared to be happy with each other.

Think about why I am telling you about St. Theresa. She had a problem, and she dealt with it the best way she knew. To combat her ill feeling for that nun, she showed her kindness and saw Jesus in everything that the nun did. Theresa explained there were times when she absolutely despised being around that woman, but the nun never knew it.

Maybe if Theresa had confronted the situation with that nun, matters could have been rectified and they could have enjoyed a deeper relationship together. Maybe a happier existence could have developed if the two nuns had talked things out.

I am not trying to second guess St. Theresa or any other holy person who adopts the attitude she did. I am merely asking you to look at the confusion in this example. Nothing was said between the two nuns, and even two other nuns thought everything was "peaches and cream" between them. I'm even convinced Our Dear Lord admired the perseverance of Theresa, but He let her have her own free will, and Theresa dealt with her problems the only way she knew how. St. Theresa exerted tremendous humility, but she could have spared herself some unnecessary grief. I do not know if anything could have changed the situation, and maybe I should not even use that example, but I have learned from situations like that. I learned how to deal with things in a more adult manner, and still please my God, as St. Theresa did. I could never be compared to St. Theresa. I'm not even in the same league as her, but I do struggle with the same things she did, and that's all I am trying to convey.

DEALING WITH CONFUSION

Many times in my life I have been confused. Ideas, teachings, dogmas and even my own thinkings have caused me frustration. When I get confused, I deal with things differently than I used to. I still have my little idiosyncrasies. I still have insecurities. I can still ruin my day all by myself. That still hasn't changed. What has changed is I do not suppress my feelings anymore. That doesn't mean I run around being obnoxious, inconsiderate or belligerent with others, but I try not to let things get out of hand.

When a situation is causing me problems and I am not sure what to do, I devise a plan to confront that problem, but I do it while keeping in mind the other person I am dealing with. I try not to be selfish. I try not to act like a little kid who doesn't get his way. I try to be Christ-like. I try to see it from the other person's point of view. This is hard to do.

Let me give you an example. When I have a problem with someone, especially if it is an emotional one, I go to that person and tell him or her exactly how I feel. I do not use the "Bull in the China Shop" approach anymore, because that kind of behavior never got me anywhere. It only made matters worse. I now sit and listen, and even pay attention, to what is being said without compromising my feelings or the other person's. I try to work out a plan to handle the problem when it comes up again. That sounds easy, but believe me, that's not always the case. However, there is less confusion and less misunderstanding in situations when problems are dealt with in this manner. You also have to be aware that when the other person comes to you with a problem bothering them, you have to give them the same consideration. Remember, life is a two-way street. Don't adopt the attitude that you are right until proven wrong.

In the past, I gave absolutely no consideration to anyone who didn't think as I did. I had no use for them. If you didn't do what I wanted, I'd eventually write you off and get you out of my life. I am sure I lost many friendships because of that attitude. Now, when someone is causing me strife, I pray about that person. It's not always a long, drawn out prayer: sometimes it's short. Then I talk to that person about what's wrong, when the situation presents itself.

Perhaps this sounds as if my life is one big happy time, day after day, with no problems. That's not the case. I have merely found a way to combat daily problems in a better way. Sometimes it takes me a little longer to see the light. This is when Christ eventually steps in and saves the day for me.

Think about someone you are having difficulty with and how that person annoys you. You could do the admirable thing and bite your tongue and let your relationship with that person wind up dissolving, and sometimes that is what should occur. You could let it cause you immense pain, or you could try my suggestion. Remember, this is only a suggestion. This method may not work for you in every situation.

First, I would ask God, in prayer, to guide you with the Power of the Holy Spirit. Ask Him to give you the words to say. Next call and ask the person to have lunch with you, or take a walk with you. Use a method comfortable for the two of you. When you meet with that person, discuss what difficulties you are having with him or her, and stick to the point. Do not wander off on some obscure tangent, because that is easy to do. Next, ask that person to explain his or her side of the problem. Listen and don't interrupt. Then both of you logically devise a plan to see what can be done to alleviate any further confusion. This procedure sometimes falls flat on its face, but I have found most of the time the problem is resolved or the relationship breaks up. Either way, the confusion is gone, and that's the point of the exercise.

What do you do with this mess?

Many times, the hardest prayer petitions I hear are those that have confusion entangled in them. Here is a list of some I have heard.

a. I'm going to get an abortion, because when my father finds out I'm pregant, he's going to kill me.

b. My husband beats me unmercifully, and he hits my kids, too. I really love him. Should I stay with him?

c. My wife was unfaithful to me, and I don't know why she did this to me. I've always been a loving companion to her. I will never be able to face her again.

d. I can't stop my addiction to pornography, and I masturbate constantly sometimes seven or eight times a day.

e. I can't stand my husband anymore. I hate him; he's not the same man I married 20 years ago.

f. My son told us he's gay. I'm humiliated. What am I going to do?

g. I haven't been going to Communion because a priest 30 years ago told me that since I got divorced, I was not allowed to receive the Sacraments.

h. I met a boy at college. He is in the seminary. We love each other, and now he can't make up his mind whether to marry me or become a priest.

i. I'm 52 years old. I've been with my company for 26 years, and now they tell me they don't need me.

What am I going to do now? I've given them the best years of my life.

j. My mother-in-law had a stroke, none of my wife's six brothers or sisters want to get involved, so she's coming to live with us. It's not fair, we've only been married two years.

k. My 30-year-old daughter has cancer. She's had two operations and 26 chemotherapy sessions she doesn't want anything to be done to her anymore. She just wants to die.

l. I feel so bad I want to end my life. No one would even miss me.

When I delved into each one of those situations, confusion reigned. Misconceptions abounded. Chaos was the order of the day. Go back and read them again. I bet you know someone who fits into at least one of the slots. How many of them do you fit into?

I could spend 30,000 pages giving you answers on how to solve the above problems, but that's not necessary. All I want you to do, especially if any of the above fit you, is to examine closely the true nature of the problem. Could some of the situations be averted? Can some of them be fixed? Are some of them ruined beyond repair?

Confusion occurs when we don't assess a situation correctly or when we don't know what response or action to choose to resolve a problem. When we feel confused, we can't lose if we turn the problem over to God. That should be our first step. When the problem doesn't require action on our part, we should ask God to take care of the situation, bless us with correct interpretation of the problem and give us peace of mind.

However, if action is required on our part, the confusion takes on another quality and we must make choices and do something. If we simply turn the problem over to God and allow the problem to drift on and on, we are engaging in denial. If your spouse is drinking too much, missing work, asking you to call his employer and say he's sick when he's actually hung over, those are important signs that action must be taken. You can put the problem in God's hands and ask for peace about it, but you must make some hard choices and act! You could confront the drinker. You could join Alanon. You could refuse to lie for him and ask him to move out until he quits drinking. You could move out yourself or ask him to go to counseling. You could continue to lie for him, beg him to stop drinking, threaten him, throw away the liquor bottles, cry copiously, or blame yourself for not being a good wife. Putting your problems in God's hands because you are scared and confused is not an act of faith, it is an act of fear.

Yes, you should turn the problem over to God and let Him handle it, but that is only the first step. Ask God to instill in you the power of the Holy Spirit. Then ask for discernment so you can hear Jesus when He speaks to you. Also, ask for discernment so you can understand when Satan tries to confuse you. Ask the Holy Spirit to strengthen your faith, so you have the courage to do whatever Jesus will asks you to do. Lastly, ask the Holy Spirit to give you wisdom, so that even in the face of ridicule and persecution, you will persevere.

When you turn a problem over to God, you must leave it in His hands. God will never interfere in your free will. Those two points have to be clearly understood, so there is no confusion between you and God. Let's examine these two things.

Leaving your problem in God's hands is hard to do, because we all have a tendency to take it back. What does that mean? Prayer sometimes gets canceled or delayed because we want to help God with the task we laid before Him. You CANNOT do that! He knows what you want, (Matt. 6: 6) and He knows when to give it to you. You shouldn't alter this process by offering your assistance.

People pray and ask God to grant them a specific petition, then when it doesn't happen in the next day or two, they think maybe He didn't hear them, so they pray again about it. It's as if your son asked you for five dollars to buy something, and you are thinking in your mind that you will give it to him the next day, before he leaves for the store, so you tell him Okay. The child knows you are going to give him the money, but he doesn't know when, so in his mind he thinks it will be that day. At the end of the day, when he doesn't get the money, he asks you again. By that time, the child is becoming anxious. Your response might be, "Didn't I tell you I would give it to you? Be patient!" The next morning comes; he still doesn't have the money; and he asks you again. You remain silent and look at him. When the afternoon comes and the money still isn't in your child's hand, he gets even more nervous. He asks you again. You look at him and say, "NO!" The child's face registers utter disbelief.

I know I am over simplifying, but apply that example to a petition you might place before God. Develop the same scenario. Can't you see how your petition may be handed back to you with a the same resounding, "NO!"

The second point I asked you to consider is this: God will not interfere with your free will, or anyone else's. If you are praying for your spouse to stop drinking, I feel certain God will not make him or her stop, until your spouse makes that conscious choice. When that choice is made by your spouse, God will help.

Some of you could say, "St. Monica prayed for her son, St. Augustine, for fourteen years, untill he was finally converted and stopped his evil ways." I'd have to agree with your example. It took that long because St. Augustine wasn't ready, and God didn't interfere with his free will. Legend has it that St. Augustine converted because he was told his mother had been praying for him for that long, and he couldn't believe it. It was not until then that his heart softened, and at that point God was able to touch him. God saw where St. Augustine was and He responded to his heart softening. Today, St. Augustine is considered one of the great theologians of the church.

Try not to let confusion reign supreme in your life. You must also take into consideration that when confusion abounds, Satan will be there to help it along. Don't let this happen. Go to God. Confusion is never in God's plan for you. Trust that implicitly.

CHAPTER 10

FANATICISM AND OTHER DETOURS FROM YOUR SPIRITUAL GROWTH

"Don't let anyone criticize you for what you eat or drink, or for not celebrating holidays and feasts or new moon ceremonies or Sabbaths. Don't let anyone declare you lost when you refuse to worship angels, as they say you must. They have seen a vision, they say, and now you must. These proud men (though they claim to be humble) have a very clever imagination. But they are not connected to Christ, the Head to which all of us who are His body are joined; for we are joined together by his strong sinews we grow only as we get our nourishment and strength from GOD."

Collosians 2: 16-19

When people get enthusiastic about their spiritual process and growth, they can lose perspective or get out of balance. When that happens, the door is wide open for fanaticism. People frantic in their search for healing can be susceptible to the influence of fanatics or extremists.

What exactly is meant by the term "fanaticism?" What one person considers fanaticism can be, to another simply devotion or commitment to a cause. To prevent confusion, I want to define the terms.

Webster's dictionary defines "fanatic" as a person with an "extreme and uncritical enthusiasm or zeal, as in religion, politics, etc." The key word is "uncritical," because that will lead us into trouble. People join all sorts of cults, jump into projects with both feet without looking first, get taken in by cons and wind up suffering hurt and loss because they don't look carefully at what they are undertaking. It's easy to do, and not merely because some people are stupid or easily taken in. I prefer to think being uncritical is a condition of the heart and spirit that makes a person vulnerable to extreme ideas.

FANATICISM IS A SPIRITUAL CONDITION

If you think about it as a spiritual condition, fanaticism comes into focus as a way to avoid looking too closely at things we prefer to idealize. We can be fanatical about anything, healing, God, love, morality, even diet and exercise! Have you ever been around someone fanatical about health food? Exercise? Politics? Religion? You'll know them when you meet them, because they eventually pull the conversation around to the subject of their fanaticism, and they will speak about it with tremendous passion. Nothing wrong with that, but can you get them off the subject? Did you get the feeling that something was wrong with their zeal? Your heart might be trying to warn you. Did they want to convert you to their way of thinking? How did they try to do that? Did they use strong arguments and suggest that your life will not be all right unless you do it their way? Be careful.

The subject of fanaticism is one Christians should approach humbly. The history of our religion is full of fanatics who lost their perspective and blazed a passionate trail across the horizon that turned out to have destructive elements. What kind of people launched the Crusades, the Inquisitions? Were these people who sacrificed greatly for their cause or were they destructive fanatics? Our interpretation of history frequently depends on which side of the fence we're sitting. This book could get sticky if I got into specific examples, and because I probably can't handle too much more controversy than what I've already taken on, I won't push all those hot buttons. That's not the purpose of this book. I do not plan to tell you who I think the fanatics in the world are versus who I think are the committed wonderful people. The purpose of this chapter is to give you, the reader, a gentle urging to be thoughtful and careful about whose guidance and advice you follow. Including mine!

One of the ways you can protect yourself against fanaticism is to examine the motivations of the persons drawing you to their ideas. Do they want your money? Do they want your time and energy? Are they demanding something from you? Are they pushy? Do they listen to you or do they only want you to listen to them? Do they want to take away your freedom to choose and think for yourself? Spiritual guides and helpers of any kind should not put a price on their prayers or spiritual guidance. They should not beat anyone up with their beliefs. The example of Christ is the best one to turn to in this regard. He accepted support as it came, but he didn't charge money to pray with people. He was gentle in his dealing with people's spiritual paths. He talked with them, told them stories, shared Himself with them. He didn't strong-arm anyone. He just asked them to come to Him. He exuded love and care. He wasn't wishy-washy. He was passionate and strong in what He presented to people, but He respected and cared for the person's spirit.

Remember the story of the rich man who walked up to Christ and said, "Master I want to follow you, what do I have to do?" Jesus told him to sell everything and follow Him. What did the man do? He simply looked sadly at Christ and walked away. He realized he was not willing to sell everything he had. Did Jesus chase him down and plead with him? Did He stop the man? No. He simply let the man walk off. (Matt. 19: 16-24) If we don't have the example of Christ chasing people and beating them up emotionally with religion, why should any of us allow others to do this to us?

Some people would disagree with my assessment of Jesus and make the argument that He was, indeed, a fanatic. Didn't He make extreme demands on the disciples to leave their jobs and families and roam the countryside with Him? (Mark 6: 7-

11) I may surprise you by saying I won't try to argue on these points. If you perceive Jesus this way, I would invite you to be open to the broader picture of Him presented in the gospel. He <u>was</u> passionate and challenged people's ways of thinking. He <u>does</u> make demands of us when we say we want to follow Him, but He only does it when you decide with your heart and commit yourself to Him.

Trusting Jesus is one thing. Trusting the spirituality of people is another. There is surrender involved in spiritual activity of any kind, including healing, but a certain amount of caution and common sense should precede your surrender, especially when it involves others. Remember the TV ad where the person takes a sip of the product being advertised and falls backward into a swimming pool? It's a wonderful image of refreshment and abandoning inhibitions, but it would be a very different picture if the pool had no water in it. Be sure to take a look before you leap.

PEOPLE WHO ARE HURTING MAY BE VULNERABLE TO FANATICISM

If you are reading this book, the chances are good that you are seeking some kind of healing. Chances are also good that you have come across at least one person who thought they knew better than you how you could get that healing.

Sometimes other people are a tremendous source of information and help, and not everyone who wants to help others is fanatical. However, if you come across a person who is pushing and manipulating you in your time of need, you must find strength to resist. If you are in need of healing, you may be in a vulnerable position that makes it more difficult to handle the games fanatics play. Use the same good sense in dealing with those people as you would use dealing with a pushy salesperson trying to sell you something you aren't sure about. Give it time. Think it over. Don't make a commitment until you are sure about it. If something sounds too good to be true, it probably is. Be assertive. If someone pushes you, assert your need for time to think about it and your right to make up your own mind. It is your right. If you decide to do something and the other person does not agree with you, assert your right to direct your own life! Laws in this country give us three days to back out of most sales contracts. Why do you suppose that is so? Three days is ample time to think about your decision and discuss it with others. This space of time will assure you that your choice will not be ruled by impulse.

If you do find yourself in the position of considering an important decision involving healing or spirituality, keep in mind that your heart, body and spirit may be yearning for an answer, for fulfillment, for release. You may be in physical pain. You may be in a state of anxiety and mental distress. You may simply want out of something causing you to despair. If someone comes along and offers you an answer to your problem, keep your head, ask around, do some research, then make your decision after you have all the facts.

Don't be afraid to go against the crowd and do something a "little different," if that's what you decide is the right thing for you. Goodness knows I'd be the last one to tell you never to go against the crowd! I direct people toward avenues of healing that are considered by many to be out of the ordinary; however, I believe strongly in respecting each person's beliefs and decisions. Ask yourself whether the person with whom you are considering aligning yourself is actually respecting your right to make up your own mind. Ask yourself if your own motivation for following them is healthy. Ask yourself honestly if you are operating out of a desire to answer your problem with a simplistic approach. Ask yourself if you really want that person to make the decision for you so you won't have to take any responsibility for it. Ask yourself if you're agreeing with them because you're afraid to confront them and tell them you disagree. Reflect on what you want to do and why, pray about it, and then STAND UP FOR WHAT YOU BELIEVE! This examination of your belief system may be hard to do, but it will help you grow and develop confidence in yourself and your ability to act in your own best interests.

Many people join cults because cult members convinced them they had the answer. In one case, a young woman was living on a compound owned by the cult and was instructed to have no contact with her family. Because she was over 21 at the time, the arrangement was perfectly legal and appeared to be by her free choice. However, when she made the decision to leave the cult, the members exerted tremendous pressure on her to stay. Her observation today, now that she has been away from the group for more than a year, is that she was hungry for a way to live her life and make it more meaningful. She was so in need of belonging to a group that she bypassed clear thinking to have her needs fulfilled. Her heart was hurting and her spirit was hungry. She wanted the promises of the cult to be true, so she didn't carefully look at their motives. Before long, they had her working for them with her extensive computer skills, giving them her money and recruiting new members.

That woman now sees that the price of belonging and being accepted by that group was high. Cult leaders require members to do everything they ask without questioning. In the process, members relinquished many personal freedoms and eroded their access to families, friends and jobs. That price became too great for our friend. Finally, she experienced the scary and painful process of pulling away from the cult, a process that might have been avoided if she had "looked before she leaped."

SPIRITUALITY AND SENSATIONALISM: USE YOUR HEART AND YOUR HEAD!

In my travels, throughout North America, I now meet or hear about a visionary in almost every city I visit. Frequently, people approach me in a prayer line and ask me if I know "so-and-so," in that city, who has been receiving messages from God. Sometimes people call the churches where I am going to be and make appointments for me to meet with the alleged visionary. Occasionally the people claiming to receive the messages simply show up at the church during the healing service and want to discuss the apparitions they have been receiving.

I am not ridiculing those visionaries nor the people who attempt to involve me with their cause. However, I have learned to be cautious about these matters. I have found discernment is crucial in deciding whether I should pay attention to anyone claiming to have supernatural experiences. I treat all these cases with caution. I listen and consider what I am being told. I try to avoid making judgments and simply remain open to possibilities. I keep my focus on my own ministry, and I pray, so I am not swayed by those sensational claims, messages and predictions. I can appreciate the position the Catholic Church has taken regarding apparitions, locutions, visions and other miracles. The Church may seem to some to move slowly in validating supernatural spiritual events, but a calm, steady consideration of those matters helps lessen the chance that a fanatic or purely sensational event will adversely influence people.

BE CAUTIOUS ABOUT PREDICTIONS OF CALAMITIES

Some of the visionaries I hear about are predicting impending doom for the entire planet. Most claim that the so-called "end-times" are here. Some visionaries even predict calamities that are supposed to occur in specific places. Some of these people have given dates and places of events that never occur. A few years back, a visionary predicted a terrible earthquake would occur in Tennessee. It did not happen, not even a tremor. However, the individual received a great deal of publicity and sold many books. More recently, another visionary predicted an earthquake in the South. When it did not take place, It was said it was because many people prayed and God relented.

A man who moved away from the city where he was living because a visionary predicted terrible calamities for that city. The visionary claimed the events would occur soon, and the individual decided he wanted to be in a safer place. Can we trust such predictions? Shouldn't we be wary of people who urge us to base major life decisions on their predictions, rather than trusting in God.

I saw this occur in another situation where a visionary was involved. The visionary was receiving messages from Jesus and His mother. This person was being instructed to tell everyone, supposedly, that certain Catholic beliefs were the only true teachings sanctioned by Heaven, and if certain things weren't changed, catastrophes would befall us all. Many people followed this person, and I have met a few of them. The unfortunate thing about this is that the people following this visionary did nothing but live in fear of impending disasters. They worried about when things were going to occur and, in the process, they missed the abundant life Jesus had for them. What was even sadder, the people who believed in this visionary became very critical of those who would not listen to the predictions.

Another visionary reportedly was told by the Virgin Mary that the only true Mass in the Catholic church was the Latin Mass. There were also instructions that petitions should be sent to the Vatican and the Pope that all Masses should be done in Latin. If those instructions are true and Heaven is telling us the Latin Mass is the only official one, then what about all the Masses said since the change occurred by the Magisterium of the Church, with the arrival of Vatican II. Are they invalid?

When I talked with the visionary, on closer inspection, it was apparent the desire for Latin Masses, along with other things, were the want of that particular person. The person was disillusioned with what was going on in the Catholic church today, and wanted things to be like they used to be. Was the person really receiving messages from Heaven or was this merely a personal mental frame of mind being inflicted upon us? I don't know. I see only the end result of what has happened to the people involved with that visionary. Even the priest who is the spiritual adviser to the person has been ridiculed by his superiors and peers, because most of the predictions made by the visionary have NOT come true.

Another visionary told everyone that on a specific day, the messages that were being received would cease. That pronouncement caused a panic. Rumors started flying, and things were blown out of proportion. When serious dissension started to occur with the rank and file, ironically, Heaven rescinded the "ceasing" and the messages kept coming on prescribed days. Was this Heaven's doing, or was it that of the visionaries? Did Heaven change its mind, or did the visionary? This is where everyone has to be careful. There is a fine line to be walked with matters of this nature. One thing you can use as a barometer is you will recognize them by their fruits. (Matt. 7: 15-20) If there is always turmoil around certain happening's caution should be exerted.

In a different vein, there was someone who had the unpleasant experience of being contacted by a "friend of a friend" to buy health supplements when her son developed cancer. When the mother said she wanted to think about it, the saleswoman said she would send her some samples and a video tape at no charge. When the woman received the samples, she tried them. She watched the video. Something didn't seem right about the presentation. It was proclaiming too loudly that this was a sure-fire answer for a cancer cure. She mailed the video back to the sales representative and received a prompt phone call. When the mother again told the saleswoman she did not want the products, the saleswoman asked her why she would not want what was best for her son. Those tactics put undue pressure on the mother who wanted her son to be healed yet who did not believe the products were all they claimed to be. "I felt guilty, even though I knew better," she said. "I found myself thinking, 'What if this could make him well, and I'm not giving it a chance because I don't want to spend the money?' I know it was crazy, but I wanted him to get well so much. I wanted to believe there was some magic potion that could effect a cure." She didn't buy the products, but her example illustrates people's vulnerability and the unscrupulous tactics some people will use out of their fanaticism and/or desire for monetary gain.

Even in the area of spirituality, I have found people who are as intense and manipulative as the most aggressive salespeople. People who insist you can have anything you want if you have enough faith are actually providing a shallow and materialistic solution to the need for healing or spiritual well-being.

How many times have you prayed for something with a fervor so strong it hurt? How many times have you prayed many days, or even weeks, and your intentions were never answered? How many times have you sat in church and pleaded with God to hear you? How many times have you thought God was not listening? How many times have you cried yourself to sleep, almost in despair because your petitions weren't being answered? Were these the times you didn't have enough faith? My Resounding answer to this is: NO, in big capital letters.

Those strong-willed individuals who inflict their individuality on you, in my estimation, are wrong. Try not to be swayed by anyone telling you anything that drives you deeper into "Spiritual Depression." When somebody tells you the Lord "Put it upon their Heart" to enlighten you, it may not be true. They may believe it's true, but they may be wrong.

I have known specific people and prayer groups who inflicted their brand of spirituality upon those who went to them to seek help. Be careful of individuals who insist you do things their way to obtain your spiritual wants and needs. Fanatical insistence can destroy a person's prayer life. I have seen it happen.

Over the years, I have come across many methods and styles of praise and worship. Some of them I was able to do, and some of them I was not, but that didn't mean they were wrong. It only meant that I was uncomfortable with them. I know many Ukrainian prayers, and I can truly give homage to God by saying them, but I would never insist that someone else pray with me in Ukrainian. First, they would not be able to understand the prayer. Second, they would feel uncomfortable in trying to enunciate foreign words. This is the type of thing I mean when I say be careful of insistence. My Ukrainian prayers aren't bad or wrong. They would not be the prayers that everyone would want to use to pray.

There are many methods, styles and ideas of praise and worship that receive criticism. The criticism is wrong. God doesn't care how we give Him honor and glory, or how we pray. All He cares about is that we do it. Jesus says, "Where two or more are gathered, I am there." He also tells us we must be in ACCORD when praying with someone else. He says, "Two people standing in accord with my Father, asking the Father for anything, my Father will give it to them." (Matt. 18: 19-20)

Most methods and styles are not wrong; They simply make some people uncomfortable. Here are statements from people who criticize some techniques.

a. They made me try to speak in tongues, and I felt silly.

b. They made me lie on the floor and pray in front of the tabernacle.

c. I avoided the Healing Service because I was afraid of being prayed over and then falling down.

d. I was told to bury a statue of a certain saint in the ground to receive a specific prayer intention.

e. I don't like to worship with Charismatics because they dance around and sway during the service.

f. I was told if I broke a religious prayer chain letter I would meet with tragedy.

g. Someone told me the Lord put it upon their heart to tell me how I should be doing things.

This list could go on and on and on. I know you get my idea!

I was invited to pray with a prayer group. By the end of the evening, I was uncomfortable. I was being forced into praying in a style that I was not accustomed to. My lack of comfort didn't make their style wrong, but the more I sat there, the more uneasy I became. That aggravation was not worth the trouble. Some of you could say that is Spiritual Warfare. I watched the prayer group, in time, become filled with dissension, strife and turmoil. Members joined and left the group continually. I am not being judgmental towards the group. I simply saw what started out to be a good thing dissipate into nothing. It finally dissolved.

Don't be intimidated by any type of shallow theology and cheap grace. Sometimes God and your spirit know you will experience important learning and be blessed by some life experience, including illness. In my opinion, this is why we should pray for the Perfect Will of God to enter into each situation. However, we can ask God to answer our petitions, to open His merciful Heart and satisfy us.

ILLNESS COMES IN MANY FORMS

Do not assume illness is a punishment. Do not assume God wants us to offer up as a sacrifice every bad thing that happens to us. Sometimes He wants us to ask for it to be taken away. Sometimes we get sick because we are pushing ourselves unnecessarily, and He wants us to slow down. After we rest awhile and learn our lesson, we usually regain our health. Do not assume we should hang on to every bad thing in our lives and shoulder it as a cross. These things require discernment to understand and move through. Christ even asked, in the garden of Gethsemane, if His cup could be removed from Him but, if not, that the Father's will be done. (Luke 22: 42) If Christ experienced darkness of the Spirit and asked for his Father's help, why would we not do the same? I believe the Father considered the prayer of Jesus as He does ours, and His decision was that a greater good could be achieved through the Crucifixion. If the answer was to "name it and claim it" and only to experience abundant life in a positive, happy way, as some proclaim, would not Christ have refused the cross as a painful and negative experience? Admittedly, it takes great patience, faith and trust to ask God for what we want, tell Him what we need, surrender ourselves to Him and believe miracles can happen.

Hmmmm. Surrender. There's that word again. Earlier, I was saying you shouldn't surrender your free will to fanatics and cults? That you should approach those who claim to have "THE ANSWER" with caution? Then, I sneaked that word "surrender" into the last paragraph and you're wondering, "How in the heck do you know for sure when you're surrendering to God and when you're wrongly throwing away your free will?" What's the difference between "surrender to God" in a conversion experience and "surrender to the Widget salesman" who convinced you to buy 50 widgets, become a widget salesman yourself and badger your friends and relatives into becoming widget salesmen? Truth is there is not much difference. In both cases, you believe you have come upon an answer and someone is drawing you toward their circle and asking you to jump into it with both feet. A preacher or a salesman, they're both into persuasion, right? Of course, the spiritual experience of religious conversion is different from the emotional experience. I believe part of discernment is learning to separate these two phenomena.

When you are on an emotional high, you might feel euphoric, on top of the world. Your rational faculties and your judgment are pushed back, sometimes a little, sometimes a lot. You are ripe for persuasion. Most people function this way, and most salespeople (the successful ones) take that knowledge into account when they make their pitch. You want to say yes. The whole process is seductive. The last thing they want to hear is, "You know, I want to take a day or two and think about this." Why do they dread hearing this? Many times your rational judgment will have more opportunity to erode the momentum of your impulse. What is the difference in the case of a Spiritual High? In my opinion, a spiritual high can be similar. The rational faculties are pushed back and an emotional rush often occurs. Have you ever experienced the rush of emotion during a spiritual retreat? It can be wonderful! I had these experiences in Medjugoje, many times. You shouldn't have to examine and guard against your emotions all the time, but be careful what you do with them.

How many people have felt moved to go into a religious vocation after a strong, emotional, spiritual experience? What kind of advice would you give them? Ponder it, pray about it, and explore it. Don't decide right away. Not because their experience wasn't authentic; it might have been a truly authentic, wonderful emotional experience! However, you could make a mistake if you base a major life decision on such an experience. That is why priests and nuns have many years between the time they enter into their called vocation, and the time they take their final vows.

Take this example: A loved one is involved in a serious automobile accident, and you panic. Your emotions get away from you. You fall on your knees, and you begin to wail. You tell God, if you save my loved one from death, I will go into a religious order and become a priest or a nun, or I will build You the biggest hospital ever for automobile accident victims. When you examine this scenario, doesn't it appear to be foolish? Many people fall into this trap. They make rash promises to God that they will never be able to keep. I once promised God I would do something if He granted me a petition. He did, but I never was able to complete my part of the bargain, because it was unrealistic. It was irrational emotional behavior that caused this petition. Do you think God will hold me to that promise? Probably not, what I should say is I sure hope He doesn't.

What would you do if your son or daughter came to you pleading that you give him or her $35.00 for something they really, really wanted. Zealously, they promise you they will clean the house for one whole year. They will also care for, feed and groom the dog for the rest of its life, and for good measure they will never disobey you ever again. Would you hold that child to those promises? No, you wouldn't, so why would God hold you accountable for the same type behavior.

Deep spiritual experiences do sometimes have these emotional qualities, but they eventually subside. When the emotions are exhausted or simply not active in the experience, how do people usually describe what has happened? Sometimes they say they cannot describe it in words. Sometimes they use adjectives like peaceful, moving and deep. The Bible says the angel Gabriel visited the Virgin Mary and told her she would conceive by the Holy Spirit and bear a son who would be the Savior. (Luke 1: 26-31) She responded with awe and said she would serve God. ("Be it done to me as you say.") Sometimes people miss the description of her emotional state right after this happened: "And Mary pondered these things in her heart." (Luke 2: 19) She was only about 14 years old. She was not married yet. She had no context for the meaning of the Annunciation. Don't you imagine she was struggling to understand those things? It doesn't say Mary continued to prepare for the birth of Christ. It doesn't say she ran out and told everyone all about it. She pondered things in her heart. The time must have been one of reflection and wonder for her.

In the years I have spent in my spiritual awakening, I have tried valiantly never to inflict my thinking upon anyone. I have tried to make people aware of certain ways to obtain healing through Jesus, but I never asked them to adhere to my personal spiritual beliefs, because sometimes they differ from those of others. I could get fanatical about what I think people should do. I could insist they believe in Rymniak's Rules for Healing. Please be aware that there are NO Rymniak's Rules for Healing. If there were, and if I did make you adhere to them, how many times do you think I would be effective? Probably not many times at all. I am sure God would intervene. He would probably ask me what I was doing. If He saw me trying to tell the world how to live, He might not want me to work for Him anymore. Pay attention into whose hands you place your spiritual well-being. Make sure you are comfortable about the ways you are being prayed with and about the means that are being used.

CHAPTER 11

THE OCCULT

OCCULT, the Webster's Dictionary says it means HIDDEN, not able to be detected.

Whenever we think of the occult we don't think of it as undetectable. The first thing we think of is evil. The word occult even sounds mysterious to me. Doesn't it to you?

Don't think about the Satanic Church, which obviously brings up the thought of evil in our minds. Think about the definition of Occult and apply it to Satan and his followers. Being hidden and not noticeable is their primary concern. You rarely hear about the Satanic Church until someone stumbles across carcasses of dead animals in the back yard of a boarded-up house. Then upon entering the house you see writings on the wall and makeshift altars. Then the media gets involved, and it's on the 11 o'clock news, and then that's it; you never hear about it again.

Is there a Satan in the world? You better believe it. If you don't think so, then I think you ought to back up three steps and reassess your thinking. He's alive, he's out there, and he's going to try to destroy you if he can. His best trick is deception. He's the master of lies. His best angle is trickery. His best plans are illusions. He's the best magician known to man. He's the ultimate confuser, and I'm sure you can add many things to this list. You get the idea.

The one thing that I try to refuse to give Satan is power over me with all the above things. I try not to give him any power. I hear people attribute everything bad that happens to them as coming from Satan. Don't blame the Devil all the time. If you do, you give him more power over you than you should, and he will take it.

The famous comedian Flip Wilson had a comedy routine that always started with the words, "The Devil made me do it." Then he spent several minutes telling jokes about stupid and idiotic things he did, and blame them on the Devil. Do you do that? Do you give Satan more power than he deserves? Are you hiding behind every frustration as being the fault of the Devil? If you are, then he's getting more credit than he deserves.

I hear people praying by casting out evil spirits, as an answer to every problem. Sometimes that is the way to pray. Jesus even prayed like that, but He first discerned an evil spirit was present and then He cast it out. He didn't pray by casting out demons for every healing that he did. Even when He admonished Peter, He told him, "Get behind me, Satan." (Matthew 16: 23.) He was speaking figuratively. He knew Peter wasn't possessed by Satan. Peter's thoughts disturbed Christ. I hear people praying by casting out the demons of flat tires, of a one-time headache, of brown spots in their lawn, their child's gold-fish dying, and all kinds of other silly things.

Satan did not give you a headache this morning. He didn't make your child's pet die. Sometimes those things happen. If Satan hears you giving him credit for those happenings, he'll take it. Don't get on his play-ground. If he lures you onto his turf he'll beat you. One of the first military strategies known to man is to fight your enemy on neutral ground, not on his territory. If you do, you'll lose almost every time.

One of the best ways Satan can get you is when you are standing in front of the mirror, early in the morning. Especially, when you get to be my age, you start to dislike what you see. You notice the gray interspersed through-out your hair. You see those lines and furrows getting deeper in your forehead, and around your eyes. You see pockets of fat building up under your chin. You even step closer to the mirror so you cannot see the rest of your pathetic body. This is how he'll get you. He'll lower your self-esteem. He'll make you feel unworthy. You may even dress in black when you go out of the house because it makes you look thinner. If the Talk Shows haven't destroyed you by noon, your grandchildren by three, your own children by five, then in walks your spouse at supper time, and you're ready to hit him with a pot.

Men are not excused from all of this, either. Think about this scene. He comes home from work, and all he wants to do is eat dinner. He has a beer and sits down to watch TV. His wife has, what he considers, 32 things for him to do. He says something to her, and she snips back at him. I even hear the story that he gets up and smacks her. She runs into the bedroom. He storms out of the house, goes down to the bar with his buddies and gets half looped. He comes home at one o'clock in the morning. The bedroom door is locked, and he winds up sleeping on the couch. This is where Satan has them, and if you don't think this is Satan at his best, you got another "think" coming.

Are you going to let Satan grab you the next time the above scenario starts to develop in your day? The most powerful way to combat this is to invoke the protection of the angels. They are strong spiritual entities and we seldom avail ourselves to their power. Use the name of Jesus; the name of Mary, his mother, the saints; or whatever power-to-be that is Divine, and Satan will flee every time. Don't be afraid to call upon the power from above. Usually, this simple spiritual demand thwarts the power of Satan and causes him to scurry.

Is Satan powerful? Can he overtake you? Can he possess you? Sometimes he can, but possession is a strong word. Even in the church, an exhaustive examination of a person is done before any form of Exorcism prayers are said.

Sometimes the investigation takes months, before the decision is made that a person is truly possessed. The better term to use, and it is appropriate in most cases, is "Under the Influence." This again goes back to the thinking that Satan causes confusion, disharmony, disruption, and deception. He seldom possesses us; he only has a strong influence on our actions.

I was in a church in Louisiana, and a woman asked that a fear be taken away from her. I asked her what the fear was, and she told me the Devil was tormenting her.

When I hear that type of petition, and I frequently do, I do not rush in and start rebuking Satan. I will ask more in-depth questions before I start praying with people.

I asked this woman how she knew Satan was tormenting her. She told me she sometimes sees two tiny red eyes looking at her, especially in the night. I must admit I do become suspicious with this type of story, and I know I shouldn't. So, I listened to the lady and did not truly give her my undivided attention. She continued with the story, and because many people were still waiting in line, I cut the woman's story short. We prayed so Jesus would cast Satan away from her. I also prayed for protection by angels. As she started to walk away, she said, "Can I call you and talk about this some more?" I handed her my card. I told her she could call anytime. I thought I would never hear from her again. Two weeks later, much to my surprise, she called.

I listened to her story again, but this time it was more detailed. She told me of all kinds of unusual happenings. She told me that some nights she could hear gruff, deep-throated laughter in the hall-way, outside her bedroom door. She repeated the phenomenon of the two red eyes that kept appearing. She even shared with me that the night she was coming to the Healing Service, several things thwarted her, and she almost didn't make it.

She told me it took her almost 10 minutes to start the car, and after almost giving up totally, she tried again and the car engine turned over. Where the story gets scary is that she told me that as she was driving to church, by herself, she looked into the rear view mirror and saw the two red eyes looking at her. She said she smelled a foul odor in the car. She even said that something appeared to be in the back seat, and it pulled her hair. At one point, it grabbed the seat and shook it so much she had to stop the car.

I listened to her and, at one point, I thought, "Boy, this would make a great Stephen King novel." She stopped the story once and said, "Paul, I bet you think I'm crazy, don't you? I bet you think I'm making this all up." Her comment snapped me back into reality. I thought, "This woman sounds too serious to be a mental case." So I listened more intently from that point on.

She told me that after I prayed that night in the church, she felt much better. As she drove home, she wasn't bothered by the two red eyes in the car mirror. When she got home, however, all Hell broke loose.

As she was preparing for bed, she felt a cold chill grip her. She smelled the same foul odor she had noticed in the car. She looked, by chance, in the mirror on the wall, and standing in the corner was a dark ominous figure with two red beady eyes. It started to laugh at her in the same gruff laughter she also heard in the car. She didn't know what to do. She told me she almost called me, but she was afraid to, so she jumped in bed, and curled up and was going to endure the rest of the night. Nothing else happened that evening, and she finally got to sleep.

I continued to question her about all of this. I asked her to think of any possible thing she had done in her past that would bring on this type of foolishness. She kept saying "no" to everything I asked. I asked her if she ever consulted a fortune teller. She never went to one. I asked if she ever played with a Ouija board; she said no. I explored every possibility, and I kept coming up dry. I finally said, "Have you ever called upon the help of Satan or invoked his name?" There was silence on the phone. I had to ask if she was still there, because it dragged into a full minute.

The woman finally responded, with a horrific tone in her voice. "Oh my God, I did once." I asked her to tell me about it. She continued with the story, and as she did, she kept stopping and saying, "Oh, my God, Oh, my God. I can't believe this. I can't believe this."

She said about eight years, prior, she bought a puppy for her then 10-year-old son, and the two of them became inseparable. Then one day, the woman went to the store and took her son with her. The dog had only been around about a month, but they noticed that when they arrived home, they didn't hear his customary barking. Even when they entered the house, they noticed stone silence. Both of them put down the groceries they where holding. They searched the house, but could not find the dog.

Friends, neighbors, family, and eventually, the police were all called. No one had seen the animal. The boy was devastated. He went to sleep that night crying. The search went on for several days. The family devoted every free moment to finding the dog. The woman prayed constantly for the dog to return. Days went into a week, and the woman came to her wit's end. One night, in a fit of despair, and after praying to God, she burst into tears and cried out, "Satan, even if you're listening and can help, please do so. We just want the puppy back, and we don't care who does it."

Saying that, she could hear her son screaming at the top of his voice, "Mommy, Mommy, come here, come here!" The woman ran to the kitchen where her son was, and the puppy was standing outside the screen door. As she told the story she continued to say, "I can't believe I didn't remember this; I just can't believe I could have done this." she also said, "Paul, I bet you think I'm crazy." I listened, in utter disbelief, at what she told me.

The woman asked me, "Do you think the Devil could have brought back the dog?" I told her I couldn't say for sure, but I told her I thought we should pray about it. She said she would like that.

I asked if she was alone in the house, and what room she was in. She told me she was in the bedroom, and her husband was down stairs watching TV. I told her to tell her husband we would be praying, and he should check on her in about 10 minutes. She yelled down to him. He said Okay.

Think about what was uncovered in the story. You can imagine how I felt after listening to her tale. I believed her. We started praying. About two to three minutes into the praying, the woman became frightened and started to scream. She told me the two red eyes were looking at her from across the room. The room had gotten cold. The smells in the room became almost unbearable. She told me she wanted to run from the room. I prayed harder.

I could hear her terror on the other end of the phone. I was tempted to hang up and call her back, to give the woman a chance to get to her husband. I suggested that, and she pleaded with me not to stop praying. I continued.

I came to a part in the prayer when I asked Jesus to banish Satan away from, not only the room, but from the lives of that family. I could hear the woman give one more scream, and then I heard nothing. I stopped praying. I yelled into the phone to the woman, asking if she could hear me, and I got no response.

Finally, after about five minutes, I heard the woman's soft, groggy voice tell me she felt exhausted. She kept talking low, as if she didn't have the strength to speak. I asked her if she was Okay, and she told me, "Yes." I asked her what was happening. She said when I asked Jesus to make Satan leave, the two red eyes in the corner of her room started yelling at her, telling her to hang up the phone. It told her that if she didn't, he was going to hurt her. She had buried her head in a pillow she was holding on her lap, and she almost dropped the phone. She was still terrified. She said as I continued to pray she felt the "Being" in the room come at her, and when I asked Christ to banish him, there was an explosion in the room, and then everything got quiet. The coldness left the room, and so did the foul smell, and then there was total silence.

I asked again if she was Okay. She said she was, and she was going to hang up. I told her to call me again if anything happened. Two weeks went by. She called to say that since that evening, she was never again bothered by the two red eyes or anything else. She contacted me again about three months later, and again about eight or nine months after that, and she said she was free from the torment she had experienced.

So let me ask you, is there a Satan? Can things that almost seem like a Hollywood movie occur in your life? Is there evil out there? I would have to say, "Yes, there is."

I do not want to minimize the seriousness of the situations that some people get themselves into with different practices. Practices as fortune-telling, crystal balls, psychic readings, Channeling, Ouija boards, tarot cards, astrology, numerology and palm-reading. There are many more I could mention but these are the biggest in todays society.

Of the nine things listed in the preceding paragraph, I got caught up in one of them, and it almost ruined my life. I still think about things I did with a certain fortune teller, and I shudder.

When I was in my mid-thirties, I stumbled on a fortune teller who had tremendous power over me. I'm not saying she was Satanic, but what led me to do what I did was surely in that realm. I'll call this woman Lucy. She told someone else at a seance that she wanted to know who "Paul" was. This other person couldn't recall right away, but her friend sitting next to her said, "You know a Paul who owns a travel agency," and this person said, "Oh, yeah." Lucy said, "Tell Paul I want to talk to him."

When this person told me, I became curious. The person gave me Lucy's phone number. I put it in my pocket and went back to my store. Later, I found the note in my pocket, looked at the number and laid the paper on my desk, pushing, out of my mind, the thought of calling her. I disregarded it as nonsense.

Two weeks later, I found the phone number on my untidy desk, and I thought, "What the heck, this can't hurt anything." I dialed the number, and a very soft, matronly voice said, "Hello."

I said, "Is this Lucy?"

She said, "Yes, is this Paul?" My curiosity was piqued. I was had.

She knew it was me on the other end of the phone before I even gave her my name. If she knew who I was without ever being introduced, what else could she know? She told me she wanted to see me. My only objection at that point was that the woman would try to get money out of me, and even a prediction of the future wasn't worth getting taken for a ride. I told her I wasn't going to pay her anything, and she nonchalantly said she didn't care. She said she didn't want my money, but to come see her. In all the years I knew her, she was true to her word. She never asked me for money, and I never gave her any. I was hooked.

The first time I met with Lucy, I was surprised to find a sweet, grandmother-looking lady. She was about five feet tall had short red hair and wore glasses. She was rather pudgy and huggable. She asked me to sit down and take off the school ring I always wore. She twirled it on her right index finger as she spoke, and she repeated that ritual each time I saw her. Twirling the ring was a point of contact, she said, which helped her reach outside this dimension. She could see the past, as well as the future, and she was almost unerringly accurate. She wasn't a fake psychic like the ones who tell you vague information that could fit anyone. Neither did she tell me information she could have gotten from someone else, a trick some fortunetellers use. She told me things nobody else could know about me, and this both scared and intrigued me.

As time went on, her predictions about the future began coming true, and I became tied to her to advise me about my everyday life. This was a gradual process for me. I began by calling her occasionally when I had a problem or an important meeting coming up. Her foreknowledge was so accurate and helpful that I started calling her more often. Finally, I was calling her almost every day. Some mornings I woke up and the first thing I did was reach for the telephone on the nightstand. I wanted to call her before I even got out of bed; that's how bad a hold she had on me. I didn't see it as a problem at the time. I thought she was a tremendous help to me.

To this day I do not believe Lucy purposely did anything Satanic. Some would argue with me, I know, and I could be wrong, but I believe some people have psychic gifts and those gifts are not necessarily evil. The problem with having that power is that some people can misuse it. These psychic gifts are supposed to help people with life decisions. What they really do is erode a persons ability to make decisions on their own.

For those of us who believe in God, following psychics is not only wrong, it erodes our faith in God. I observed this erosion of faith in God and even in my own ability to manage my life. Although Lucy never took money from me, I brought many people to her who paid her large amounts of money. This was the tradeoff for Lucy. She and her psychic ability held me captive for almost four years. I spoke with her the last time in the early 80s, and she told me I would never see her or talk to her again. I never did. She went out of my life as mysteriously as she came in.

Several years passed and I forgot Lucy. One day I was watching television. One of the sports announcers was interviewing a psychic who predicted the outcome of a football game. She said a major player would be hurt, but that his team would win, anyway. Sure enough, Sunday came and the game was played. The team she picked won, and the quarterback broke his arm. I remembered what she had said and even remembered her name. I thought about going to see her. I looked her up in the phone book and called her. I made an appointment to see her that day.

When I walked into the room where she held her sessions, I was impressed that it was filled with religious articles. She had paintings of Jesus and Mary, candles, crucifixes, and pictures of saints. I have since learned this is a common practice of fortunetellers. I felt at ease. I thought this encounter would be more spiritual than the ones I had with Lucy. She told me I was going to be successful and prosper, and she began to tell me things that would ease my fears about my life. Then she stopped abruptly and said, "But there's one thing I'm not sure I should tell you about." She looked at me quizzically and said, "Something bad is going to happen to you." She shook her head and rolled her eyes and seemed disturbed by what she "saw." "It's too terrible. I'm not going to tell you."

I begged her to explain, but she kept saying "No." I became agitated because she wouldn't disclose her vision. I got up, tried to laugh it all off, and left. I told myself she could have been making a ploy for me to come back again, with more money, of course. She could be wrong, I thought, but I remembered the football game and the quarterback with the broken arm. If she could see that, maybe she could see something coming in my future, too. Fortunately, I never went back to see this woman or any other psychic, again.

Since then, a few things have happened that could have been the unfolding of her prediction. Were they what she saw, or yet will another catastrophic event befall me? Even today, I struggle with those foolish thoughts. The difference is I trust God, and I know He will protect me.

The next time you want to get involved with fortunetellers, think about Paul Rymniak, and how he almost lost himself. Especially, if you want to call those pyschics on television. PLEASE DON'T.

DABBLING IN THE OCCULT

Mary had experiences with the occult that were less dramatic, but perhaps more typical of what can happen to the average person. In her adolescence and through her college years, She was interested in occult practices. On the surface, dabbling with the occult appeared harmless, but she now realizes this pastime could have led her into trouble.

"When I was in junior high school, my friends and I loved to play with the Oujia board. At slumber parties, someone always asked the "spirits" to answer our deepest questions.

Does Jeff love Lois? Who would Suzie marry? How many kids would they have? All this was harmless and never led to anything scary. It intrigued me, and if I had the availability of information about the occult and the related paraphernalia kids have today, I think I would have pursued it more in depth. Some of my interest was caused by normal adolescent development. I had natural curiosity about spirituality and the supernatural. I wanted to know about the future, and I wanted to believe I had some power over its outcome.

By the time I went to college, the general public was showing an increasing interest in the occult and metaphysics. I investigated those subjects through books, groups and classes and saw them as a means of self-discovery and self-understanding. I wondered if God existed. I sought God through those non-traditional methods, because I had never been able to develop spirituality through attending church and Sunday school. Although I went to church every Sunday all the way through high school, I quit going once I got to college. My motivations were good. I wanted to find God and understand myself. I was not a Satanist. I didn't want to do voodoo on anyone.

Many of the things I explored and learned about at this time of my life were helpful and are part of my spirituality today, such as meditation. However, I am focusing right now on the things that stand out in my mind as unwise and potentially detrimental. To give an example, I began using tarot cards when I was a sophomore in college. I had been given a reading that got me excited, and I began learning about the practice through the person who did my reading. I got myself a set of tarot cards and began learning how to read them. Books and paraphernalia were easy to buy then, even in the small Ohio town where I attended college.

I don't claim to be psychic, but as I began using the cards, I got feelings beyond the rote interpretations in the books. For example, if a card represented romance, I became adept at expounding upon what that might mean for that specific person. I didn't have to know the person to do it. I'm not sure to this day why I was so effective, but something was definitely happening. Was I developing "psychic powers," or was I simply developing an ability to give people bits of information and watch them rush in with a few details and eagerly ask me for more? Probably the latter, but something else began to happen that concerned me.

One day I didn't have anything to do. I went to a place at the college to "hang out." I made myself comfortable and sat down on the floor of the student lounge. I had my tarot cards with me and laid them out on the floor. Soon someone came over to me and asked what I was doing. When I told her, she asked, "Would you do a reading for me?" Her friends stood around. As they watched, they began asking one by one if I would do readings for them, too. Soon I had a small line of people who wanted me to read their cards. I spent the entire evening performing and felt rather like a celebrity as individuals walked away, many of them wide-eyed with expectation about my predictions.

A few days passed and I began seeing some of the people for whom I had done readings. They wanted to know more. They had friends who wanted readings, too. What started out as fun, because I was being sought out, soon began to feel uncomfortable. I realized people were coming to me for answers to their life problems, and I knew that I didn't hold the answers for them. I thought, "These people are using me like a crutch." Today I would word it differently. They were using me to avoid the pain of life and looking for easy answers, rather than developing skills to manage their lives. They were also trying to avoid responsibility for making life decisions. It didn't feel right, and I stopped it. Today I would add they weren't putting their trust in God."

For those of you who have never been involved in the occult in any way, we congratulate and encourage you to continue to stay away from these practices. You may have lost some regard for us after reading this chapter, but we chose to put this in, even though we will undoubtedly lose some of the luster from our halos, in your eyes. We hope you won't think we're so silly that you are tempted to toss the book. We took the risk of being totally honest, because we believe strongly that **SOMEBODY OUT THERE NEEDS TO READ THIS.** If it's not you, please bear with us. **IF YOU FEEL WE ARE SPEAKING TO YOU, WE HOPE YOU ARE PAYING ATTENTION!** If you want to be at Peace, put your trust in God not psychics, Ouija boards or any other means that claims to predict your future.

STORIES ABOUT THE OCCULT

I have to admit I am not an expert in the field of Satanism, but I have had experiences in that area. Some of the situations are frightening.

I was in a church in the West. The next person in line was a woman who was in her 50s. When I asked her name and what she wanted, she turned around and pointed to her crippled and deformed young daughter who was being held by her elderly aunt. The mother told me her daughter, who I will call Jane, was 29 she had been treated for Muscular Dystrophy for the last nine years. The doctor was becoming discouraged because there was no progress being made with her treatments. Knowing that the woman was Catholic, the doctor went as far as to suggest they consider the church as a means of helping Jane, because he felt her condition could have stemmed from something demonic rather than something physical. Rarely does a medical practitioner, make such a decision.

The woman was at her wits' end. She did not know what to do. She had seen the notice in the church bulletin about the Healing Service, and she attended, in hopes that her daughter's progressive illness could, and would, be abated.

I didn't know what I was going to do. I could see that it would be difficult for the young woman to come up the steps of the main altar for me to pray with her. I told the mother I would go down to her daughter, about 15 feet away. As I started down the steps towards Jane, I saw her tense up, and I thought it was just a nervous reaction to my coming towards her. I raised my hands to place them on her head, and at the same time started to close my eyes and bow my head. When I almost touched on her, she did the strangest thing. Without warning, she punched me in the middle of my chest. Because I had my head bowed and my eyes closed, the punch surprised me.

Startled, I jumped back looked at Jane, and much to my surprise she was standing straight up. She showed no signs of any infirmity. She looked perfectly normal.

The mother immediately started yelling with screams of delight, thinking her daughter had been healed. As I started to go back towards Jane she saw me coming and put her arms up in front of her face. At this point, her voice dropped from a high pitched tone to a deep guttural one. She sounded as though she were growling. She kept saying, "Get away from me! Get away from me! Get away from me!"

As she spoke, her face became contorted. She started to snarl like an angry dog. I was frightened, but determined to pray with her. I stepped forward towards her and she drew back her hand to punch me again. This time I grabbed her and embraced her. I drew her close to me and prayed. I think I said every prayer I knew about Spiritual Warfare, and I invoked every Saint I could think of to intercede. Jane became furious, and she began thrashing around. Her yelling grew in intensity, and she got extremely loud.

I backed away from her, because she was uncontrollable. As I did, I noticed she was standing erect and without any sign of a problem or physical dysfunction. Her mother kept saying, at the top of her voice, "She's healed, She's healed, She's healed."

She walked off under her own power, beside her mother. I watched as she sat down. She looked very much healed. I was amazed, but I wasn't convinced she was healed. Jane, her mother and aunt hugged and kissed each other. I went back to praying with the other people.

About 30 minutes or so passed, and the three women still sat in the far pew to my extreme left. Everything appeared normal. I finished praying with someone, and I told the next person to wait one minute. I wanted to go over to Jane and her mother to say good-bye. I was about 40 feet away. As I neared, Jane put her hands back up in front of her face and yelled again. I stopped dead in my tracks. I was not going to repeat the incident again. I simply waved at the mother and told her I was sorry for any embarrassment the incident may have been caused her. She just smiled back at me and waved.

I think she was happy her daughter looked normal. She didn't care how, why or who was responsible. Her daughter was healed. I went back to the front of the church and resumed praying with people.

After a short time, I noticed Jane appeared to be shrinking back into her Muscular Dystrophic state. Her body looked as it did when she first entered the church. She looked crippled and deformed. Her mother noticed also, and I could see streams of tears running down her face, because she was realizing her daughter was not healed. She knew that something else had to be done, because the problem had returned.

I watched as Jane's mother and aunt put her into a

wheelchair and rolled her out of the church. What had happened? Here was a young woman crippled, then she appeared to be healed, and then she was crippled again. What was all that growling? What was all the hollering? What had happened?

Did Jane have demonic problems? Did Satan have a grip on her? I think so, but I never have been able, and never will be able to give qualified answers in this area. To the best of my understanding, I think Jane was possessed and under the extreme influence of the Devil.

I was not able to follow up on Jane. I never knew what happened to her. Since that time, I have seen many happenings of the same kind, and I am convinced Satan roams the world seeking to ruin the souls of many. He's out there, and he's alive.

Even more amazing was the second encounter I had with the dark side, also in a church out west. I had been praying with people for an entire evening. It was about one o'clock in the morning, and I was almost finished. The church was predominantly Hispanic. I do not speak Spanish, so I had several interpreters at this service.

As the line was dwindling, I noticed one individual near the end. He made a strong impression on me. I could see he was in need of a good scrubbing, and his clothes needed washing. He looked as if he hadn't bathed in two weeks. He was wearing a cloth poncho, the kind with a hole in the middle, where you put your head through. Around his waist was a belt with a pouch on it for carrying things. His shoes had holes in them, and one of them exposed two of his small toes. He looked grungy.

As he stepped in front of me, I asked his name. He looked at me quizzically. The interpreter realized he couldn't speak English, so she asked him his name. He told her it was

Carlos. I told the interpreter, whose name was Maria, to ask Carlos what he wanted Jesus to do for him. Maria did. Carlos replied he wanted Jesus to heal us first. Maria told him we were happy to receive his prayers, but she asked him again what did he want from Jesus for himself. This time he said he wanted to pray for his friends who were drug addicts. Maria told him we would do that, but she asked him the third time what he wanted for himself.

This time Maria listened and then told me that Carlos wanted Jesus to make the voices in his head stop. I told Maria to ask him what the voices were saying. Carlos rattled off several sentences, and Maria looked at him totally shocked. I asked her, "What did he tell you?" She said the voices were telling him to take the knife out of his waist pouch, and stab me as many times as possible.

I lunged forward and grabbed Carlos by his head. I placed my hands on the cheeks of his face, and I prayed. Other people around us who had heard what Carlos said joined in the prayer. As I prayed, I felt a tremendous surge of heat shoot through my hands.

After several minutes, Carlos slumped into my arms and against my chest. I never let go of his face. I tried to balance him. It became awkward and strenuous trying to hold him up, so I helped him over to the first pew and sat him down. When I removed my hands from his cheeks I was shocked. On his cheeks, where my hands had been, it looked as if someone had taken a pen and outlined my handprint on his face. Remember when you were in first grade and the teacher made you put your hand on a piece of paper, trace its outline and then color it? On each of Carlos' cheeks was the outline of my hand, and it looked as if someone had taken red paint and colored it in. I almost laughed. I told Maria that maybe we should revive him. We did not want to break the Resting in the Spirit he seemed to be doing, but it was late in the evening, and everyone wanted to go home.

As Carlos came to, he shook his head as if he had been in a deep sleep and kept looking around. After a while, he regained his composure. He had a gigantic smile on his lips, and he seemed to be in a happy mood.

I noticed my hand prints on his face were getting redder. Carlos finally, with some prompting, got up and left the church. The hand prints did not go away for the duration of his stay. Everyone was happy to see him leave. When the full realization hit me, I got scared. I realized this man could have killed me or severely hurt me.

I called Maria several weeks later to ask her if she had heard what happened to Carlos. I couldn't believe my ears. She told me Carlos had been a member of the Satanic Church, and he was scheduled to be ordained as a high priest. Jesus must have touched Carlos, because he had quit the Satanic Church, went back to his own church and started going to Mass every day. Carlos had called Maria to tell her.

Several months later, while I was in Phoenix, Arizona, Maria came to help interpret at a Healing Service I was conducting. I asked her how Carlos was doing, and she told me he was fine. She saw him every day, and he was a changed man. Thank God.

I have seen many more incidents like the ones involving those two people, but nothing as dramatic. Most of the time, people simply tense up perhaps scream. Sometimes they slump to the floor, rigidly lie there and moan and groan. Sometimes they fall to the floor, thrash around and have to be restrained. Most people in this state become abnormally strong, I never really try to restrain them, I hold them and protect them from harming themselves. In all of this, I still think most of these people are only strongly influenced and not possessed.

When someone steps in front of me in church and tells me about tremendous depression or anxiety that makes them tremble when they talk, or severe panic that causes them to become frozen, I normally pray for Jesus to protect them from Satan. Some of these people may be mentally ill. Sometimes fanaticism causes the same symptoms. Sometimes the person's own insecurities drive them to react the way they do. I realize all of that, and I go back to the statement made earlier that you do not want to give Satan that much power, but strong discernment should be used in making such an assessment.

STEALING YOUR PEACE.

You can tell Satan is at work if there is an uneasy feeling around you. I'm not talking about "Twilight Zone" material. I'm talking about that feeling you get when you're not at peace with yourself. This feeling is definitely Spiritual Warfare. If you have assessed the situation and find everything around you is great and you can say to yourself, "I shouldn't be feeling like this, nothing is really wrong," then Satan is probably at work.

If you assess the matter and you find yourself confused about something, or if it seems everyone around you is in turmoil, you can bet it's Satan. This sequence does not occur in everything, as I have mentioned, but be aware that maybe something else is going on, and pay attention to it.

PAINTING EVERYTHING BLACK

Every now and then, I get myself into thoughts and mind games, and I start "Painting Everything Black." This doesn't sound all that bad, but if you were around me when I started this you would see how bad it gets. I don't do it as much as I used to, but I still have the ability to perform this feat.

What do I do when I Paint everything Black? I am going to make up an example of how I paint things black. This **DID NOT** happen to me, it is merely an example, but it proves a point.

I am sitting watching a video from my Disney collection...I'm watching Bambi....up comes the part about Bambi's mother getting killed...I think...How cruel. Killing some poor animal like that...It's inhumane...how different is that from how people treat each other...My friend is just as cruel to me in the way he treats me...If he does it to me one more time, I'm going to let him have it...He's not going to make fun of me anymore....I hate his opinionated thinking....He's like our Pastor....Our Pastor could help more people than he does...He only helps those that he wants to....I really hate that. Our Pastor should be sent to live with some poor people in other countries...Some of those countries have people running them who are as bad as that religious fanatic I ran into on my last trip...Boy, was he a jerk, telling me that Florida was going to fall into the sea...Where does he get off warning people to move out of Florida...That's as bad as those professional athletes who cry all the time about not making enough money...They all make 20-million-dollar salaries....I can't make that much money in a lifetime...Where do they get off acting like that? All they're doing is holding all of us sports fans hostage....they're all terrorists....just like those people who killed 200 people with that explosion the other day...What's worse those terrorists who did that heinous act were women....I hate them all....They should be shot....I hate all women.

After all those dark thoughts run through my mind, in walks some woman who says, "Hi, Paul, how are you doing?" With rage in my heart and my trusty emotional paint brush in my hand, already dipped in black, I look at her and say, "I hate you!"

Isn't that the silliest stuff you've ever heard? Yes, it is, but how many of you do the same thing? Could you write a script like the one above? I'm sure most of you could. Do not do this! The world does not need any more painters splashing black paint on everything. Don't be as foolish as I am sometimes. The way I was thinking in the above hypothetical scene is how I can spiral down, like water in a toilet. Once you flush it, the water spins around and takes everything down with it. This is how Satan can get you. He will watch you begin you own thought process. He'll make you dredge up something out of your past, and then he'll sit back and let you do the rest. When you come to an uncontrollable anxiety, he flushes and you're gone.

I tell you all this with what may appear to be a flippant and comical attitude, but when it hits me, I'm not funny. When the spiral grabs me, I can be panic stricken, emotionally freeze for several hours, and then I am good for nothing. I'm lost. I don't want you to think I'm a raving maniac, and I fall apart all the time. I don't really do that. I am trying to make the point that I am human, and I still fall down. I have developed skills that let me come out of that kind of foolishness and not stay stuck. I seek Spiritual help, and I talk things through with people. I am not that proverbial "bull in the china shop" that I used to be, but it took work to get to that point.

As I have said, I try to discern between Spiritual Warfare and just plain things going wrong in my life. I try not to give Satan extra credit for anything, but I am keenly aware he's always looking over my shoulder, ready to whack me. Be careful! He's looking over your shoulder, also. Don't let him whack you, either.

CHAPTER 12

YOU'RE HEALED NOW WHAT?

You're healed now what? It doesn't seem as if this question should even have to be asked. One thing that I have noticed in the years of my ministry is that most people do not follow up their healing with Prayers of Thanksgiving, and I think this is sad. I'm not saying that everyone is like that, I'm only suggesting that the greatest majority of people forget to say Thank You to God for the things that he gives us. This is even found in the Bible. Jesus went into a village and saw ten men who had leprosy. They all begged to be healed, and almost instantaneously all ten were cleansed. Jesus tells them to go to the priests to be examined, and when one of the ten realizes he is healed, he comes back to tell Him Thank You. It even says that he threw himself at the feet of Jesus. Jesus then asks the man where were the other nine? The man couldn't answer Him. (Luke 17: 11-19) Don't you think Jesus was dismayed with the whole situation?

How many times have you done something spectacular for someone and they treated you as if it was your duty to do it? For those of you who have children, you know what I'm talking about. I know they have done that to you. Didn't it make you feel bad? How do you feel on birthdays or anniversaries when you're forgotten by someone important to you? Well, that's the frustration I think Jesus felt.

I want everyone to understand what I'm going to say. I am not likening myself unto Christ, but I think I know how He felt. When I see someone a year or two after they got a healing and they say, "I came back this time, because the last time you were here, I was healed of this, or I was cured of that." (Or you fill in the blank.) I will immediately ask them if they prayed Thanksgiving Prayers to Christ. Most people will look almost embarrassed. They will bow their head, sometimes, in shame, and tell me, "No I didn't I guess I should have, huh?" Not everyone is like that; some people do tell me that they Thank Him every day.

I guess the most exasperating thing I have found is that about 75 per cent of the people I talk to who get healings honestly forget how it was before. Most of them, after a few years, even forget the whole situation they where in. Even worse, some of them go right back to complaining about how bad they have it.

I have talked to people who have had a beautiful healing, and almost immediately they ask for more, shortly after their first problem was taken away. I know some of you are sitting there saying, "Jesus tells us He will fulfill all our needs, you only have to ask." Should it be constantly? I know it is not in the Bible, but isn't there an adage somewhere that says the Lord loves those who help themselves?

Many times I think we have a tendency to want everything the way we want it, without any consideration to how Christ wants it. We sometimes pray hard for things that we want, thinking if we had things that way, or if we had this much money we could get out of the hole, or if only she would do this, or if only he would do that, and on, and on, and on. I don't think we are ever truly satisfied with the way things are in our lives. We always have a tendency to want more. Why is that? Why can't we be satisfied with the way our lives are? Why do we always have to strive for the great American dreams - house - big car - lots of money?

I meet people from every walk of life. Rich, poor, various ethnic backgrounds, various religions, etc., and after a while, everything starts to look the same. The faces, the churches, the clergymen and the cities all start to run together. Everyone thinks their problems are unique. Let me tell you, they're not! The same problems exist everywhere, and seldom do I find people who are happy, and if I do, there is always someone, or some group, there to cut them down. We strive for happiness, and when we get it, are we truly happy? Most of the time the feeling is fleeting.

Stop and think about the last time a major crisis occurred in your life. Think more about how you felt when it was over, whether it was good, bad or indifferent. Did this crisis, after it was taken away, change things? Yes, I'm sure it did. Did you then become free of pain and torment? Did the rest of your life become one big happy time? It probably did not. Life is usually a series of brush fires you have to keep putting out, one at a time, and that job never ends.

Has God blessed you in some special way? Have you been healed of some physical problem? Has God answered a prayer petition for you? So, where do you stand with Him now? Can you truly say you're pleased with the way things are going in your life? I hope so. What's the point to all of this? It's simple. Don't force things. Let God do it. Matthew 6: 34 says, "So don't be anxious about tomorrow. God will take care of you tomorrow, too. Live one day at a time." How true, how true, how true.

SLOWING DOWN

I think one of the biggest factors to missing what I talked about in the opening of this chapter is the so-called Rat Race of Life we get ourselves into. Sometimes it is merited, and sometimes it is not. Some of us still have young children who must be raised. Some of us are entering school, not knowing where we are going. Some of us are finishing our education and are about to embark on a career. Some of us are worried about losing jobs. Some of us are losing our identity in relationships. Some of us are at a crossroads and have to figure out what to do, and maybe that will cause pain. Worst of all, some of you might be suffering with terminal illness, and death may be eminent. Do you fit into any of these categories? I am sure most of you fit in somewhere. In every one of the above, one thing must be done. A decision must be made.

Are you going to make that decision, or are you going to let God do that for you? Are you going to consult others, or are you going to consult God? Are you going to seek the aid of friends or family, or are you going to seek God? Are you going to put your trust in others, or are you going to put your trust in God?

This is where I think we all fall down, when we don't go to God first. We wait until things get bad, then we run to him, usually screaming. Listen to what the Lord says in Jeremiah 17: 5-8: "Cursed is the man who puts his trust in mortal man and turns his heart away from God. He is like a stunted shrub in the desert, with no hope for the future; he lives on the salt-encrusted plains in the barren wilderness; good times pass him by forever. Blessed is the man who trusts in the Lord and has made the Lord his hope and confidence. He is like a tree planted along a riverbank, with its roots reaching deep into the water - a tree not bothered by the heat nor worried by long months of drought. Its leaves stay green and it goes right on producing all its luscious fruit." This passage is strong. It's almost scary to think about this when we apply it to our own lives. I hope I am not instilling the wrong kind of fear into your heart, because that is not my intent.

Has God been working in your life and you do not realize it? Is He telling you something, and maybe you're not paying attention? Did you seek something, and did He let you find it? Did you ask for something, and did He give it to you? Did you knock on the door, and did He open it for you? Did He open His Infinite Merciful Heart to you in some way?

HOW DID YOU RESPOND?

How did you respond? How are you responding right now? Where are you with your relationship with God? I hope you will not be the idiot I can be sometimes. If you got something from Christ in the past, especially if it was a tremendous gift, how have you handled it? Was it a healing? Was it an answer to a petition? Was it a blessing? Did something you have wanted for a long time finally come your way? Now that you have it, are you happy?

This was made evident to me with this example: I was at a church and at the end of the evening, a woman told me an experience she had during the Healing Service. The woman who was 70 years old, graciously volunteered to be in charge of selling my tapes, so she spent the whole time, that evening, in the back of the church.

She told me that all of her life she always wanted to see an angel. I looked at her with a smile. She told me that during my talk, she saw my body become encased in a light, but the light was not blinding. She told me that as the light blocked out my body, everything else in the church still looked the same. She could see everyone. There were approximately 1,000 people there that evening. She could see the altar. She even looked around to make sure that light was not coming from some other source in the church, but this was not the case. I have to tell you that I had no extraordinary feeling while I was standing in front of the church giving my talk while this was, supposedly, going on. Rarely do I feel anything while I am speaking.

The woman was standing in the back, so she had a good view of the entire interior of the church. As she stood there, she was compelled to look at the light. All of a sudden, she saw a face look out from behind the light. It was the face of a beautiful person. She could not tell if it was the face of a man or a woman. The face looked as if it were peeping out at her from around the light. She said she became excited, and didn't know what to do. She was the only person in the vestibule of the church, so no one was around for her to ask if they could also see what was happening.

She told me she stared at the face. It even smiled at her several times. The thought came into her, "Is this an angel? Could I be getting my wish?" She didn't know for sure. She stood there frozen, because all of a sudden, from behind the light, the face she was looking at showed her half of its body. It was wearing a long gown of some sort, tied with a long cord around its waist. She was mesmerized. She could see what appeared to be a person almost six or seven feet tall standing there looking at her.

She said to herself, "If you are an angel, show me your wings?" Without hesitation, a gigantic wing fluttered out from behind the persons body. It flapped it slowly and gently, and the person smiled kindly at her. She told me she stood in a trance looking at the creature. She didn't know what to do.

Suddenly, the wing retracted, the person stepped back, the face took one last look at her, smiled, and stepped behind the light. The light vanished, and she could see me standing at the podium. Everything was normal again. She told me she began to cry tears of happiness, and they did not cease for quite awhile. She kept mulling over the question, "Was this the angel I prayed to see all my life?"

I must admit, when people start explaining things like this to me, I become a little uneasy, not because I question their credibility, but it amazes me that these things could happen. We kept talking about her experience for quite a while. I even made her repeat the story again. She did, and it came out the same way the second time.

The other factor that leads to my uneasiness, in situations like this, is that I become skeptical of things of this nature that I cannot explain. With this matter, I had to believe the woman saw what she did. Who was I to question a spiritual experience like that one. I had felt nothing at the time it went on.

I do not want any of you to think I'm something special that angels, or any other divine beings come out because of my presence somewhere. I do not believe that for a minute. People also tell me they see Jesus, they see His Mother, they see Saints...they tell me all kinds of things. I can only trust they are not conjuring up in their minds some image so they can feel good, and then on top of it, dragging me into it.

I also do not want to sound ungrateful. Maybe I was part of a spiritual happening for someone. I shouldn't interfere with the beauty of God when it comes to matters of this nature.

The story doesn't end here. With my own foolish pride, I said to her, "I envy you. I wish sometimes I could have something happen to me like that." The woman shocked me with her reply, and this is the whole point I'm trying to make. She said: "How can you say that? You have something bigger happen to you all the time that's better than what just happened to me. You get the chance to feel Jesus Christ come through your hands when you touch someone, and then see that person get healed." The woman humbled me. I didn't know what to say to her.

Even though I do feel that Christ uses me, I never feel special. I really don't want to, because I do not want my pride to get away from me. I don't want to fall prey to this kind of thinking, but the woman had a point.

I used a good portion of this book to explain many wonderful healings. I see Jesus work wonders. I get to see the power of God, and I'm thankful. The point is that sometimes I want more. Sometimes what I have is not enough. Do you ever feel that way?

Have you prayed for a specific need and received it? Have you had a healing occur in your life? Have you gotten a prayer request filled? If you have, did it fulfill your wants and needs? Did you really benefit by the results of your prayers? Has your life really changed? Did the granting of your petition really make things turn out the way you wanted?

Most of the time, when I see people get what they want they say: "Maybe I should have asked for my petition differently. Maybe I should have omitted this when I asked Jesus to help me. Maybe I really should have told him to give it to me in greater quantity, then I wouldn't have to bother Him again." Everyone struggles with these things. That's why I caution people to be careful what you pray for because, you might get it.

So, are you healed? Now what!? Because I have made the effort to write this book, I have had the chance to go back and to talk to some of the people who have gotten dramatic healings. I also have, over the past year, paid more attention to following up on those people that write me telling me about an answer they received to prayer, and a common denominator emerged.

I found that the more dramatic the healing was, the more turmoil people found themselves in. Let me explain. When I checked with those individuals that got free of cancer, had their sight return, had their hearing come back, became free of having to use a wheelchair or experienced any other healing of this enormity, I found they had a sharp decrease in their Spiritual Life. I find that interesting.

I found that while they had the problem, or affliction or disease they had a prayer life. They designated periods of the day to interact with God. They made sure that prayer was a part of their day. Then after the problem was taken away and things returned to a state of normalcy, their prayer time diminished. It suffered severely, and eventually it ceased. Why is that? What's even worse is other problems that never concerned them became monumental, all of a sudden. Things that never bothered them before became thorns in their sides. In some cases, these new problems became greater than their former ones.

You see, sometimes we forget how intensely we were praying, initially, for the things we needed. We forget how we were focused on Jesus, during the time of our trial. We forget how ritualistic we were with our praying methods. We simply forget how it used to be when things were really bad, and I'm sometimes the biggest offender.

When I first started in this ministry, I had nothing. I was limited in what I could do. I had one phone that was separate from my home line. I had an electric typewriter that constantly needed repairs. I had a desk and a chair and that was it. Many years later, things have changed. I have several phone lines, one of which is an 800 number people call me on from all over North America. I have a sophisticated computer system, and I can operate it. That's a miracle in itself. I have six tapes that I sell. I visit about 120 churches a year conducting Healing Services. I publish a newsletter that reaches thousands of people. You're reading a book I wrote. I even had my own religious TV show, which Mother Angelica appeared on, and I'm existing financially on the generosity of people. Am I telling you this to impress you? **HEAVENS NO**. I'm telling you this to exemplify my point.

When I started I prayed hard for these things to come, and there were times when I wanted to chuck it all, but I stayed rooted in my prayer life. The only reason I am existing today is that I still am rooted in that life. It's the only way I know to survive, but I realize I will still have hard times. I realize things will not always work out the way I want. I am going to have horrendous days full of strife. Any kind of success takes hard work and discipline. Even praying.

So, I'll ask you again. Have you been healed of some affliction? Did you avert a serious problem? Have you had a prayer petition answered? If you have, the thing to remember is how you received the answer to your prayers. Don't forget the answer came from GOD. Don't forget to thank Him. Most of all, Don't quit praying. Prayer is the answer to the question posed at the beginning of this chapter:

"You're healed - Now what?"